J.M.G. Le Clézio

# J.M.G. Le Clézio

## *A Concerned Citizen of the Global Village*

Keith Moser

LEXINGTON BOOKS
Lanham • Boulder • New York • Toronto • Plymouth, UK

Published by Lexington Books
A wholly owned subsidiary of Rowman & Littlefield
4501 Forbes Boulevard, Suite 200, Lanham, Maryland 20706
www.rowman.com

10 Thornbury Road, Plymouth PL6 7PP, United Kingdom


First paperback edition 2014



British Library Cataloguing in Publication Information Available

**Library of Congress Cataloging-in-Publication Data**
The hardback edition of this book was previously cataloged by the Library of Congress as follows:

Moser, Keith A.
J.M.G. Le Clézio : a concerned citizen of the global village / Keith Moser.
p. cm.
Includes bibliographical references and index.
1. Le Clézio, J.-M. G. (Jean-Marie Gustave), 1940—Social and political views. 2. Globalization in
literature. 3. Consumption (Economics) in literature. 4. Material culture in literature. 5. Social values
in literature. 6. Social justice in literature. I. Title. II. Title: Citizen of the global village.
PQ2672.E25Z768 2013
843'.914—dc23
2012033870

ISBN : 978-0-7391-7205-6 (cloth : alk. paper)
ISBN : 978-0-7391-9759-2 (pbk : alk. paper)
ISBN : 978-0-7391-7206-3 (electronic)

To Kelly, Zoey, and Chloë
With love that transcends all borders

# Contents

# Contents

# Acknowledgments

First of all, I would like to thank my beautiful wife Kelly for her unwavering support throughout the entire writing process. I am also truly indebted to J.M.G. Le Clézio for allowing me to interview him in Albuquerque, New Mexico, as part of this project. Furthermore, I would like to express my sincere gratitude to every colleague with whom I have had the pleasure of collaborating since I entered the profession. Without your support, this book would have never been possible. On a final note, I would like to thank Justin Race for believing in this interdisciplinary project and for his enthusiastic encouragement every step of the way.

# Acknowledgments

# Introduction

## *J.M.G. Le Clézio: A Concerned Citizen of the Global Village*

Although J.M.G. Le Clézio's diverse and complex literary corpus has been oversimplified by misinformed critics[1] as nothing more than a naïve ethical system that resembles "boy scout" political correctness, the stark realism of certain works clearly negates these criticisms (Thibault *Métaphore Exotique* 11). The narrator of a recent documentary produced by BBC World News accurately affirms that the 2008 Nobel Laureate in Literature is "acclaimed for literature that conveys the splendor of the world but that also examines its brutality."[2] During this same interview, Le Clézio elucidates that existence is "full of very extraordinary moments and very terrible moments and the very thing together makes a life." Echoing the presence of this nuanced belief system in the Franco-Mauritian author's fiction, Isabelle Roussel-Gillet asserts, "la magie s'inscrit en contrepoint de l'horreur du monde" / 'The magical is counterpointed by the horror (s) of the world' (11; my trans.). The writer's balanced worldview underscores both the searing pain of the human condition and what it means to be thrown into the chaos of existence in a drastically altered urban landscape in addition to intense moments of life-affirming ecstasy that sustain the subject and sometimes compel him or her to live otherwise. Indeed, perhaps no other contemporary author is able to depict the profound anguish experienced by ephemeral beings in the modern globalized world as realistically as the 2008 Nobel Laureate in Literature.

This specific study will focus on the multifaceted representations of globalization in Le Clézio's extremely varied *oeuvre* from 1963 to the present. Additionally, this investigation seeks to enrich the wealth of literary criticism devoted to the Nobel Laureate by exploring the interlocking power structures created and maintained by what Le Clézio terms the *Happy Few* for the systematic and hegemonic exploitation of the marginalized and disenfranchised inhabitants of the global village. Although Le Clézio is not a didactic thinker as he even expresses his distrust of any type of dogmatic ideology that claims to possess definitive answers for life's greatest mysteries, his narratives often pose disconcerting questions related to the realities of the increasingly interconnected and interdependent modern world. In her aptly named monograph entitled *Le Clézio, peintre de la vie moderne,* Marina Salles describes the writer as an artist that is astutely cognizant of the grave problems that afflict contemporary society. Given that the complex phenomenon of globalization is undoubtedly the most important present and future subject that concerns all of humanity, it is hardly a surprise that Le Clézio's narratives, public discourses, and press articles concretize this profound apprehension. Furthermore, reiterating a contention that is reminiscent of many other researchers in the diverse field of global studies, Langman and Morris assert that "globalization is the dominant hegemon of the present age" (n.p.). As a well-informed and perceptive author, Le Clézio often expresses his disquieting anxiety concerning what the realization of the global village means to all material beings across the planet.

It should be noted, however, that the author avoids proposing simplistic solutions to complicated issues. Yet, having the courage to be inquisitive in the face of alarming and mounting evidence related to globalization represents perhaps the first step in the creation of a meaningful dialogue that could potentially alter the current course of the world. For Le Clézio and many other writers, this deep conviction represents the dire significance of literature and of the humanities in general. In reference to the pragmatic importance of the human sciences in an educated and knowledgeable society, Roland Barthes contends that "literature is the question minus the answer" (qtd. in Spencer 48). In an interview with the journalist Adam Gopnik, Le Clézio reiterates Barthes's assertion. As the Franco-Mauritian author affirms, "Literature is contrary to knowledge and affirmation. Literature is a series of questions" ("Every Word Contains the World" n.p.)

Although Barthes, Le Clézio, and many other contemporary thinkers reject the notion that artists possess a type of prophetic vision which allows them to ascertain definitive truths concerning the nature of reality, they also emphasize the practical significance of literature given its ability to foster critical thinking skills and to (re)-conceptualize how human beings perceive their role in society and their relationship to the natural environment. In spite of the current trend in Western society to devalorize other disciplines besides math and science, many researchers have noted that the humanities are more critical than ever in today's modern world in desperate need of a radical paradigm shift. In the wake of recent scientific discoveries that cast doubt upon former preconceived notions concerning the universe and which underscore questions of sustainability related to our ecological footprint, such as Commoner's first law of ecology and quantum contextualism, it is the imperative mission of the human sciences to articulate a new worldview that more accurately represents current knowledge and undermines outdated, disproven theories. Underscoring this crucial role and denouncing the pervasive anti-intellectual climate in the United States in which the worth of a given discipline is based solely on its direct contribution to our materialistic consumer society, Daniel Shanahan declares, "Our fundamental goal as language professors is to expand and enrich the lives of our students and the society in which they live. Our dedication to this goal [...] has sustained our commitment to humanistic study even when it exists [...] on a bleakly unreceptive landscape" (170 –171).

Given the urgency of the problems that the global village must begin to confront together, such as widespread pollution, climate change, the loss of biodiversity, and the rapid depletion of the earth's non-renewable resources, the era of academic overspecialization must come to an end as researchers from different areas should collaborate and exchange their expertise in an effort to create a more sustainable and equitable society for the future of humankind. Instead of suffering from "insularity and defeatism" engaged in philosophical disputes that have no practical correlation to quotidian reality or worse still playing self-indulgent semantic games designed to demonstrate one's intellectual superiority (Robert Weisbuch, *Chronicle of Higher Education*, 26 Mar. 1999: B4), Thomas Dean and many other theorists have stressed the necessity to "reconnect the disciplines" (n.p.). For this reason, this specific study will be quite interdisciplinary in nature as it will take advantage of any valid theory that contributes to the major global discussions of our time.

In an effort to overcome the aforementioned rigid academic divisions, this exploration will delve into research from the diverse fields of traditional literary criticism, ecocriticism, interculturality, sustainability studies, and basic economics. Given that many scholars have identified the ecological crisis as both the most important and complex issue of the present age, this investigation is a response to the summons extended by colleagues from all disciplines to collaborate and exchange ideas. Although our knowledge of the intricate nature of the biosphere will forever remain fragmentary, posing disquieting questions and working together is the first step to creating viable solutions. As Joseph Stiglitz muses in *Making Globalization Work*, "how can we marshal the cooperation of all to solve our most pressing global issue? [...] No issue is more global than global warming: everyone on the planet shares the same atmosphere" (166). Moreover, it should be noted that Stiglitz's profound environmental concerns motivated him to dedicate an entire chapter of *Making Globalization Work* to proposing proper economic incentives, such as a pollution tax, to combat this issue. In this section entitled "Saving the planet," the Nobel Laureate affirms, "Global warming is too great a threat to the well-being of our planet for us to just ignore the crisis and pray that a resolution will eventually emerge" (183). This passionate call to action resembles the efforts of ecocritics to cross traditional disciplinary boundaries.

In the apparent foundational text of ecocriticism in which he justifies his literary "experiment," William Rueckert (1978) asks the reader: "How can we move from the community of literature to the larger biospheric community which ecology tells us (correctly, I think) we belong to even as we are destroying it?" (85). Rueckert's alarming questions still remain unresolved decades later and the field that he launched continues to mature and diversify. In her essay entitled "The Hitchhiker's Guide to Ecocriticism," an eminent modern ecocritic Ursula Heise cites the "steadily increasing urgency of environmental problems for ever more closely interconnected societies around the globe" (505). Although Le Clézio is clearly aware of his limitations as a writer, as demonstrated in the "autocritique" sections of his novel *Le livre des fuites*, the author's deep ecological concerns echo those of Stiglitz, Rueckert, and Heise. In his analysis of the text *Terra Amata*, Roland Racevskis summarizes, "With its consistent attention to the most minute particularities of physical existence and its presentation of the concerted apprehension of these details as a new way to approach the earth, *Terra Amata* pursues this literary objective, inherited from the Renaissance, with the urgency of a late twentieth-century response to our society's potentially self-destructive detachment from Terra" (408). Similar to the frustration and anxiety expressed by other discontents of the global village, Le Clézio's narratives remind the reader that the status quo is not only inequitable and unjust, but it is also untenable from an environmental standpoint.

Furthermore, as Racevskis notes, an essential aspect of the Franco-Mauritian author's entire literary project is to (re)-conceptualize the relationship between humanity and the rest of the universe to which all material beings are inextricably linked as part of the same cosmic forces that originally created and which continue to sustain abundant life on this planet. Not only must we reunite the disciplines, as Thomas Dean suggests, but we must also reconnect ourselves to the natural world from which we originate in order to protect the cosmos from the destructive impulses of modernity that incessantly exploit its resources as mere commodities that reflect the maximization of profit. For this reason, Le Clézio's diverse protagonists often attempt to eliminate all of the artificial barriers which contemporary society has erected that imprison the modern subject in a sterile inauthentic universe in which he or she no longer has a direct primordial sensorial contact with other forms of matter.

In reference to the crucial role of the humanities in an increasingly interconnected and interdependent world that has wreaked havoc upon the earth, Kate Rigby declares,

> as our world becomes ever more ecologically impoverished [...] we need writers and artists who can draw our attention to the beauty, complexity and potential fragility of the earth, mediating the 'voices' of nonhuman others, whose being and meaning we can never fully comprehend, and, perhaps inviting us to join in their heteroglossic song (16).

In the landscape of contemporary French literature, it is perhaps Le Clézio who best concretizes this profound cosmic sensibility. The Nobel Laureate's varied narratives foster a more ecocentric way of thinking as they expose both the perils and limitations of homocentric logic. Moreover, texts such as *L'Extase Matérielle* and *Terra Amata* underscore the importance of ecological humility. Similar to all other sentient beings, the Franco-Mauritian writer reminds us that we are thrown into the chaos of existence through no choice of our own and for no apparent reason. All life forms endeavor to survive and to thrive in spite of the inherent mortality that is inscribed in the genetic code of each distinct species. Additionally, ecologically engaged and poignant works, such as *Pawana,* underscore the importance of protecting the delicate web which ensures that the natural cycle of life and death will continue. As Rigby correctly highlights, although a more intimate communion with the universe facilitates a greater understanding of an individual subject's place in the cosmic whole, the undeniable alterity of this sacred entity cannot be fully appropriated. Yet, in spite of the obstacles that prevent the human species from realizing a perfect marriage with the natural world, the path to spirituality and to a type of pragmatic knowledge for Le Clézio's protagonists entails reducing the distance that separates us from other particles of matter to the greatest extent possible.

In this specific exploration of how an evaporated dream could be (re)-envisioned to create a more egalitarian, harmonious, and sustainable global society through the lens of one of the most important contemporary authors of our time, chapter one will provide a conceptual framework for understanding the nuanced representations of globalization in Le Clézio's diverse literary repertoire. After delving into the original ambivalence of McLuhan's notion of a global village in addition to his misguided humanistic aspirations, the first chapter will examine the current state of the modern world using an interdisciplinary approach. Chapter two will focus on how the Franco-Mauritian author's narratives attempt to give a voice to marginalized and disenfranchised communities all across the planet. Elucidating Le Clézio's predilection to bear witness to injustices suffered by ethnic and moral minorities, Jean-Xavier Ridon affirms that the writer's works "sont habités par de nombreuses voix marginales, par des êtres qui semblent exclus de notre modernité [...] Le Clézio investit cette part d'ombre de notre époque où les identités minoritaires sont amenées à se taire" / 'are inhabited by many marginal voices, by people that seem to be excluded from modernity [...] Le Clézio exposes the ugly underbelly of our age where minorities are silenced' (39; my trans.). By highlighting the complexity and richness of indigenous cultures that are for the most part removed from the global conversation, Le Clézio valorizes the unique contributions of all civilizations insisting that an intercultural, authentic dialogue, grounded in mutual respect, could potentially benefit all of humanity. Moreover, the author decries the abuses of a capitalistic system in which unscrupulous individuals justify their exploitation of anything and everything for monetary profit.

Chapter three will explore Le Clézio's astute observations related to the pervasive ideology of consumerism that is indicative of the modern world. In reference to the materialistic values that define the contemporary global village, Langmann and Morris affirm, "Consumerism is the sustaining religion of globalization, the new opiate of the people with malls as their churches" (n.p.). Langmann and Morris reiterate that the mentality which maintains that the "goods life" is the ultimate path to happiness permeates Western society (n.p.). However, it is evident that for many of Le Clézio's protagonists, the endless pursuit of wealth and unbridled consumption does not provide them with any lasting appreciation of human existence or any deeper type of meaning. For this reason, Fredrik Westerlund describes the writer's early seminal works as a "critique mordante de notre société occidentale" / 'scathing critique of our western society' ("*Les Fleuves dans l'œuvre Romanesque*" 72; my trans.). Moreover, in the context of the first stage of Le Clézio's literary production, Claude Cavallero asserts, "Dans la mouvance du *pop art*— dont Le Clézio sent proche—l'époque était à la contestation, à la remise en cause du consumérisme, à la dénonciation outrée des maux de la société urbaine" / 'The *pop art* movement to which Le Clézio seems linked was a period that challenged and contested consumerism while indignantly denouncing the evils of urban society' ("J.M.G. Le Clézio et le sable des mots" 122; my trans.). Although many scholars have analyzed the profound transformation that occurs from the author's early narratives to his later texts, it should be noted that Le Clézio has never wavered in his concerns related to the eroding of traditional values by the hollow virtues of consumerism. This section will also investigate the intricate interconnected systems of hegemonic domination, such as the media, created by the corporate giants to sustain their supremacy.

Chapter four will probe the holistic nature of Le Clézio's de-centered humanism that extends to all other living creatures. By combating what he terms the "genesis myth," the author's fiction allows the reader to (re)-conceptualize a *post-materialist* world through the lens of philosophical materialism and cosmic humility. Similar to David Ehrenfeld in *The Arrogance of Humanism,* the Franco-Mauritian writer demystifies the universal values of Renaissance humanism and envisions a more biocentric ethic. The final chapter will explore forms of resistance to the aforementioned monolithic culture systematically imposed by conglomerates through the elaborate structures that they have created to ensure their continued governance of all corners of the globe. Despite the powerful forces of modernity that have already completely eradicated many minority languages and ways of life, some people are actively fighting back in the hope that another world is possible. In his recent text *Raga,* Le Clézio recounts the efforts of an indigenous community to maintain its autonomy and traditional identity in the face of globalization. However, the author unequivocally asserts that creolization/hybridity is a positive phenomenon given that every civilization has something to contribute to the entire human family. Finally, intercultural research also offers invaluable insights into the continuing struggle to create a more egalitarian, peaceful, and democratic global village.[3] As Le Clézio himself explains in a recent interview entitled "The World Has No Center" in the context of how human beings are able to empathize with others and the role of intercultural narratives in terms of honing this emotional faculty,

> I think that literature is essential because you create interculturality through imagination. Literature in the 21st century is the only place to understand the other, because literature is about compassion for humanity [...] I mean the capacity of understanding others and being aware of their connection to you. But, in order to be compassionate, one should be able to understand the human condition, to understand another culture's point of view, to see the meaningless of "otherness" (80–81).

In addition to the writer's undeniable compassion and respect for the downtrodden and their unique cultural contributions, this study will elucidate that Le Clézio's empathy and sincere effort to understand "the Other" extend to the entire biotic community.

## NOTES

1. See Zanganeh, Liza Azam. "Une œuvre mal comprise aux Etats-Unis." *Le Monde*, 11 October 2008: 23.
2. www.youtube.com/watch?v=S7Y8KgTdnzk.
3. A personal interview with Le Clézio entitled "Doubting Must Be the Beginning of Wisdom," in which the Nobel Laureate delves into all of the aforementioned issues at great length, serves as the postscript to this interdisciplinary study. On a personal note, I am truly grateful that the author was willing to take time out of his hectic schedule to meet with me at his personal residence in Albuquerque, New Mexico.

# ONE

# The "Global Village"

## *An Evaporated Dream Turned Nightmare*

### THE ORIGINAL AMBIVALENCE OF MCLUHAN'S VISION AND ITS EUPHORIC RECEPTION

The researcher Marshall McLuhan coined the term the "global village" in the 1960s to explain how technological advances would continue to place divergent cultures in intimate contact like never before. This notion would soon deeply resonate with both the general public and in academic circles. However, in spite of the initial enthusiasm related to this prediction, McLuhan was originally quite ambivalent concerning the significance of this term or what it could one day encompass. As Rico Lie affirms, "It is unclear what the origins are of this concept. It is also unclear what McLuhan actually meant by it" (57). This nebulous vision of a more closely interconnected and interdependent global society would also become indicative of larger humanistic aspirations related to a more just and egalitarian world. Many people expressed the sincere hope that the realization of this dream would even lead to a greater understanding and acceptance of other ways of life.

McLuhan's contention that traditional geographic boundaries would be effaced thereby thrusting a myriad of unique cultures into daily contact appears to have come to fruition. Underscoring the quotidian intercultural communication that is emblematic of contemporary society because of inventions such as the Internet and social media networks, Tracy Novinger asserts, "In our world of expanding technology and shrinking geography, people of different cultures have increasing frequency of contact" (ix). Echoing similar sentiments to those of the intercultural theorist Novinger, Calloway-Thomas, Cooper, and Blake note, "the global economy links people in desert and rural isolation in Mongolia via Worldwide Internet with those in urban areas of Minnesota" (174). Given the undeniable utility of certain devices that allow someone to interact with another person that lives on the other side of the world, the possibilities for meaningful dialogue in addition to economic and cultural exchange seem to be limitless.

Moreover, euphorically announcing the dawning of a new era, the mainstream media associated McLuhan's vision with the neoliberal fallacy that deregulated free enterprise would create a new society that would benefit all of humanity. Articulating both this fervor and the appropriation of this dream by transnational conglomerates wishing to extend their domination to the furthest reaches of the globe, Richard Pickard explains, "The international media simply does not tire of telling us that the world is metaphorically shrinking, that the grandest predictions of Marshall McLuhan are coming to pass in our time. The media's membership in multinational corporate society is of course the impulse toward this shrinking, so such enthusiasm is hardly surprising" (95). As Pickard clearly underscores, increasing corporate ownership of the mass media casts little doubt upon the true intentions of such messages. Given that international corporations have derived unprecedented profits from the inception of a worldwide market, they logically attempt to control public perception of the powerful forces of globalization that have impacted the entire planet.[1]

## FULFILLMENT OF A PROPHECY AND THE CRUSHING WEIGHT OF REALITY: CONCEPTUALIZING THE CURRENT SITUATION FROM AN INTERDISCIPLINARY PERSPECTIVE

Although perhaps everyone agrees with Pickard's assertion that the global village has indeed become a reality, the alleged shared benefits of this interwoven and diverse community are in question. In other words, even if modern technology quite literally places the entire world at one's fingertips, this phenomenon is not necessarily a benevolent force from a social or economic standpoint. Indeed, a considerable amount of research suggests that financial inequalities and ethnic discrimination have only continued to intensify as traditional boundaries have been erased. For this reason, researchers like Claudia von Werlhof and Samir Amin have speculated that contemporary capitalism and its values are in crisis.

This mentality, grounded in studies that reflect disconcerting trends, explains the increasing skepticism and even cynicism of theorists that examine the nefarious effects of the actualization of the global village. Summarizing his initial fears related to McLuhan's evaporated dream, Dean Barnlund ponders,

> What is in doubt is whether the erosion of cultural boundaries through technology will bring the realization of a dream or a nightmare. Will a global village be a mere collection or a true community of men? Will its residents be neighbors capable of respecting and utilizing their differences, or clusters of strangers living in ghettos and united only in their antipathies for others? (27).

After carefully analyzing the state of the modern world, Barnlund concludes, "events of recent decades provide little basis for optimism. Increasing physical proximity has brought no millennium in human relations. If anything, it has appeared to intensify the divisions among people rather than to create a broader intimacy" (27). Although the romantic universalism espoused by McLuhan and promoted by the media is appealing, it does not correspond to the dire conditions of the marginalized and disenfranchised inhabitants of the global community. In fact, neoliberal globalization has created a far greater disparity between an ever shrinking affluent minority that controls nearly all of the capital and those whose aspirations are deliberately and systemically stifled beneath a glass ceiling. Furthermore, as Barnlund notes, intimate, intercultural relationships, fostered by the development of a veritable world economy, have perhaps even created more prejudice, intolerance, and injustice.

Reiterating Barnlund's frank assessment concerning the disquieting realities of the current situation, Tracy Novinger underscores, "Our global village is turning out to be an unstable and often unfriendly place, with ethnic nationalisms taking center stage [...] Individuals and organizations struggle to cope with problems in living and working with people of other cultures on a daily basis" (8). Similar to other intercultural theorists, Novinger wonders if the world was prepared for these types of quotidian encounters. It is perhaps naïve to assume that merely placing people in an atmosphere in which they are forced to confront fundamental cultural differences will automatically create a more harmonious human family. The concerted efforts of multinational corporations to train their employees in "intercultural sensitivity" concretize the failure of such presumptions.

In her article entitled "We Are Not the World," Sue-Im Lee highlights the resistance to the universal logic of the global village that now permeates contemporary literature. In reference to the aforementioned unity that was supposed to arise from McLuhan's humanistic vision, Lee states,

> The best encapsulation of the globalist "we" is [...] the concept of the "global village." Since Marshall McLuhan famously used the term in the 1960s to foreshadow a new world order, one in which the electronic communications medium overcomes and diminishes the physical and temporal distance that separates the world's inhabitants, "global village" has been the dominant term for expressing a global coexistence altered by transnational commerce, migration, and culture (502).

After elucidating what McLuhan's notion now symbolizes in its everyday sociolinguistic usage, Lee importantly notes that "interdependence is certainly no guarantor of equitable relationship" (512). Although many people living in developing countries have little choice but to participate in the global village in order to survive, those who suffer from acute poverty are often exploited as a mere commodity by transnational entities that seek to maximize profits by means of cheap manual labor. This debasement of humanity is antithetical to the idealism which posited that the quality of everyone's life would improve because of the interconnectedness that is emblematic of the global financial system. Although the most prosperous countries and the world's elite might depend on the continued and incessant manipulation of the disadvantaged inhabitants of this planet for the realization of their materialistic aspirations, this relationship is characterized by unequal relations of power. For the marginalized members of human society, McLuhan's dream is more like an ironic caricature that feeds rapacious consumerist desires and justifies the exploitation of the weak by those who have access to certain privileges at the expense of the Other. As this study will establish and as the author readily admits in his Nobel acceptance speech, a major aspect of Le Clézio's literary project is to give a voice to disenfranchised individuals that have been silenced by the ruling majority which the author describes as the "happy few." By posing alarming questions, the Franco-Mauritian writer denounces those who claim to represent all of humanity and to possess definitive answers to the major issues that all cultures must confront together.

The profound concerns of intercultural theorists such as Barnlund and Novinger in addition to those expressed by J.M.G. Le Clézio in his diverse fiction explain why the initial enthusiasm related to the notion of a global village has waned given the unpleasant realities of the current situation. Although globalization was theoretically supposed to unite the entire human family, violent protests, such as the one in Seattle organized in opposition to the World Trade Organization in November 1999 and the various "Occupy" movements, concretize the uneven and undemocratic profits generated by the major conglomerates that dominate the contemporary economic landscape. As the giants of industry have been growing expeditiously, acute poverty has also drastically increased in both third-world and developed countries. For this reason, even mainstream economic theorists, such as the 2001 Nobel Laureate in Economics Joseph Stiglitz, have noted that neoliberal globalization has not "delivered the goods," but rather it has created a more elitist society that serves the interests of a tiny sliver of the population (Koechlin 258). Stiglitz also reiterates that the global economic system, as it is currently being managed by the world superpowers and organizations such as the International Monetary Fund and the World Bank, is an undeniable disenfranchisement to an alarming number of people that are not even granted access to basic needs like health care and education while transnational corporations are reaping record profits. The nightmare scenario envisioned by intercultural theorists, such as Dean Barnlund, is becoming more painfully evident and difficult to ignore.

Although Stiglitz is a renowned lifelong economist that has held numerous important public offices for politicians such as Bill Clinton, many of his works, such as *Globalization and Its Discontents* and *Making Globalization Work,* have a humanistic tone which is similar to that of several of Le Clézio's narratives. Highlighting that the global village as it is currently being mismanaged by a miniscule social elite to maintain their privileges is both unjust and undemocratic, Stiglitz, like many artists, exposes and decries the deliberate and systematic exploitation of the majority of humanity for the benefit of a few. For this reason, Kaushik Basu describes *Globalization and Its Discontents* as "a diatribe against the injustices of global finance and politics [...] this too is a book where an academic [...] cuts loose from the binds of his discipline and assesses the world with passion, concern, and also disappointment" (885). In addition to emphasizing the interdisciplinary nature of Stiglitz's efforts to foster a dialogue related to the greatest issues faced by human beings across the planet, Basu also underscores that the Nobel Laureate is "popular globally for championing the cause of the disadvantaged and dispossessed" (885). As the next chapter will establish, this predilection to denounce human exploitation and social injustice also pervades Le Clézio's fiction.

Whereas the Franco-Mauritian author does not propose any solutions related to the complex phenomenon of globalization, Stiglitz outlines possible alternatives that could improve the quality of life for billions of people around the world based on sound economic principles. As Basu notes, "while he lashes out at market fundamentalism he is fully aware of and never downplays the importance of markets and incentives [...] he makes it clear that he is no anti-globalizer" (886). In the last section of *Globalization and Its Discontents* entitled "Toward a Globalization with a More Human Face," Stiglitz clarifies his nuanced position as follows: "Today, Globalization is being challenged around the world. There is discontent with globalization, and rightfully so. Globalization can be a force for good [...] But for millions of people, globalization has not worked. Many have actually been made worse off" (248). As this passage clearly illustrates, Stiglitz's impulse to write is motivated by both his hopes and frustrations related to globalization and the future of the human race. In this vein, similar sentiments of injustice, affirmations of hope, and a valorization of the dignity of human life compel both Stiglitz and Le Clézio to voice their unsettling concerns, albeit in different contexts.

In stark contrast to many other economists that analyze the strengths and weaknesses of markets in a detached and purely analytical fashion that is divorced from larger humanistic questions, the academic discipline of economics appears to be inseparable from fundamental ethical principles for Stiglitz. In the preface to *Globalization and Its Discontents,* Stiglitz explains, "Economics may seem like a dry, esoteric subject but, in fact, good economic policies have the power to change the lives of these poor people" (xi). Given the nature of such declarations, Basu labels *Globalization and Its Discontents* as "Stiglitz's breaking rank with the establishment" in addition to a "morally courageous book, one in which the author does not flinch from taking on the powerful and the established" (886; 899). For Stiglitz, the fact that a privileged minority lives in the lap of luxury while millions of others are vulnerable to starvation on a daily basis is morally unacceptable.

Likewise, Le Clézio's fiction, public discourses, and recent initiatives such as the *Fondation pour l'interculturel et la paix,* reflect these same concerns. However, a salient difference exists between their respective humanistic projects. Whereas Stiglitz expresses his disdain for the manner in which world markets have been managed and proposes significant changes to the system that will more equitably distribute the benefits of globalization thereby reducing human anguish, Le Clézio is clearly cognizant of his limitations as an artist. In an affirmation of both his sincere desire to help those that suffer from famine and his understanding of the frustrations of the literary profession, the author confesses in *L'Extase Matérielle,* "Les pauvres m' émeuvent [...] Que faire pour eux? Qui sont-ils? Comment partager leurs souffrances [...] Y a-t-il vraiment quelque chose à faire pour les autres [...] Et pourtant, quand je les rencontre à l'improviste, dans la rue, ou quand je les trouve endormis à côté des poubelles, hommes et femmes pareils à de vieux sacs troués, j'ai honte" / 'Poor people move me [...] What to do for them? Who are they? How (can I) share their suffering? [...] Can we really do anything for others? And nevertheless, when I encounter them by chance on the street or when I find them asleep next to trash cans, men and women like old garbage bags with holes, I am ashamed' (75–76; my trans.).

Moreover, in *Le Livre des Fuites,* the writer undermines the significance of the novel itself in the "autocritique" / 'autocriticism' sections. After pondering "Est-ce que cela valait vraiment la peine d'écrire tout ça [...] Je veux dire, où était la nécessité, l'urgence de ce livre [...]" / ' Was it really worth writing all that [...] I mean, where was the necessity, the urgency of this book,' the author repugnantly groans, "Est-ce que j'écris pour les hommes, ou bien pour les mouches?" / ' Am I writing for human beings, or for flies' (54–57; 58–61). Despite Le Clézio's undeniable skepticism concerning the role of literature in society that resembles the pervasive cynicism of Stig Dagerman, his narratives bear witness to crimes against humanity that are never questioned in the modern world. As this study will attempt to elucidate, perhaps a veritable interdisciplinary dialogue that combines the contributions of those that expose and draw attention to injustice and those which endeavor to offer possible solutions to multifaceted problems that plague contemporary society is the first step in imagining a better world.

Many other researchers from divergent disciplines also agree with Stiglitz's contention in *Making Globalization Work* that "For much of the world, globalization as it has been managed seems like a pact with the devil. A few people in the country become wealthier [...] but ways of life and basic values are threatened" (292). In a scathing indictment of market fundamentalism which has created a society in which inequality abounds, Jodi Dean affirms, "neoliberalism is an economic and political program benefiting the top 1 percent of the world's population as it sends billions into poverty" (67). Echoing Dean's astute observations, Ian Boyd and Margaret Boyd assert that globalization, at least in its current shape, "builds paths to the top for some and digs holes for others" (125). Robin Leichenko and William Solecki [2] also express similar sentiments concerning the inability of neoliberal globalization to keep its promise that it would eventually create a society in which everyone would derive immense benefit from its financial system.

Similar to Dean, Claudia von Werlhof summarizes the unequal distribution of power and privilege that is indicative of the contemporary global village as follows: "While a tiny minority reaps enormous benefits from today's economic liberalism, the vast majority of the earth's human and non-human population, and the earth itself, suffer hardship to an extent that puts their very survival at risk" (94). Although the gross domestic product (GDP) of many developed countries has exploded since the inception of policies that emphasize free market capitalism, it should be noted that this wealth is now concentrated in fewer hands than ever before. This disturbing trend explains why poverty is on the rise as corporations laugh all the way to the bank. Moreover, as von Werlhof notes, the current financial system does not just exploit humanity, but it also places a material value on the entire cosmos.

In his brief essay entitled "The Fall: Original Sin and Free-Market Capitalism," William Pfaff not only reiterates the failure of neoliberalism in terms of maximizing prosperity, but he also explains why this outdated ideology remains so pervasive in Western society. As Pfaff asserts,

> Unregulated free-market capitalism may be said to have killed itself by greed, vanity, and excess, all amply evident before and at the death scene. But the ultimate guilt must be attributed to the vacuity and perversity of market ideology, which contradicts human nature. In this, it exactly resembles the U.S. foreign-policy ideology that democracy will eventually triumph over all else. Regrettably, this is an illusion, clung to in political, academic, and government circles. It is stubbornly adhered to because everyone would like to think it's true, since it's very reassuring to Americans and an uplifting idea (7).

Pfaff underscores that although it is a romantic notion to believe that Adam Smith's invisible hand will magically steer us into the direction that most benefits all of humanity, there is no evidence that this imaginary supernatural force even exists at all. Furthermore, without proper regulations to protect those at the bottom of the social ladder from continued exploitation by the elite, the alarming gap between the rich and poor will continue to grow expeditiously.

In *Globalization and Its Discontents*, Stiglitz deconstructs another comforting ideological notion that has dictated American-style capitalism since the 1980s. In an effort to justify the morally reprehensible financial inequalities generated by neoliberal practices, the doctrine of "trickle-down economics" was born. As Stiglitz explains, "many of its proponents would argue that the best way to help the poor is to make the economy grow [...] Eventually, it is asserted, the benefits of that growth trickle down even to the poor" (78). Although this logic still garners much support amongst the general public and is supported by the titans of industry that control the media, this ungrounded, misplaced faith has been thoroughly debunked. Noting how the quality of life for the average American began to erode due to excessive deregulation, Stiglitz elucidates, "Growth in America in the 1980s provided the most recent dramatic example: while the economy grew, those at the bottom saw their real incomes decline" (78). Moreover, in an assertion that is reminiscent of Rousseau, Stiglitz adds, "Part of the social contract entails 'fairness' that the poor share in the gains of society as it grows, and that the rich share in the pains of society in times of crisis" (78). As the recent government bailouts related to the global recession confirm, the concept of social justice appears to be entirely removed from the neoliberal agenda. Offering a concrete example of this indifference in the context of the earlier East Asia Crisis, Stiglitz muses, "It just 'happened' that the IMF was able to find $150 billion to bail out the banks but could not find $1 billion for food subsidies for the people who were thrown out of jobs" ("Globalization and the Economic Role" 10). This decision reflects the priorities of those that control the global financial system and which manipulate the masses by means of effective propaganda that reinforces their dominance.

Given all of his aforementioned deep concerns related to the state of the global village, it is hardly a surprise that Stiglitz concludes both *Globalization and Its Discontents* and *Making Globalization Work* with an ethical summons to action that he extends to the reader. This attempt to appeal to the affective sensibilities of the public after exposing injustice and human suffering is reminiscent of the literary projects of many contemporary authors including Le Clézio. However, it should be noted that Stiglitz's apprehension related to globalization leaves little room for interpretation in comparison to a novel, short story, or a poem. Urging the reader to no longer be complacent and complicit in the current exploitative financial system that debases much of humanity, Stiglitz adamantly declares, "If we are to address the legitimate concerns of those who have expressed a discontent with globalization, if we are to make globalization work for the billions of people for whom it has not, if we are to make globalization with a human face succeed, then our voices must be raised. We cannot, we should not, stand idly by"[3] (252). As Stiglitz expresses, those that find themselves in a privileged position need to muster the courage to speak for those that have been silenced and therefore cannot protect themselves. For the same reasons that many artists have used a pen or a brush, Stiglitz articulates his anxiety related to the desperate situation in which many men, women, and children find themselves in this interconnected and interdependent world.

In addition to the harsh realities that so-called common citizens of a given country must confront which explain why the euphoria related to McLuhan's misguided humanistic dream, appropriated and lauded by supporters of neoliberalism, has vanished, a plethora of researchers from many distinct disciplines have noted that the global village is an even more unwelcoming place for immigrants in search of a better life. Upon their arrival in the host country, both legal and irregular immigrants often discover that the "promised land" is more like a private country club reserved for the "happy few." After scrutinizing "McLuhan's much celebrated liberal idea of the 'global village,'" Pauline Barber reaches the following conclusion, "In the first instance, globalization is not global, its processes are uneven" (207). Given that the only gainful employment which is often available to immigrants seeking more prosperity and security in the developed world offers little monetary compensation or material comfort, these disenfranchised individuals often lead a very precarious existence that marks them as easy prey for human exploitation. In exchange for long hours of sometimes physically debilitating manual labor, immigrants typically receive a miniscule salary that prevents them from starving but forces them to live in the same type of deplorable conditions that they were trying to escape in their country of origin. After denouncing "the grim working conditions of migrant domestic workers who take care of the world's 'dirty work,'" Barber also posits that "Migrants working overseas are often situated in a different, usually hostile culture resulting in an ethnically charged social environment" (209; 210). Not only do immigrants struggle to survive in unfamiliar cultural settings by performing necessary tasks that no one else is willing to do, but they also face xenophobia, prejudice, and ignorance that prevents easy integration into a new society. Although corporations deliberately exploit their vulnerability to maximize profits for shareholders, immigrants rarely receive a fair share of the wealth that is almost entirely funneled to the top. Moreover, instead of being recognized for their invaluable contributions to the global financial system, immigrants are often used as scapegoats for social, political, and economic problems that plague a given country.

In his meticulous exploration and categorization of diverse migrant populations, Stephen Castles identifies the same fundamental ethical issues as Barber. After affirming that "International migration is an integral part of globalization," Castles describes what he terms a "migration industry" comprised of "recruitment organizations, lawyers, agents, smugglers and other middle people. Such people can be helpers and exploiters of migrants" (271; 272). Whereas certain individuals wish to help these uprooted diasporic communities, less scrupulous people and especially corporate entities are waiting to line their own personal pockets with the sweat and tears of the disenfranchised. Although many migrants are aware that they are being taken advantage of by their employer, they often have little recourse but to accept the indignities that are imposed upon them. Explaining the dire predicament of both migrant and traditional immigrant workers that must in essence tolerate all sorts of inhumane treatment, Castles remarks, "Even legal immigrants are so dependent on finding and keeping employment that they hesitate to complain about abuses" (276). Moreover, even if displaced individuals that find themselves in a hostile environment wanted to decry this injustice, it is unlikely that anyone would be willing to listen. As Dean Barnlund and others originally feared, illustrated by their skepticism related to the humanistic vision associated with the concept of the global village, the intimate contact facilitated by the processes of globalization has not created a more understanding and compassionate human family.

Confirming that Barnlund's disconcerting questions have been answered and deconstructing neoliberal fallacies of a utopia in which everyone's quality of life improves because of the implementation of free market ideology, Piyasiri Wickramasekara cites the urgency of creating "a truly global labour market that can deliver the promised win-win scenarios" (1261). Similar to Barber and Castles, Wickramasekara notes that "Above all, irregular immigration is a protection problem, since migrant workers become vulnerable to extreme violations of their human and labour rights" (1253). Given that companies which exploit disenfranchised individuals are able to undercut other business thereby gaining an edge in the market because of the almost nonexistent salaries that migrants are forced to accept, little motivation exists to alter the current status quo. As Wickramasekara explains, "It is a problem of unfair competition as well, with advantages going to enterprises using workers in irregular status at cheap wages" (1253).

In her essay entitled "Ethical Capitalism and Its Cultural Logic," Nicki Cole notes that capitalism has always thrived because of its propensity to justify the incessant appropriation of anyone and everything for monetary profit. It is perhaps in this context that the unfounded doctrine of trickle-down economic ideology should be understood. Skillfully manipulating the masses into believing the notion that they should accept the rare crumbs that fall from the table of luxury at which the privileged few enjoy the fruits of their sumptuous feast is perhaps a logical continuation of the history of wide scale human exploitation that includes slavery, colonialism, and sweatshops. As Cole elucidates, "Capitalism was built on the backs of slave labor and nearly slave labor across the globe [...] This fact is alive today in the composition of the global population of poor people, and also in the way in which they are addressed and dealt with by those in power in the world" (n.p.). When one form of exploitation, such as slavery or colonialism, is deemed illegal, capitalism will always find something or someone else to fill this void. For this reason, Gayatri Spivak condemns the very notion of the global village as nothing more than "colonialism's newest trick" (qtd. in Lee 506). It appears that immigrants, documented or otherwise, have become the contemporary emblematic figure of human exploitation.

In the context of Le Clézio's narratives, such as *Désert*, *Poisson d'or*, "Fantômes dans la rue," and "le passeur," chapter two will highlight the evolution of this phenomenon. As these poignant texts underscore, instead of finding opulence and material comfort at their fingertips, a glass ceiling often prevents immigrants from escaping harsh and violent living conditions in urban ghettos, exploitative hiring practices, racism, ignorance, and xenophobia. Despite the materialization of McLuhan's prediction that the world would become more intertwined than ever before, immigrants often realize that the global village is not always a friendly place willing to share its prosperity with others. It is even more difficult for clandestine immigrants to be accepted and to thrive in a foreign environment which is distrustful of their very presence.

As Bruno Thibault notes in his analysis of the profound philosophical, spiritual, and social alienation of Le Clézio's first protagonist Adam Pollo, "le pessimisme de Le Clézio est évident dans la conclusion du *Procès-Verbal*" / 'Le Clézio's pessimism is evident in the conclusion of *The Interrogation*' ("Le Chant de l'Abîme" 42; my trans.). The pessimism to which Thibault refers is the crisis of the self that the modern subject experiences which often compels the writer's diverse protagonists to flee modern society in search of an alternative lifestyle. Le Clézio's characters often suffer from the artificial barriers that the modern world has erected which separate humanity from the rest of the cosmos. Given their profound sentiments of detachment from the material universe that creates and sustains all life, human and otherwise, the author's characters often struggle to free themselves from both the ontological shell of being and the inauthentic nature of modern civilization in an attempt to understand their small place in the cosmic whole more fully.

The anguish of many Leclézian protagonists, ensnared in a complex manufactured labyrinth and uprooted from their original source of happiness, is indicative of the phenomenon of urban dystopia outlined by other contemporary writers. Describing this trauma expressed by modern literary narratives, Joan Hamilton elucidates, "Only when mechanization began to sever our ties with nature did writers invent new forms to try to repair the damage" (n.p.).[4] As Leichenko, Solecki, and numerous other researchers have documented, it should also be noted that the ongoing processes of globalization are inseparable from those of urbanization. Revealing statistics that confirm this hypothesis, Leichenko and Solecki affirm, "According to most estimates, more than half the world's population already lives in cities [...] individuals are leaving the rural countryside [...] in pursuit of a better quality of life [...] heightened by the potential of gaining access to consumer goods associated with globalization" (244). Yet, the reality that numerous Leclézian protagonists discover is paradoxical to these materialistic aspirations as they are condemned to live in sinister ghettos that are characterized by destitution, desperation, and violence. The unfortunate individuals that reside in these urban spaces across the globe give testament to the fact that the neoliberal dream is more like a narcissistic fantasy that justifies and minimizes gross inequalities. Additionally, free market ideology dogmatically attempts to eliminate the possibility of meaningful reform to the financial system. As von Werlhof affirms,

> For a good twenty years now we have been told that there is no alternative to neoliberal globalization and that in fact, none is needed [...] Some go so far as to suggest that neoliberalism and its globalization—meaning a specific economic system that developed within specific socio-historical circumstances—is nothing less than a law of nature. In turn, "human nature" is supposedly reflected by the characteristics of this economic system: egotistical, ruthless, greedy and cold. This, we are told, works toward everyone's benefit (94).

For many of Le Clézio's protagonists that suffer from abject poverty, neoliberal globalization has failed to create the promised "win-win" situation in Wickramasekara's terms. For this reason, many of the author's protagonists are indigenous peoples for whom the global village appears to have little to offer as they continue to live as they have for generations in harmony with the natural world. Moreover, although numerous Leclézian protagonists reside in metropolitan areas, the majority of these individuals live on the periphery of a society for which they have much disdain.

However, as chapter five will investigate, it is perhaps Le Clézio's most recent texts, such as *Raga* and *Ourania* that offer the most realistic viable alternatives for re-envisioning a more humane global community. Furthermore, these narratives are indicative of the anti-globalization movement that continues to gain momentum in the face of harsh realities that are becoming more difficult for the shielded elite to conceal. Michael Bosia underscores that organized opposition to globalization did not end with the aforementioned Seattle protests. Indeed, it continues to mount in both prosperous countries and in the developing world, as evidenced by the global nature of the "Occupy" movements. As Bosia elucidates, "the contest over globalization and its alternatives, or *altermondialisation,* has produced in France one of the most powerful movements of the alternative Left, often with a politics hostile to neocolonialism" (70–71). Bosia highlights the efforts of associations, such as Act Up Paris and the ATTAC, in addition to those of political figures like José Bové to ensure that all citizens of France including legal and clandestine immigrants have access to basic needs like health care. These endeavors concretize the fact that the neoliberal ideology which drives globalization has undoubtedly disenfranchised far too many people across the entire planet. Moreover, given the gravity of the situation that continues to deteriorate, many people refuse to accept the notion that no alternatives are possible as they actively endeavor to explore other options that could deliver more egalitarian results.

## DEMYSTIFYING NEOLIBERAL MYTHS RELATED TO PROSPERITY AND HAPPINESS

The neoliberal view of happiness posits that contentment is the personal concern of each individual. As long as a given autonomous agent possesses everything that he or she desires, there is little motivation to worry about anyone else. As Grant Duncan underscores in his investigation of the attainment of "happiness in an age of advanced consumer capitalism," "The neoliberal version of deregulation and globalization relied more on the heritage of Adam Smith and Friedrich von Hayek who see justice as liberty and policy as the maximization of economic efficiency. Happiness for them is the private concern of the individual" (85; 105). This self-centered and egotistical mentality has resulted in the creation of a superficial, materialistic society in which the accumulation of monetary wealth is the only "virtue" that is valorized.

However, the so-called modern man does not always derive pleasure from the incessant pursuit of these hollow values. Based on data obtained from the emerging field of happiness research, Duncan asserts,

> Recent research on happiness has modified the notion that the individual is always the best judge of what maximizes his or her own welfare, finding that people frequently mis-predict the utility to be derived from future income or consumption […] Happiness researchers thus characterize the materialistic culture of affluent societies as an economic treadmill, driven largely by social comparisons and status envy, but not necessarily leading to anyone's benefit (97–98).

For this reason, Le Clézio's protagonists often flee the modern world in search of a more harmonious and authentic existence. Many of the Franco-Mauritian writer's characters, such as Alexis in *Le Chercheur d'or*, discover that other natural treasures far outweigh the ephemeral riches for which they had been previously longing. After wasting years of his life engaged in the chimerical quest to unearth the unknown Corsaire's treasure, Alexis is finally struck by the epiphany that he has failed to value what is truly important. Likewise, Lalla in *Désert* will ultimately reject the possibility of both fame and fortune in the modern world, as she chooses to return to the Sahara desert and to resist integration into the global village.[5]

Highlighting another reason why discontents of globalization endeavor to modify or even to escape entirely from mainstream society, Duncan notes, "One of the features of happiness in the modern era [...] is the ideal that happiness is and should be attainable by everyone—and a certain sense of injustice if it appears that not everyone reports improved happiness" (86). Recent protests against the governing agencies that manage the worldwide financial system and anti-globalization efforts reflect this philosophical principle which is at the core of the social fabric in many affluent cultures. Moreover, increasing global social inequalities and restricted access to basic needs, such as health care and education, explain the profound malaise that is at the heart of demands for drastic reform of the current financial system.

Duncan and other researchers also assert that the neoliberal definition of happiness is inseparable from consumerism. Underscoring ideological messages in Western society for a subject to "consume" and to "desire more," Duncan explains, "Capitalism, rather than providing for happiness and satisfaction, manufactures an ever-widening field of desire and innovative ways in which commodities create invidious distinctions, and hence ever-widening gulfs of resentment, dissatisfaction and anxiety" (95). Given that success is almost entirely defined by the amount of material possessions that a person owns in Western society, this pervasive mentality creates a voracious appetite that is never appeased. This cancerous attitude which erodes traditional values explains the unhealthy competition that urges each individual to "keep up with the Joneses" in a conditioned, misguided effort to maximize one's happiness.

In her examination of "Y generation" attitudes related to basic questions of consumption and sustainability, Margee Hume also underscores the relationship between neoliberal ideology and the indoctrination of the masses by consumerist propaganda. Hume offers the following definition, "Consumerism is a term used to describe the effects of gathering and purchasing material possessions to increase happiness and social position" (386). Similar to Duncan, Hume affirms that Western culture propagates the simplistic notion that frivolous spending and acquiring all of the latest luxury items will automatically translate into greater happiness. Moreover, Hume reiterates that children in prosperous, materialistic societies are imprinted by birth with this zeal to garner respect in the community in which they live by possessing more than their fellow citizens.

Echoing the concerns of Duncan and Hume in reference to the exportation of the American suburban dream throughout the entire global village, Leichenko and Solecki underline,

> This package of a new and better life is also increasingly linked to the ultimate expression of one's consumer aspirations [...] this vision which Sklair (2002) terms the "ideology of consumption" is not only received by emerging middle-income urban inhabitants [...] but also by poorer urban residents and inhabitants of many remote rural areas, who receive these images via Western television programming and other forms of mass media (246).

As Leichenko and Solecki note, the shallow, superficial values of consumerist ideology are being sold to the entire world by idealistic images of products that place luxury within everyone's reach. In the context of developing economies, Leichenko and Solecki maintain, however, that "At present, achieving this 'better life' is a reality for only a small [...] percentage of LDC[6] residents (typically less than 10 percent)" (246). Although globalization is a phenomenon that has perhaps touched the entire planet, its processes are not truly "global" because they are quite uneven as evidenced by the research conducted by contemporary economists such as Stiglitz. The ideology of consumption might be seductive, but its messages resemble the sardonic farce of dangling a carrot in front of a starving person by a string given that these romantic fantasies are illusory and inaccessible for billions of people.

Despite fundamental issues related to inequality and injustice that are emblematic of both affluent countries and the developing world, as highlighted by Leichenko and Solecki, Robert Sack observes that consumerism is inseparable from the ongoing effects of globalization. Underscoring this undeniable reality, Sack affirms, "We live by consuming mass-produced goods whether we wish to or not. We are consumers in a consumer society" (643). In this same essay entitled "A Consumer's World: Place as Context," Sack asserts that the modern world is comprised of bureaucratic, consumer republics whose main function is to regulate and promote consumption. Offering a concrete example of the pervasive ideology of consumption that is intertwined with the neoliberal view of happiness, Dannagal Young notes that "In post–September 11 America, consumers were often confronted with messages urging them to consume for the explicit purpose of strengthening the U.S. economy [...] President Bush publicly issued statements encouraging Americans to travel, to fly, and to spend" (50). Instead of purely mourning the victims of this great tragedy, American politicians and the conglomerates that control the mainstream media informed U.S. citizens that perhaps their most important duty of all was to purchase mass-produced goods. This public appeal for frivolous spending during such a time of tremendous loss essentially proves Lizabeth Cohen's theories related to what she terms a "consumer republic." According to Cohen, the global financial system is predicated upon the premise that the incessant cycle of fulfilling materialistic, hedonistic desires must never be interrupted.

As Duncan, Hume, Leichenko, Solecki, Sack, and Young have all noted, the historian Gary Cross's assertion that "consumerism was the 'ism' that won" rings more true with each passing day in a more compact world in which the neoliberal dream has been appropriated by billions of people around the globe that wish to live the idealistic images which inundate their television and computer screens (qtd. in Young 51). Similar to Young, Wan-Hsiu Sunny Tsai has astutely observed and documented the relationship between patriotic propaganda and the ideology of consumption. Summarizing the findings of a qualitative study entitled "Advertising and the Patriotic Consumer Citizen," Tsai explains, "Consumerism constitutes a main vehicle for affirming one's citizenship [...] In general, American consumers tend to believe that consumption has collective, cumulative, and positive impacts on the demand-driven economy, while saving is downplayed as an individualistic matter unlikely to benefit the economy" (43). The data derived from Tsai's interviews confirms Cohen's hypotheses related to what she terms a "citizen consumer" or a "purchaser consumer." According to consumerist logic, not only does the endless acquisition of the latest mass-produced goods translate into a more luxurious lifestyle, but it also stimulates the economy allowing others to experience the same material comforts. The unequivocal messages of the mainstream media, dominated by powerful conglomerates, constantly reinforce the notion that self-indulgent spending is a philanthropic act that benefits society. For this reason, the model citizen purchases newer versions of the same gadgets that he or she already possesses in addition to acquiring the latest technology in an effort to improve his or her own existence and to contribute to a healthy and stable financial system.

Similar to Young, Greg Dickinson explores the ideological discourse related to consumerism and civic responsibility that followed the September 11th tragedy. In the weeks after the terrorist attack, Dickinson observes, "In the wake of September 11, 2011 corporations moved swiftly to assert the relation between consumption and citizenship [...] Advertisers utilized this identification to argue that enacting consumption was a central mode of practicing patriotic citizenship. The advertisements [...] served to create consumer citizens through the civic duty of shopping" (271). It should be noted that Dickinson and many other researchers have identified transnational corporations as the driving force of modernity and its global economy.

Moreover, Dickinson underscores the ethical dilemma of the predominant worldwide conglomerates in the days that immediately followed September 11th. Multinational businesses were placed in the difficult predicament of promoting consumption that would keep the monetary cycle flowing without offending the delicate sensibilities of shell-shocked Americans during a period of tremendous distress and uncertainty. As Dickinson elucidates,

> Advertisers faced particular difficulties in confronting the post–September 11 environment. Shopping in the context of the life altering, mortal attack seemed a banal and selfish action. Selling seemed in even worse taste [...] At the same time, consumption was and is crucial to maintain the health of advertisers specifically and the economy more generally, a point eventually acknowledged explicitly in buy-American and travel more campaigns. How corporations responded to the attacks was crucial to not offending taste while keeping the dollars flowing (272).

In a climate of paranoia and fear, advertisers had to express an image of unity in the face of disaster in addition to restoring consumer confidence which was vital in order to avoid an economic landslide. A clever and calculated ruse allowed transnational corporations to express their sense of loss and solidarity while simultaneously encouraging consumption. Suddenly every major business was now selling images of the American flag to a public in need of articulating its anguish. As Dickinson explains, "Buying and wearing images of the flag became one way of being patriotic. This patriotism is enhanced by the fact that a portion of the proceeds from the purchases is donated to relief efforts" (280). Dickinson's concrete example illustrates that the ideology of consumption deliberately attempts to create citizen consumers that are guided by an incessant impulse to purchase. When presented with a moral or simply a pragmatic obstacle, capitalism will create what it deems to be an appropriate outlet for consumption which will allow consumers to express their sense of pride and belonging to a given culture. Given that the commerce of death in the form of exorbitant funeral expenses is a billion dollar industry, it should come as no surprise that nothing is sacred in a global village controlled by corporate titans that are willing to exploit anyone and everything for monetary profit including human misery.

Echoing the concerns of Duncan, Hume, Leichenko, Solecki, Sack, Young, and Dickinson, Langman and Morris affirm that "While globalization is the dominant hegemon of the present age, consumerism has become the basis of its wealth" (n.p.). As Langman and Morris establish, globalization is inseparable from the ideology of consumerism because the world is becoming more interconnected and interdependent due to the continuing expansion of multinational corporations. Similar to Young and Dickinson, Langman and Morris also reiterate that "consumerism is one of the major means through which hegemonic ideologies are promulgated. Advertising is designed to directly encourage consumption, while much of the media representations of reality directly affirm the superiority of the 'goods life' achieved through that buying" (n.p.). Like Duncan, Langman and Morris note that the images of happiness and success portrayed by the mainstream media and in popular culture reinforce the pervasive notion that the "goods life" automatically equates to the "good life."

In his first film, *The Joneses,* which has been accurately described as a "biting satire on competitive consumption," director Derrick Borte deconstructs the simplistic ideology of consumerism and its cancerous impulses ("Consumerism triumphs in *The Joneses*" n.p.). The title is an obvious reference to the aforementioned phenomenon of "'keeping up with the Joneses." Donald Munro refers to Borte's initial cinematic effort as "a seething, darkly comic meditation on our national obsession with accumulating stuff. Though the bland title might suggest just one more programmed family brainwashed into a highly efficient consumption machine, there's delicious depth here. This slick satire is quite a bruiser in terms of bashing America's motto of Buy, Buy, Buy" (n.p.). As Munro affirms, the somewhat banal name does not accurately represent the film's originality or its destabilizing realism.

The premise of Borte's first cinematic work is quite simple. The Joneses are an artificial family unit or a "cell" that was systematically constructed by an unidentified entity representing corporate interests in order to market specific goods and services to all facets of a given community. In fact, every family member, including the two children, has been trained to flaunt his or her possession of certain products in an attempt to manufacture desire thereby increasing revenue for the company that makes a particular item. After little more than a few weeks in their new home, the Joneses have so successfully manipulated their neighbors that everyone envies the idealistic image that this fictitious family represents.

Although the basis of Borte's film might at first appear to be merely a product of a creative imagination, the viewer quickly realizes that what is transpiring on the screen is not very different from what is happening on a daily basis. This epiphany is disconcerting because it forces the viewer to reflect upon how public perception and even entire belief systems are framed by advertisers whose only concern is to maximize corporate profits. In a recent interview with Charlie Wachtel in which he explains the impetus that compelled him to create *The Joneses,* Borte explains, "One night I was in bed with my wife and we were watching a show about self-marketing that showed an alcohol company which hired models to go out to bars and order repeatedly the same drink [...] So I thought it would be interesting to use this as a hook set up against the backdrop of a stealth marketing program" (Wachtel n.p.). Given what has already been exposed related to the dubious nature of stealth marketing designed to manipulate the masses covertly, Borte's cinematic work renders the viewer uneasy because it is not far-fetched enough to be disconnected from reality.

In spite of its aforementioned originality and alarming realism, *The Joneses* has suffered from a mixed reception. For instance, several reviewers have criticized Borte for being too indulgent of modern society and for not taking his satire to another level. However, the abrupt, dramatic climax of the film leaves little doubt concerning the director's intentions. Attempting to emulate the model of a purchaser citizen espoused by Steve Jones (David Duchovny) and the respect that he has earned in the community, Larry Symonds (Gary Cole) quite literally becomes a victim of consumerist excess. Although Larry is unable to afford everything that his neighbor Steve owns, the superficial image of success and happiness that Steve projects is too seductive for Steve to ignore. Thus, the covetous neighbor buries himself in debt before symbolically committing suicide by attaching himself to an expensive mower that he recently purchased as he drives into his pool sinking to the bottom. In reference to the evolution of Larry's growing jealousy which culminates in tragedy, Munro explains, "A strong subplot involving an envious next-door-neighbor, Larry [...] and his flailing wife [...] provides a dark undercurrent for the film, and Borte makes an emphatic statement on the downside of shopping till you drop" (n.p.). The ending of *The Joneses* could be interpreted as a metaphor that represents a global society that worships material possessions and is slowly drowning in a pool of capitalistic greed.

After his envious neighbor tragically takes his own life, Steve Jones realizes that his glamorous lifestyle does not provide him with any type of meaning or lasting happiness. For this reason, Steve declines a lucrative offer to become the head of a household for an elite family unit specially designed to reach the coveted "icon status" in this stealth marketing scheme. Similar to many of Le Clézio's protagonists, Steve is struck by the revelation that human treasures are more important than monetary ones. After his chimerical quest to buy happiness fails, Steve also convinces his former imaginary wife Kate (Demi Moore) to quit her job and to take a chance on a more authentic existence together with him.

Steve's epiphany resembles that of Leclézian characters, such as Alexis in *Le Chercheur d'or* and Jacques in *La Quarantaine*, because he embraces what the Other has to offer while simultaneously rejecting an empty existence governed by monetary aspirations. Although earlier in the film, Steve professes that "whoever dies with the most toys wins," Larry's life was ruined and completely engulfed by this unending zeal to compete for social status. In *The Joneses*, Steve discovers that even though "consumption is depicted as the shortcut to happiness and well being" in Western society, materialistic obsessions often hinder one from being cognizant of what brings fulfillment and satisfaction (Crawford 115). The incessant pursuit of shallow, consumerist virtues can be an obstacle that prevents fundamental needs, such as feeling connected to another person, from being actualized.

## THE ENVIRONMENTAL TOLL OF SHORT-SIGHTED ANTHROPOCENTRIC CONCERNS

Since the path to happiness is purely an individualistic endeavor in Western society that feeds a rapacious appetite for material comfort, the ruthless exploitation of everyone and everything for the actualization of one's own personal consumerist aspirations is not problematic whatsoever. Yet, American-style free capitalism is not truly gratuitous in terms of both the human and environmental toll that it has inflicted upon the world. The extreme avarice and lack of concern for anything else besides money that is emblematic of the modern era has led to what many scientists now affirm is an unprecedented global, ecological crisis. Moreover, the anthropocentric and egotistical notion that human beings are the center or the great miracle of existence itself has resulted in a catastrophic loss of biodiversity, disconcerting pollution levels, rapid depletion of the earth's nonrenewable resources, and climate change that has destabilized cosmic equilibrium creating lethal and frequent natural disasters that have affected the entire planet.

Given the gravity of the ecological calamity that has forced the global village to engage in a dialogue, as evidenced by the Kyoto Protocol and the Copenhagen Summit,[7] scholars from various subjects are crossing traditional disciplinary boundaries in an effort to contribute to the conversation regarding what is undoubtedly the most urgent contemporary issue of our generation. For this reason, Joseph Stiglitz dedicated an entire chapter of his publication *Making Globalization Work* to "saving the planet." Moreover, Stiglitz has also expressed his ecological concerns in recent public discourses and documentaries. Explaining the current predicament, the Nobel Laureate in Economics passionately asserts,

> The world is currently engaged in a grand experiment, studying what happens when you release carbon dioxide and certain other gases into the atmosphere in larger and larger amounts. The scientific community is fairly sure of the outcome, and it is not pretty [...] If we had access to a thousand planets, it might make sense to use one to conduct the same experiment, and if things turn out badly—as I believe this experiment will—move on to the next (161).

Although Stiglitz readily admits that a degree of uncertainty exists concerning exactly what continued environmental degradation could mean for the future of the biosphere and all of the organisms that call it home, the renowned economist emphasizes that maintaining the status quo simply because we do not possess all of the answers is unacceptable. Moreover, Stiglitz underscores that the global implementation of proper economic incentives designed to protect the earth could both eliminate unnecessary ecological risks and foster greater prosperity. The "tragedy of the commons" is avoidable if preserving the planet is made profitable to corporations and a system of worldwide governance enforces certain regulations. In other words, the simplistic dichotomy of civilization versus nature is misleading. By providing tax breaks to transnational entities that respect the ecosphere and conversely levying penalties against those that refuse to engage in environmentally safe practices, carbon emissions could be drastically reduced.

Similar to artists that express profound concerns related to the possibility of an ecopocalypse,[8] Stiglitz asserts that the "world is writing the script for its own doomsday scenario" (174–75). The Nobel Laureate reiterates, "global warming is too great a threat to the well-being of our planet for us just to ignore the crisis and pray that a resolution will eventually emerge" (183). Deconstructing the comforting notion that technology will one day solve our energy addiction and other related ecological issues, Stiglitz cautions that the growing body of scientific evidence concerning the environmental crisis is too alarming to fall on deaf ears. Summarizing humanity's worst fears, Stiglitz affirms, "We are getting early warnings about global warming loud and clear. But we have yet to respond" (186). This unequivocal call to action which concludes the chapter "Saving the Planet" creates a somber tone which is reminiscent of Le Clézio's short story "Pawana." If this summons, based upon decades of disconcerting empirical data, is once again ignored, then perhaps the sterile wasteland of "Punta Bunda" represents the future of the entire cosmos. [9]

As evidenced by the rapid emergence of ecocriticism in worldwide literary circles, Stiglitz is not alone in his unsettling concerns related to the environmental toll of neoliberal globalization. Attempting to define the diverse interdiscipline of ecocriticism, Thomas Dean offers the following explanation: "Ecocriticism is a study of culture and cultural products (art works, writings, scientific theories, etc.) that is in some way connected with the human relationship to the natural world. Ecocriticism is also a response to the needs, problems, or crises, depending on one's perception of urgency" (n.p.). Dean's comprehensive, all-encompassing definition is the most relevant to this specific investigation because a salient feature of Le Clézio's entire literary corpus has been to explore, delineate, and re-conceptualize the rapport between humanity and the remainder of the material universe. Moreover, as Dean notes, much ecocritical writing is motivated by the same disquieting anxiety expressed by researchers from other disciplines. Furthermore, ecocritical approaches to interpreting literature provide a conceptual framework for understanding the environmental distress articulated by contemporary authors, such as Le Clézio.

Decrying the pervasive neoliberal worldview that justifies the exploitation of everything and everyone for the actualization of individualistic consumerist aspirations, the ecofeminist Claudia von Werlhof highlights "the material crisis that many of us remain unaware of; namely, the annihilation of matter through its transformation into commodity, which we, in delusion, call 'materialism' [...] The original richness of mat(t)er [...] is now giving way to a barren wasteland that will remain unrecognized by many as long as their belief in 'progress' blocks their views" (100–1). Whereas philosophical materialism emphasizes the notion that everything is comprised of matter and thus the path to deep spirituality involves reducing the distance that separates us from other material life forms to the greatest extent possible, economic materialism entails the systematic appropriation of the entire planet for the sole benefit of humanity. Materialism in Western society is predicated upon the notion that human beings are the center of the universe, therefore the rest of the biosphere only exists to help us live more abundantly.

Numerous ecocritics identify this anthropocentric lack of concern for anything outside of oneself as the veritable origin of the environmental crisis. In what has become a seminal work of literary criticism, the biologist David Ehrenfeld in *The Arrogance of Humanism* dissects human exceptionalism by reminding the reader that every material being, human and otherwise, is inextricably linked to the same cosmic forces that created and which continue to sustain life. In a contention reminiscent of Le Clézio's notion of the "genesis myth,"[10] Ehrenfeld explains the homocentric worldview that "the features of the natural world—mountains, deserts, rivers, plant and animal species [...] have all been arranged by God for certain ends, primarily for the benefit of humanity" (7). Ehrenfeld reiterates, "Thus the idea of using a Nature created for us, the idea of control, and the idea of human superiority became associated early in our society" (7–8). Moreover, Ehrenfeld notes that the human belief in "our ability to manipulate the earth in any way and to avoid paying any ultimate penalties for this manipulation" lies at the heart of the ecological crisis that fellow scientists had already begun to observe when this book was first published in 1978 (8).

If human beings are the only important forms of matter whose existence is valorized, then there is little motivation to protect other organisms. Despite "false and misleading" dualities that somehow inexplicably create a schism between humans and the rest of the universe, Ehrenfeld as a scientist affirms that all sentient beings have the same origin (10). For this reason, the environmentally engaged researcher poignantly concludes his essay with the following indictment of modern society:

> Last night I listened to one of my favorite pieces of early baroque music. It reminded me [...] of the sea pounding relentlessly on a dark beach where I have spent many nights waiting to watch the giant sea

> turtles, last of their noble race [...] The music saddened me [...] because I know that it could not have been written in my time; there has been too much progress [...] It saddened me because it reminded me that in my century nothing is totally free of the taint of our arrogance. We have defiled everything, much of it forever, even the farthest jungles of the Amazon and the air above the mountains, even the everlasting sea which gave us birth (269).

Asserting that it would perhaps be impossible to discover a natural landscape that has not been forever altered by the forces of globalization, Ehrenfeld laments the increasingly heavy ecological footprint of humanity that has already irreparably destroyed much of the original beauty of the cosmos. In addition to the deep regret that Ehrenfeld expresses related to human contamination of the ecosphere, the biologist also reiterates that a large body of evidence suggests that the sea is the locus from which all life originates. In a society in which nothing is sacred except materialistic notions of progress, it is quite alarming on both a philosophical and spiritual level that the space in which all sentient beings drew their first breath garners such little veneration or even respect.

Building upon Ehrenfeld's ideas approximately two decades later, Louise Westling affirms, "Ever since David Ehrenfield's *The Arrogance of Humanism* twenty years ago, the realization has been growing that a paradigm shift is needed in the so-called developed world [...] The need for change must be defined against the basic notions of human superiority we inherited from Renaissance humanism" (4). Attempting to undermine the credibility of certain humanistic principles and the outdated scientific premises upon which this logic was constructed, Westling reiterates, "Cartesian philosophy and Newtonian mechanics of the Enlightenment era grew out of such notions, but the mechanistic model of the universe was thoroughly debunked in the earliest decades of the twentieth century, even though dominant rhetorics fail to move away from it" (4). Westling contends that science far from placing human beings on a pedestal as members of a privileged species attests that we have the same intrinsic right to exist as anything else. Proposing a more de-centered ethical system that valorizes not just humanity but the entire material universe, Westling muses, "An ecological humanism would restore appropriate humility, absorbing the lessons of quantum physics and emphasizing cooperative participation within the community of planetary life" (4). The scientific principles to which Westling refers explain Aldo Leopold's "land ethic" which is predicated upon the notion that all creatures share the same common space in a vast interconnected and interdependent web. Moreover, as chapter four will elucidate, modern ecology in part explains the cosmic modesty expressed by the narrator of *L'Extase Matérielle*. Since human beings are thrown into the chaos of existence into a given material form like all other organisms on this planet, any type of cosmic hierarchy, albeit perhaps comforting, is illusory.

Echoing the sentiments of both Ehrenfeld and Westling in the context of fostering global citizenship including responsible stewardship of environmental resources, Michael Tarrant asserts that "Dobson's (2003) concept of an Earth Citizen (as someone who holds environmental virtuous values and acts in an environmentally responsible manner) [...] suggests that participation in study abroad programs can promote global citizenship by modifying beliefs about environmental conditions and influencing proenvironmental behaviors" (434). Similar to Westling, Tarrant notes that a shift from a more anthropocentric to a more ecocentric way of thinking is paramount to protect the sanctity of the cosmos. An earth citizen is able to deconstruct arbitrary, homocentric superiority complexes and to realize that human beings are inseparable from the material universe that spawned and maintains all life. It should also be noted that Tarrant understands that very few individuals in modern consumer republics have a direct, primordial relationship with nature. For this reason, he developed a study abroad program that reconnects his students with the earth and momentarily removes them from the artificiality of contemporary society.

Both ecocritics and researchers in the field of environmental justice like Tarrant stress the essential role of humanities "to articulate the world view that is required as much by the new physics as by ecological sciences and the increasing evidence of global problems" (Westling 4). In stark contrast to traditional scientific theories which posited that life can easily adapt to changing planetary conditions, modern research underscores the delicate chain of existence that links all substances together. If too many threads of this web are destroyed, then the earth is no longer able to sustain all of the organisms that inhabit its physical plane. This grim reality motivated William Rueckert to launch the literary movement commonly known as ecocriticism in 1978. In Rueckert's so-called initial ecocritical "experiment," the author explores the ramifications of Commoner's first law of ecology which stipulates that "everything is connected to everything else." Underscoring the disconnect between recent scientific discoveries which highlight the interconnectedness of all material organisms and outdated, erroneous ideology which still maintains human exceptionalism, Rueckert states, "In ecology, man's tragic flaw is his anthropocentric (as opposed to biocentric) vision, and his compulsion to conquer, humanize, domesticate, violate, and exploit every natural thing" (78). Similar to Thomas Dean and numerous other contemporary researchers from many divergent fields, Rueckert affirms that the urgency of the problems which inflict the global village compels colleagues to collaborate more effectively. Although science appears to have effectively disproven notions of human superiority inherited from the Renaissance, homocentric mentalities still persist in the general public which clings to obsolete belief systems. Moreover, a renewed focus on the humanities which foster critical thinking skills can perhaps lead to concrete social change in the form of more earth citizens that understand the importance of protecting the environment.

Building upon the ideas of Rueckert, modern ecocritics, such as Oppermann, Buell, and Sadner[11] assert that other scientific premises in addition to Commoner's Law beckon us to re-envision the relationship between humanity and the material universe. In reference to Jeanette Winterson's *Gut Symmetries,* Serpil Oppermann explains that "The metaphor of GUT (Grand Unified Theory) echoes the ecological principle of the interrelatedness of all things and beings" (245). Winterson also notes, "In quantum physics, this essential bond between the human and nonhuman reality is called *quantum contextualism,* in which correlated nonlocal connections exist between apparently separate particles" (246). After outlining the basic tenets of these theories, Oppermann reaches the same conclusion as Rueckert. The disproven yet still lingering dualistic worldview which separates human beings from other animals is the core of the ideology that overshadows the ecological calamity. As Oppermann summarizes, "In the present crisis of sustainability [...] the rift between human and nonhuman realities, and the fundamental essence of binary thinking prompt readers to reconsider their existence in the world as not only shaped and defined by language but also by interconnected relations to entire biotic communities. If their existence continues to be threatened, so is ours" (250). Although the extent to which humanity is willing and even capable of shifting its current homocentric vision to a more ecocentric one is debatable, much scientific data suggests that such a drastic ideological transformation is vital to the future of the human race and to the overall health of the planet. If for no other reason, Commoner's Law, Grand Unified Theory, and Quantum Contextualism urge the global community to protect the ecosphere for reasons of self-preservation.

In *The Environmental Imagination,* which is undoubtedly the most influential work of ecocriticism to date, Lawrence Buell discusses the Gaia hypothesis developed by the British engineer James Lovelock. Summarizing Lovelock's theory, Buell states, "Lovelock has characterized Gaia merely as a 'shorthand' for the theory that 'the biosphere is a self-regulating entity with the capacity to keep our planet healthy by controlling the chemical and physical environment'" (200). As Buell correctly remarks, not only does Lovelock attempt to shed light upon the invisible connections amongst all of the various forms of matter that are part of a larger cosmic whole, but he also derives moral lessons from his findings. As Buell elucidates, "personification of the planet[12] helps Lovelock bond ecology to ethics. Reminiscent of Muir, Lovelock contends that humans "live within Gaia," that other species are "our partners in Gaia," that "all attempts to rationalize a subjugated biosphere with man in charge are as doomed to failure as the similar concept of benevolent colonialism" (201). Given that the Gaia hypothesis confirms that all species have the same inalienable right to exist, nothing grants humanity the unique privilege of exercising dominion over the ecosphere. According to Lovelock's ecological premises and the ethical system that he derives from his discoveries, the appropriate relationship between humanity and the universe necessitates responsible stewardship of environmental resources. Additionally, the biotic egalitarianism espoused by Lovelock has been indicative of the cosmic sentiments expressed in the field of environmental ethics since Rueckert's foundational essay. In reference to the existential realities of the human condition, Rueckert elucidates, "man comes into being, as other creatures do and has what might be called the same species-rights as they do and is, as they are, part of an environment. When the individual's time comes and he is ready to become garbage or carrion, he is composted, recycled" (66). The first law of thermodynamics posits that energy is never created nor destroyed as matter only changes forms, thus ephemeral beings are paradoxically part of an eternal force that never truly dies to which they reintegrate themselves at the end of their fleeting existence as a particular species. Chapter four will investigate this phenomenon that explains the bittersweet epiphany related to the "gouffre serein" / 'serene abyss' which numerous Leclézian protagonists experience after re-establishing a direct, sensorial contact with the universe.

In addition to the scientific and ethical implications of the aforementioned theories, the new discipline of ecophilosophy has also emerged in an effort to re-conceptualize the rapport between humankind and the rest of the biosphere based on current knowledge of the inner workings of the biosphere. Perhaps the most salient feature of ecophilosophy is that it deconstructs Cartesian dualistic logic that appears to be entirely incompatible with recent discoveries. In an essay entitled "Dominion, Empathy, and Symbiosis: Gender and Anthropocentrism in Romanticism," Nandita Batra asserts,

> The most influential modern reinforcement of the dualist position came, of course, from Descartes, whose 1637 *Discours de la méthode* contained the notorious *bêtemachine* theory that animals were mere bodies, no more than automata. Both human and animal bodies could be considered automata, but speech and the soul separated the human from the animal. The animal body operated purely on mechanical principles, and any sounds made by the animal—including its cries of pain—were the products of its machinery (156).

Modern science (i.e., Grand Unified Theory, Quantum Contextualism, Gaia Hypothesis) effectively debunks Descartes's naïve and simplistic dichotomies. If human beings are inseparable from a larger entity that represents the origin of all life, then no meaningful distinction exists between the subject and the object. Moreover, the path to philosophical and spiritual enlightenment entails a greater understanding of one's small place in the cosmic whole.

After deconstructing Cartesian logic with scientific principles, Batra also notes that Descartes's *bêtemachine* doctrine was the subject of much scrutiny in the philosophical community even during his time. As Batra explains, "Cartesian dualism appeared on the surface to reign supreme, but several philosophers throughout Europe had been unconvinced by Descartes. In France both Voltaire and Diderot had been skeptical of the *bêtemachine* theory (with Voltaire providing proof of animal intelligence in his article on animals in (the) *Dictionnaire philosophique*" (157–158). Although Descartes's notion of the *bêtemachine* continues to be appealing because it in essence grants human beings the right to exploit other "inferior" creatures, the logic upon which this theory was founded is extremely flawed. Numerous studies have unequivocally proven that animal intelligence far surpasses the mechanistic realm.[13] It might be consoling to conceptualize other organisms as soulless automata, but this is merely idealistic wishful thinking that continues to justify the global appropriation of the entire universe for the singular benefit of humanity.[14]

In addition to outdated scientific and philosophical logic, another issue that has exacerbated the ecological crisis is the modern suburban lifestyle. Given that urbanization is inseparable from neoliberal globalization, billions of people spend the vast majority of their time enclosed inside walls of brick, concrete, and steel. Outside of these artificial barriers that society has erected for material comfort and to maximize productivity, very few individuals have intimate regular contact with the universe. This sense of displacement from the cosmic whole to which all beings are connected often afflicts early Leclézian protagonists which long for a more authentic lifestyle in harmony with the elements. The profound anguish from which Le Clézio's protagonists suffer when they reside in an urban labyrinth where no meaningful communion with other forms of matter appears to be possible is clearly evident in texts, such as *Le Procès-Verbal*, *La Fièvre*, and *Le livre des fuites*. In reference to the modern descendants of the nomadic Tuareg civilization that survive in one of the harshest climates on this planet in the novel *Désert*, Bettina Knapp notes that these indigenous peoples which have resisted integration into the global village are "better off than city people who have been alienated from nature" (703). Although traditional societies which reside in the Sahara desert live a precarious existence which can be taken away in the blink of an eye by nature's fury, at least they have not been entirely removed from the greater ontological shell of being. The attempts of Leclézian protagonists to fuse with the natural world and the efforts of many characters to seek viable alternatives to globalization will be analyzed in chapters four and five respectively.

The ecocentric trauma of being displaced from the cosmic whole that haunts numerous Leclézian antiheroes is a common theme of Romantic nature writing. As Kate Rigby elucidates, "Wordsworth was himself something of a 'reinhabitant,' seeking to develop a sense of belonging in a world that was increasingly characterized by dislocation and alienation" (n.p.). Rigby reiterates that much of Wordsworth's poetry could be interpreted as "'spousal verse,' celebrating the marriage of the poet with the place that modeled for him the partnership of humanity and nature" (n.p.). The elemental nuptials to which Rigby refers accurately describes the efforts of Le Clézio's protagonists to unite with the material universe that surrounds them. Moreover, several critics have already noted that the pantheistic communion with nature that is evident in numerous texts written by Le Clézio resembles the enigmatic ecstasy experienced by the Camusian narrator of *Noces*.[15]

However, this exploration of a faded humanistic dream in the context of Le Clézio's narratives will dispel any notions that the 2008 Nobel Laureate in Literature is an idealistic romantic or neoromantic writer. The alarming realism that destabilizes the reader in certain texts is emblematic of a larger worldview that equally highlights the aforementioned trauma from which fleeting beings suffer in the modern world while simultaneously affirming that life is indeed worth living. Although Le Clézio's protagonists often experience intense and transformative moments of euphoria because of a direct, sensorial contact with other forms of matter, natural catastrophes remind the reader that the biosphere is not always generous to humankind. For this reason, the indifferent wrath of the elements which can be a lethal force coexists with the more gentle vision of nature as a nurturing "mother" in many Amerindian belief systems. This cosmic duality and apparent paradox is also present in Le Clézio's narratives as well.

## CONCLUSION

Few people deny that McLuhan's predication of an interconnected and interdependent global village is indeed a reality, but his misplaced faith that the forces of modernity would bring unprecedented prosperity and happiness to all now seems like a cruel farce given increasing economic and social inequalities. Moreover, unscrupulous transnational corporations motivated purely by extreme avarice have appropriated McLuhan's aspirations for their own personal gain. Denying that any alternatives to the current situation are possible, the conglomerates that control the media still continue to laud globalization euphorically even in the face of harsh realities that contradict the simplistic neoliberal ideology that drives a world which is metaphorically shrinking with each passing day. Not only has consumerism failed to provide happiness for billions of poor and even affluent people around the world because of its superficial virtues, but it has also justified the large scale exploitation of anything and everyone for the actualization of one's own narcissistic and hedonistic desires. This incessant zeal has also led to what most scientists now assert is an ecological calamity of catastrophic proportions. For this reason, researchers from many divergent disciplines are uniting in a common effort to improve the situation before human beings and the other material creatures that inhabit this planet all pay the ultimate price. Paraphrasing the concerns expressed by the ecocritic Glen Love in addition to those of numerous contemporary scholars, Sheng-Yen Yu "warns that soon we will be compelled to recognize human hegemony over the biosphere as the paramount problem of our time" (91).

## NOTES

1. The media's role in the dissemination of information will be systematically explored in chapter three in the context of Le Clézio's narratives, such as *Les Géants* Moreover, the author's skepticism concerning the very concept of the global village is quite clear in the interview which culminates this interdisciplinary investigation. As the writer affirms, "I don't believe that much in the global village because as we said earlier, there is evidence of its failure. The global village seems more and more like the global market instead of a global village."

2. See Leichenko, Robin and William Solecki. "Exporting the American Dream: The Globalization of Suburban Consumption Landscapes." *Regional Studies* 39 (2): 241–253.

3. See also the last paragraph of *Making Globalization Work* (p. 292) in which Stiglitz expresses a similar plea.

4. Chapter four will investigate this complex phenomenon in relation to Le Clézio's *oeuvre* in a more exhaustive fashion.

5. Chapter three will analyze the inability of consumerist virtues to create and to sustain happiness in the context of Le Clézio's narratives.

6. LDC = Less Developed Country.

7. It should be noted, however, that the United States still refuses to ratify the Kyoto Protocol. Furthermore, the resolutions of the 2009 United Nations Climate Change Conference (i.e., Copenhagen Summit) were nonbinding.

8. A term used by numerous ecocritics, such as Loretta Johnson, to describe an ethical summons which urges the reader to reflect upon the ramifications of our ecological footprint in terms of the delicate balance related to the intricate and complex web of existence that sustains all life.

9. Le Clézio's poignant metaphor of ecological sterility will be systematically explored in chapter four. "Punta Bunda" refers to the natural wonder that is destroyed by extreme avarice in the narrative "Pawana."

10. See chapter four for a comprehensive discussion concerning this idea in relation to Le Clézio's fiction.

11. See Sandner, David. "Habituated to the Vast: Ecocriticism, the Sense of Wonder, and the Wilderness of Stars." *Extrapolation* 41 (3): 283–297.

12. Similar to other contemporary authors, Le Clézio often personifies nature in narratives like "Pawana." The Nobel Laureate's usage of this literary device will be discussed in chapter four.

13. (e.g.) Uhlenbroek, Charlotte. *Animal Life*. New York: Dorling Kindersley, 2011.

14. It should be noted that other prominent ecocritics/ecophilosophers often take aim at Cartesian dualism. (i.e. Johnson, Loretta. "Greening the Library: The Fundamentals and Future of Ecocriticism." *Choice* (Dec. 2009): 7–13.

15. (e.g.) Moser, Keith. "Rending Moments of Material Ecstasy in the Meditative Essays of Two Nobel Laureates: Le Clézio and Camus." *Romance Notes* 49 (1): 13–21.

# TWO

# Defending the Marginalized and Disenfranchised Inhabitants of the Global Village

J.M.G. Le Clézio's diverse protagonists often discover that for many people the modern world is a site of unspeakable horrors that is antithetical to global village universalism. His fiction exposes the dire, precarious situation of millions of human beings across the planet for whom neoliberal fallacies related to prosperity and happiness bear little fruit. Although numerous researchers[1] correctly assert that Le Clézio's prose is often poetic and even lyrical, perhaps no other contemporary author portrays the profound anguish of marginalized and disenfranchised individuals in such a disquieting and realistic fashion as the 2008 Nobel Laureate in Literature. In an interview with the writer Jean Grosjean concerning Le Clézio conducted by Gérard de Cortanze, Grosjean explains, "Dans le monde de Le Clézio, le paysage, le temps qu'il fait, ont une existence très forte, mais il sait aussi très bien évoquer la misère, les villes" / 'In Le Clézio's world (of fiction), natural landscapes and climatic conditions have a very strong presence, but he also knows how to evoke misery, cities' (52; my trans.). Echoing the sentiments of Isabelle Roussel-Gillet,[2] Grosjean affirms that Le Clézio's balanced worldview counterpoints simplistic interpretations of his complex and evolving *oeuvre*.

## ENDEMIC GLOBAL POVERTY AND THE UGLY UNDERBELLY OF THE URBAN GHETTO

In an interview with National Public Radio, the Le Clézio specialist Jennifer Waelti-Walters contends that given his "nineteenth-century facility with words," the author "could draw a word painting of a storm, and you'd feel as though you got wet" (n.p.). However, it should be noted that the meticulous portrait which progressively reveals itself to the reader in Le Clézio's texts is often a disconcerting creation from the hand of an artist that is astutely cognizant of the crimes against humanity that are transpiring around him. The eleven short stories that comprise the collection entitled *La ronde et autres faits divers* (*The Round and Other Cold Hard Facts*) reflect macabre realities that are indicative of contemporary society. As the title of the collection suggests, these varied narratives were inspired by true events recounting traumatic, painful experiences in which very few if any ephemeral moments of ecstasy dissipate the subject's anguish. In reference to this somber work, published by Gallimard in 1982, Le Clézio himself affirms, "tous les récits de ce recueil sont provoqués pour moi par un choc de la vie quotidienne. Ce sont des histoires vraies. Ce sont des faits divers basés sur des faits réels dont l'un s'est passé à Nice" / 'all of the narratives from this collection were inspired by a clash with daily life. These are true stories. These are news stories based on true events one of which happened in Nice' (Dormoy 131; my trans.).

Numerous protagonists of *La ronde et autres faits divers* are on a collision course with harsh realities that are emblematic of the globalized and urbanized world which will have traumatic and even deadly consequences. As Bruno Thibault elucidates, "l'écrivain met en scène dans *La Ronde* des hommes, des femmes et des enfants qui sont exclus du système et qui font l'expérience du néant social. Il met en scène les 'marginaux' et les 'immigrés' de la France aujourd'hui" / 'the writer introduces in *The Round* men, women, and children that are excluded from the system and which experience social emptiness. He presents the marginalized inhabitants and immigrants of contemporary France' ("Du stéréotype au mythe" 964; my trans.). Reiterating Thibault's interpretation of these profoundly unsettling texts, Fredrik Westerlund states, "La façon discrète, sympathique dont Le Clézio dessine les personnages engage et trouble d'une manière réaliste, cinématographique" / 'The discrete manner in which Le Clézio depicts the characters engages and troubles (the reader) in a cinematic, realistic fashion' ("La vie urbaine-mort urbaine" 73; my trans.). Instead of discovering a welcoming global community which reserves a place for the downtrodden allowing them to access the neoliberal dream, the protagonists of *La Ronde* will suffer from economic and sexual exploitation, racism, indifference, alienation, and acute poverty.

The final narrative of the collection entitled "David" recounts the adventures of an adolescent that resorts to desperate measures in an attempt to find his older brother who vanished at the age of fourteen. Not only does David endeavor to discover the whereabouts of his sibling, but he also tries to shed light upon the motivations that compelled him to run away from home. Similar to other Leclézian characters, David is struck by greater epiphanies concerning the materialistic nature of Western society as the story unfolds. The impoverished adolescent realizes that his brother's disappearance is characteristic of the current state of the global village in which desperate individuals yearn for the "goods life" that seems far beyond their reach.

Given his meticulous efforts to follow in the footsteps of his brother's fugue, David soon speculates early in his journey, "Son frère Edouard est venu par là, parce que c'était l'argent qu'il voulait, il voulait conquérir l'argent. Dans les rues sombres, dans l'appartement, dans les couloirs humides, sans lumière, la pauvreté est comme un drap mouillé sur la peau, ou pire, comme une peau sale et moite qu'on ne peut pas enlever" / 'His brother Edward came this way because it was money he wanted; he wanted to conquer money. In the dark streets, in the apartment, in the clammy, lightless corridors, poverty is like a wet sheet on your skin, or worse—like a damp, dirty skin you can't shed' (261; 199). Since their father's untimely demise in a tragic accident left their penniless mother with the responsibility of raising two children on her own, the protagonist's hypothesis is difficult to refute. Moreover, similar to his brother that appears to have intentionally vanished, David also imagines a better life outside of the shackles of poverty.

A specific incident which transpires at the supermarket is quite revealing. Although David follows various families around grocery stores as a form of cover that allows him to steal fresh food items without being noticed, his intentions are more complex than they originally seem. What these filial units represent is more important than the theft itself. While observing a particular family, David begins to daydream. Articulating this vision of an adolescent that wishes to free himself from the vicious cycle of poverty and lead a normal life, the narrator states:

> David pense qu'il aimerait bien les suivre comme ça toute sa vie, jusqu'au bout du monde, jusque chez eux. Le soir, ils rentreraient dans une belle maison claire, entourée d'un frais jardin rempli de fleurs [...] chacun aurait un lit pour soi, avec des draps ornés de dessins comme on voit [...] ce serait juste comme ça, David peut le voir en fermant les yeux.
>
> David thinks that he wants to follow them like that all his life, to the very ends of the earth, all the way to their house. In the evenings, they'd all go into a beautiful, well-lit house surrounded by a cool garden filled with flowers [...] everyone would have their own bed, fitted with patterned sheets like you see sometimes [...] That's exactly how it would be; David can see it when he closes his eyes (270; 205–206).

Given that the cost of living for a typical middle class family has exploded to the point where both parents usually need full time jobs to transform this image into reality, David's fantasies appear to be entirely illusory in the single-parent home in which he resides. With no additional economic assistance, the protagonist's mother will never be able to provide him with the luxuries to which others have access. It should also be noted that not only does David covet the financial situation of affluent families, but he also longs to be a part of a more cohesive filial unit. David would like to belong to a close-knit family with both a positive paternal and maternal influence.

Although the narrator never directly reveals the mother's profession in the short story "David," it is evident that the meager salary that she earns is not even enough to fulfill the basic necessities that her children need. Painting a clearer portrait of their dire economic situation that compelled the older brother to flee, the narrator affirms, "C'est à cause de l'argent qu'il est parti, parce que sa mère ne voulait rien lui donner, parce qu'elle lui prenait ses gains d'apprenti mécanicien, et qu'il n'y a avait jamais d'argent pour aller au cinéma, pour jouer au football, pour acheter des glaces ou jouer aux billards électriques dans les cafés" / 'It's because of money that he left, because his mother didn't want to give him anything, because she took what he earned as an apprentice mechanic and he never had any money to go to the movies, to play football, to buy ice cream, or to play pinball machines in the cafes' (259; 197). Although the reader logically surmises that David's mother implores her oldest child to relinquish a portion of his salary in order to improve their financial stability, Edouard's egotistical impulse to satisfy his own personal consumerist desires is indicative of the neoliberal ideology that pervades Western society. Given that the neoliberal pursuit of happiness is purely an individualistic journey that entails no concern for anyone else, Edouard's selfish attitude should not be surprising. As this passage illustrates, the superficial virtues of consumerism, the veritable religion of the global village, have not only eroded any sense of community, but they have also irreparably damaged traditional values that used to be the core of the family unit.

Similar to other Leclézian characters, David reaches the following conclusion concerning the materialistic obsession that defines modern consumer republics: "L'argent est sale, David le déteste, et il déteste son frère Edouard d'être parti à cause de cela. L'argent est laid, et David le méprise [...] Quand il aura de l'argent David pense qu'il le jettera par terre, ou dans la mer, pour que personne ne le trouve" / 'Money is dirty; David hates it, and he hates his brother Edward for having left because of that. Money is ugly, and David scorns it [...] When he has money one day, David thinks he'll throw it on the ground or into the sea so that no one will find it' (259; 197). The incessant zeal to acquire additional monetary wealth blinds one from realizing the repercussions of this cancerous ideology that fuels purely narcissistic visions of happiness in which one possesses more luxury items than his or her neighbors. The young Edouard, indoctrinated with consumerist and neoliberal virtues from birth, quite literally abandons his family during their time of need as he seeks to conquer the "good(s) life."

Edouard's selfish decision resembles that of Alexis in *Le Chercheur d'or* who appropriates his father's chimerical dream of unearthing the unknown Corsaire's treasure. While his mother Mam and sister Laure are left to fend for themselves in a house partially destroyed by a hurricane and because of the illusory obsessions of a whimsical father, Alexis embarks on a treasure hunt. When he collapses from heat stroke, a young Manaf[3] named Ouma saves his life and attempts to cure him of his impulse to possess and to exercise dominion over the entire universe. After Alexis's quest ends in bitter disappointment with the discovery that "toutes les cachettes sont vides" / 'all of the hiding places are empty," the protagonist muses, "Si les manafs trouveraient l'or, ils le jetteraient à la mer"' / 'If the Manafs find the gold they'll throw it in the sea' (261; 233; 262; 234). Explaining the devastation and anguish that consumerist obsessions have inflicted upon the modern world, Ouma herself declares, "Vous autres, le grand monde, vous croyez que l'or est la chose la plus forte et la plus désirable, et c'est pour cela que vous faites la guerre. Les gens vont mourir partout pour posséder l'or" / 'All of you out there, you desire gold above everything because you think there is nothing more powerful. You make war for it. People everywhere will die because of this obsession' (269; 240). As Ouma notes, individuals are willing to resort to drastic measures in a misguided effort to abandon all other concerns and to have access to neoliberal fantasies related to fulfillment and happiness.[4] Albeit in a much different context, David is struck by the same epiphany concerning Western society as Ouma.

In an effort to understand the intoxicating effects of material wealth that caused his brother Edouard to flee and which spellbind much of humanity, David will force open a cash register in a supermarket that he normally frequents in order to touch this powerful force. As an economically disadvantaged child that the narrator indicates does not even have a dollar in his pocket to purchase bread, David's crime which is the central focus of the narrative does not appear to be financially motivated. Elucidating the veritable intentions of the protagonist, the narrator affirms,

> Son cœur bat, bat, et la sueur mouille son front, les paumes de ses mains. Là-bas, au bout du magasin, il la voit bien, énorme et éclairée par ses lampes, la caisse est immobile, et il avance vers elle, vers l'endroit où il va enfin pouvoir savoir, rencontrer enfin son frère Edouard, l'endroit brûlant où est caché le message secret. Maintenant, il le comprend, il le sait bien, c'est pour cela qu'il est parti de l'appartement [...] pour arriver jusqu'ici, à l'endroit où il va pouvoir commencer à retrouver son frère.
>
> His heart races, races, and sweat moistens his brow, the palms of his hands. Over there, at the other end of the store, he sees it well, huge and brightly lit in the neon lamps, he can clearly see the cash register, standing very still; he goes toward it, toward the place where he will finally be able to find out, finally be able to meet his brother Edward,

> the burning place where the secret message is hidden. Now he understands it; he's found it; that's why he left the apartment yesterday [...] to get here, get to the place where he can start finding his brother again (277; 211).

Although such a criminal act would normally be explained as a banal event inspired by economic destitution, necessity, or avarice, David breaks the register with a stone to reach out to his brother whose disappearance caused him much pain. Not only is this vandalism and theft an attempt to reestablish a certain type of communication with his lost brother, but it is also an effort to understand why money casts such an intense curse over much of humanity.

After a physically stronger young man subdues David until the authorities arrive, the narrator reiterates, "ce n'est pas l'argent qu'il voulait, mais le visage de son frère Edouard" / 'It wasn't the money that he wanted, but (to see) his brother Edward's face' (279; 213). In this passage, Edouard's visage is a metaphor which is emblematic of seductive consumerist ideology related to prosperity and fulfillment. Behind this enigmatic mask, David hopes to uncover greater truths concerning the materialistic virtues that drive contemporary society. At the end of the narrative, as uniformed guards are approaching, the protagonist reflects upon "des murs abrupts et des vallées turbulentes de la ville moderne" / 'the steep walls and the turbulent valleys of the modern city' (281; 214). Similar to other Leclézian characters that reject the artifice of the monolithic, urbanized global village that has imposed itself across the world, David is now aware of the monetary abyss which has engulfed much of the entire planet. Summarizing the protagonist's comprehension of this inner void, the narrator concludes, "il connaît maintenant la porte qui conduit vers son frère Edouard, vers sa cachette secrète d'où on ne revient jamais" / 'now he's found the door that leads to his brother Edward, to his secret hiding place, the one you never come back from' (281; 214). David realizes that once the modern subject is totally consumed by materialistic aspirations like his older brother, one reaches a point of no return where one is lost for good in the philosophical sense. For this reason, the end of this oft-neglected short story offers no consolation to the reader because there is little reason to believe that David's family will ever reject the neoliberal dream to which only the privileged few have access in favor of a more authentic paradigm that valorizes traditional virtues.

Like "David" and several of the other narratives that comprise *La ronde et autres faits divers,* "Ô voleur, voleur, quelle vie est la tienne?" depicts criminal activities perpetrated in an urban setting. However, the unnamed Portuguese immigrant protagonist does not steal for the same reasons as David. It should also be noted that the structure of this text differs greatly from the rest of the narratives that are part of this collection. An unidentified interlocutor appears to be conducting an interview or at least engaging in a casual conversation with this mysterious thief. The story begins with the question "Dis-moi, comment tout a commencé" / 'Tell me, how did it all begin' (225; 171). This initial query prompts the main character to highlight the major events of his life that forced him into a life of crime.

Justifying that his acts are the product of necessity, the protagonist/narrator explains, "j'ai perdu mon travail, parce que l'entreprise avait fait faillite [...] Alors tout le monde s'est retrouvé sans rien, ça a fait comme un grand trou dans lequel on est tous tombés [...] Au début j'ai cru que tout allait s'arranger [...] mais il n'y avait rien, parce que les entrepreneurs engagent [...] des étrangers, c'est plus facile quand ils veulent s'en débarrasser" / 'I lost my job because the company went bankrupt [...] So everyone ended up totally broke; it was like we had all fallen into this big hole [...] At first, I thought everything was going to be all right [...] but there wasn't any work because companies hire people that don't have families, foreigners; it's easier to get rid of them when they need to' (226–227; 172). As many contemporary researchers have noted, a network of exploiters await immigrant and migrant populations upon their arrival in the host country. Both documented and clandestine immigrants are easy prey for transnational corporations seeking to maximize their colossal profits by means of a cheap labor force because they have little choice but to accept shameful salaries, grim working conditions, and discriminatory hiring practices. Moreover, when they are no longer needed to perform certain functions, these second-class or even "non-citizens" can easily be replaced or discarded entirely. In the absence of any meaningful legislation that protects these human beings which are placed in a very precarious situation, corporations have little incentive to respect basic principles related to human rights.[5]

Further elucidating how economic destitution compelled him to enter into organized crime, the narrator adds,

> Alors les mois sont passés et je n'avais toujours rien, et c'était difficile de manger, de payer l'éducation de mes fils, ma femme ne pouvait pas travailler, elle avait des ennuis de santé, on n'avait même pas d'argent pour acheter les medicaments [...] On allait mourir de faim, ma femme, mes enfants. C'est comme ça que je me suis décidé. Au début, je me suis dit que c'était provisoire, le temps de trouver un peu d'argent [...] Maintenant, ça fait trois ans que ça dure, je sais que ça ne changera plus.
>
> So the months went by, and I still couldn't find anything, and it was hard to get enough to eat, to pay for my son's schooling; my wife couldn't work; she had health problems; we didn't even have enough money to buy medicine [...] We were all going to starve to death, my wife, my children. That's what finally made up my mind. At first, I told myself that it was just a temporary thing, just long enough to get a little

> money together [...] Now it's been going on for three years; I know it'll never change (227; 172).

Although the realization of McLuhan's global village was supposed to bring unparalleled prosperity to all, individuals like the protagonist of "Ô voleur, voleur, quelle vie est la tienne?" are exploited as a human commodity that assures inexpensive products and monumental profits for businesses. Furthermore, given that undocumented immigrants often fall outside of the realm of legislation designed to protect people from exploitative hiring practices and deplorable working conditions, society does not have to worry about extending basic necessities to these disenfranchised groups such as health care and education.

After indicating that he has spent three years in this desperate situation, the narrator voices deep concerns in which he envisions no end in sight to this life of crime and misery, "les gens riches n'ont pas de considération pour ceux qui sont dans la misère, ils s'en moquent, ils gardent leurs richesses pour eux, enfermées dans leurs maisons vides, dans leurs coffres-forts. Et pour avoir quelque chose, pour avoir une miette, il faut que tu entres chez eux et que tu le prennes toi-même" / 'Rich people have no consideration for the poor, and they couldn't care less; they keep their riches for themselves, closed up in their empty houses, in their safes. And to be able to have something, even a crumb, you have to break into their houses and take it for yourself' (233; 177). Underscoring the willful blindness of those that benefit the most from neoliberal fantasies, the narrator exposes the indifference of the social elite which are shielded from the dire realities of increasing global inequality. It is easier for the privileged few to blame the victims for their own misfortune than to reflect upon the human toll of their excessive lifestyle. It is also a comforting, albeit illusory, notion to assert that everyone has a chance to fulfill the neoliberal dream.

Juxtaposing the neoliberal ideology that encourages each of us like Edouard to actualize our own narcissistic aspirations by whatever means necessary to the selfless sacrifices of the narrator of "Ô voleur, voleur, quelle vie est la tienne?," the author explains, "Déjà, trois ou quatre fois, ça a failli tourner mal, il y a des gens qui m'ont tiré dessus à coups de fusil [...] Mais une fois, c'est fatal [...] peut-être cette nuit, peut-être demain, qui peut le dire [...] C'est à elle que je pense, à ma femme, pas à moi, moi je ne vaux rien, je n'ai pas d'importance. C'est à elle que je pense, et à mes enfants aussi, que deviendront-ils, qui pensera à eux, sur cette terre" / 'Three or four times already, things almost went wrong ; people shot at me with rifles [...] But one day, it's bound to happen [...] maybe tonight, maybe tomorrow, who can say? [...] It's her I'm thinking of, my wife, not myself, I'm not worth anything; I'm not important. It's her I'm thinking of, and my children too; what will become of them, who in the world will ever think of them' (234; 177). Although the narrator realizes that the next heist could be his last, he continues to steal to support his family given that no social structures are in place to assist him in finding gainful employment. Expressing similar sentiments to those of other immigrant Leclézian protagonists such as Aminata in *Fantômes dans la rue*,[6] the Portuguese father is willing to accept severe repercussions including incarceration and even death to ensure that his family does not suffer from hunger. Perhaps this portrait of ultimate sacrifice explains why the author does not give the narrator a precise identity or even a name. The value of the enigmatic narrator's life is purely instrumental as it is defined by his capacity to help those that count on him to survive. Moreover, the mysterious immigrant's plight is indicative of the widespread nature of the "exceptions to the rule" that undermine the simplistic universalism of the global village concept and the neoliberal forces that continue to promote this ideology.

In Le Clézio's narratives, perhaps it is the ugly underbelly of the urban ghetto that best concretizes the alarming gap between the dwindling affluent members of society and the extremely impoverished. While a miniscule social elite resides in mansions with several rooms that are seldom if ever even used, the unfortunate individuals that are condemned to live in ghettos across the planet experience violence, desperation, and unsanitary living conditions that place their very survival in question. In his analysis of the novel *Désert* for which Le Clézio received the coveted Prix Paul Morand from the *Académie Française*, Bruno Thibault notes the horror that the protagonist Lalla discovers upon her arrival in Marseille. As Thibault affirms, "Au lieu d'un pays de cocagne, elle découvre un sinistre ghetto" / 'Instead of a never-never land, she discovers a sinister ghetto' ("Immigration et Individuation" 361; my trans.). Thibault reiterates, "Lalla est d'abord femme de ménage dans un hôtel crasseux: elle y fait l'expérience de la pauvreté, de la saleté et du racisme" / 'Lalla is at first a cleaning lady in a filthy hotel; here she experiences poverty, dirtiness, and racism' ("Immigration et Individuation" 361–362; my trans.). Echoing Thibault's frank assessment concerning the shock that destabilizes Lalla after her arrival in France, Bettina Knapp asserts, "The now-pregnant Lalla encounters Europe only to find the environment and living conditions in Marseille antithetical to her dreams" (705). Although Lalla is a descendant of the legendary nomadic Tuaregs that still reside in the unforgiving desert sands of the Western Sahara, she will soon realize that the precarious existence that she led in this traditional society induced far less suffering than the modern world. In spite of the quotidian confrontation with famine, drought, heat, infectious diseases, and rampant infant mortality, Lalla will reject a life of luxury and fame and return to her ancestral homeland.[7]

Before an unlikely fortuitous encounter with a photographer will temporarily make Lalla one of the most desired models in the entire world, the rending descriptions of the slum in which Lalla lives haunt the reader. Similar to other clandestine citizens of Marseille, Lalla will experience abject poverty with other disadvantaged members of society in a dangerous area of town infamously nicknamed "Le Panier." This section of Marseille, far removed from the affluent suburbs, literally radiates the pungent odor of frustration, devastation, and crime. Explaining Lalla's coping mechanism that allows her to reside in such an atmosphere, the narrator elucidates, "Il faut simplement fermer la bouche et respirer lentement, à petits coups, pour ne pas laisser entrer à l'intérieur de son corps l'odeur de la pauvreté, de la maladie et de la mort qui règne ici, dans ces escaliers, dans ces corridors, dans ces recoins où vivent les araignées et les blattes" / 'You just have to close your mouth and breathe slowly, in short breaths, to keep that odor from getting inside your body, that odor of poverty, of sickness, and of death that pervades the stairways, the halls, and all the nooks and crannies where the spiders and cockroaches live' (290; 232). Instead of discovering the promised land or a place of opportunity, most of the marginalized inhabitants of *le Panier* appear to be unable to integrate fully into a mainstream French society that does not wish to share its prosperity with others. Given that few if any lucrative opportunities seem available for these disenfranchised individuals, this inhumane slum resembles a prison with a glass ceiling comprised of neoliberal fallacies that they can imagine because of consumerist propaganda but never reach. Noting that Lalla's potential ability to climb the social ladder because of her physical attributes is indeed a rarity for those that call such ghettos home, William Thompson classifies *Désert* as an "improbable rags-to-riches tale" (710).

## THE DEBASEMENT OF HUMANITY AS A COMMODITY TO BE EXPLOITED: THE DIRE WORKING CONDITIONS OF DISENFRANCHISED INDIVIDUALS IN BOTH EMERGING AND DEVELOPED ECONOMIES

In addition to the striking economic destitution that is emblematic of an interconnected world with a rapid rate of urbanization, another salient feature of the novel *Désert* is the grim realities concerning the working conditions that Lalla confronts both in the Sahara and after her arrival in Marseille. Outlining the protagonist's motivations for leaving her homeland, Bettina Knapp explains, "At home, her aunt insists that she take a job and earn her living. She tries weaving, but cannot cope with the dark and airless working conditions forced upon her. One other alternative is left: to marry a rich old man. Lalla refuses" (705). The protagonist's encounter with the unsavory character Zora and her deplorable sweatshop is indicative of the fact that globalization has indeed impacted the entire planet. Even remote areas of the Sahara desert are not immune to global forces that take advantage of cheap manual labor and human misery to assure colossal profits for shareholders.

Although Lalla is cognizant that she is being exploited at market value by an economic system that dehumanizes her and the other girls that work in this appalling textile factory, she selflessly accepts these dire working conditions to help sustain her family. As the narrator affirms, "elle ne dit rien à cause de l'argent qu'elle doit ramener à la maison pour Aamma. Seulement, pour se venger, elle fait de travers quelques nœuds dans le tapis rouge" / 'But she doesn't say anything because of the money she's supposed to bring back to the house for Aamma. To get even, she just ties a few knots the wrong way in the red carpet' (188; 150). Lalla's frustration soon reaches a boiling point that her gestures of retribution are no longer able to contain when Zora physically abuses a young child named Mina. Although Mina is only approximately ten years old, Zora sadistically beats this feeble girl that is unable to defend herself. Lalla realizes that she will lose her job that she desperately needs but she cannot idly stand by and allow this act of violence to continue. For this reason, she exclaims, "Ne la battez plus! […] Ne la battez plus […] Lâche ! Méchante femme" / 'Stop beating her [...] Stop beating her [...] You bully! You wicked woman' (189; 150). Before the protagonist leaves this factory never to return, she breaks Zora's cane because this vile object has inflicted much pain upon far too many children like Mina.

As Knapp correctly highlights, this ethical decision to no longer remain complicit in human exploitation and debasement in addition to her refusal to marry an older affluent stranger thrusts her into contact with the modern world. Although Lalla yearns for a more prosperous life like the other marginalized inhabitants that reside in "Le Panier," she falls prey once again to "les conditions de vie très dures qui attendant les travailleurs immigrés à leur arrivée en France" / 'the very difficult living conditions that await immigrant workers upon their arrival in France' (Thibault "Immigration et Individuation" 361; my trans.). Instead of a land flowing with milk and honey for all, Lalla soon discovers that it is extremely difficult for many immigrants regardless of their legal status to procure any type of employment. Lalla will eventually obtain her first job, but this position at a grocery store is hardly one that will afford her access to the life of luxury euphorically championed by advertisers. Moreover, she will be forced to quit after the very first day given the menacing, predatory behavior of her supervisor. Painting a vivid portrait of this disconcerting conduct, the narrator explains, "tout le temps il regardait le ventre et les seins de Lalla, avec ses vilains yeux humides" / 'he was constantly staring at Lalla's abdomen and breasts with his repulsive watery eyes' (267; 212). Similar to Zora's attitude concerning the impoverished children that she in essence enslaves, Lalla's boss envisions her as a commodity that he owns since she falls outside of the realm of legal protection. Consequently, he is able to exploit her however he wishes, even sexually. After much effort and numerous failures, Lalla becomes a charwoman at the Hôtel Sainte-Blanche. Yet, as Thibault notes in his analysis of the novel, this establishment is in a polluted section of Marseille marred by violence. The reality of living and working in a dangerous, hostile urban ghetto is far removed from Lalla's original aspirations.

Although in a vastly different context from *Désert,* it is perhaps the brief narrative "La grande vie" / 'living it up' from *La Ronde* that best describes the debasing atmosphere of the modern factory in both emerging and developed economies. Similar to *Cœur brûle et autres romances,* the aforementioned English title of this short story is quite revealing and intentionally ironic.[8] Fredrik Westerlund notes that "La grande vie" conjures stereotypical images of "le luxe et la gloire que dépeignent les médias, et que dénonce Le Clézio" / 'luxury and glory that the media portrays and which Le Clézio denounces' ("La vie urbaine-mort urbaine" 76; my trans.). The two adolescent female protagonists Pouce et Poussy momentarily escape what the narrator poignantly describes as the prison-like atmosphere of the latest factory in which they work in an effort to taste the proverbial pie or to "live it up." During their fleeting fugue from the suffocating atmosphere of *Ohio Made in U.S.A,* Pouce and Poussy will stay in luxurious hotels, dine at expensive restaurants, give exorbitant gratuities, and enjoy all of the other privileges that are indicative of the life of the rich and famous before their adventures come to an abrupt end. However, the two young girls must constantly remain on the move because they vanish once the bill arrives after their limited monetary resources have been exhausted. Summarizing their experience, Westerlund asserts, "Pouce and Poussy mènent vraiment une grande vie mais leur carrière s'estompe quand vient le temps de régler les comptes" / 'Pouce and Poussy really do live it up before their dreams fade away when the time comes to settle their accounts' ("La vie urbaine-mort urbaine" 76; my trans.).

The narrator's depictions of the sinister, authoritative atmosphere that pervades the factory *Ohio Made in U.S.A.* cast little doubt upon the reasons that compelled the two young girls to run away. In addition to the "low wage/no wage salaries" that the employees receive for hours of debilitating physical work, these manual laborers are treated like machines inside this building surrounded by fences and barbed wire. Elucidating the working conditions of those that feel incarcerated inside this exploitative edifice, the narrator underscores, "Elles faisaient cela huit heures par jour et cinq jours par semaine, de neuf à cinq avec une interruption de vingt minutes pour manger debout devant leur machine. "C'est le bagne," disait Olga, une voisine. Mais elle ne parlait pas trop fort parce que c'était défendu de parler pendant le temps de travail [...] Il ne fallait pas qu'il y ait de temps mort" / 'That's what they did for eight hours a day and five days a week, from nine to five, with a twenty-minute break to eat lunch standing by their machine. 'This is a prison,' Olga, a coworker, would say. But she wouldn't talk very loudly because it was against the rules to talk during working hours [...] There was to be no down time' (154; 115–116). Given the high speed of assembly lines that are designed to maximize efficiency and the monotony of repeating the same action thousands of times per day, the subjects that are employed by factories begin to resemble the devices that they operate. Moreover, in this austere atmosphere of imposed silence, workers must constantly stay busy because, as the old adage states, "Time is money." The reader could also speculate that the twenty minute lunch break that Pouce and Poussy receive is the shortest amount of time that businesses must give their employees as mandated by law. Although the two young girls desperately attempt to break free from the chains of an economic system that forces so-called unskilled labor to accept such menial positions, it should be noted that many factories require their quasi-slaves to work six or even all seven days of the week and for shifts as long as twelve hours a day. Given the gross inequalities that are indicative of the realization of the neoliberal global village nightmare, poorly educated individuals from impoverished backgrounds have little choice but to accept these indignities or starve. Their destitution marks them as ripe for exploitation.

Reiterating the redundant nature of the tasks performed by the conditioned automates that are employed by plants across the globe, the narrator explains, "Elles racontaient toujours la même histoire, une histoire sans fin qui les entraînait loin de l'Atelier, avec ses barres de néon, son toit de tôle ondulée, ses fenêtres grillagées, le bruit assourdissant de toutes les machines en train de coudre inlassablement les mêmes poches, les mêmes boutonnières, les mêmes étiquettes Ohio made in U.S.A." / 'They always told the same story, a neverending story that took them far away from the workshop with its neon bars of light, its corrugated iron roof, its wire-grated windows, the deafening sound of all those machines endlessly sewing on those same pockets, those same buttonholes, those same Ohio Made in U.S.A. labels' (157; 118). Pouce and Poussy confront both uncertainty and danger to not only taste what solely the privileged few possess, but to liberate themselves as well from a society that reduces them to a mere commodity or a means to an end. Le Clézio reminds the reader that human beings are not warm bodies whose only value is defined by their capacity to earn money or to generate profits for others. As Sarojini Bissessur-Asgarally notes in the context of Le Clézio's fiction, "On comprend alors qu'au-delà de la civilisation moderne et matérialiste, l'homme existe comme esprit, comme âme et non pas comme une simple et vulgaire machine" / 'One therefore understands that beyond modern, materialistic civilization, man exists as a spirit, as a soul, and not as a simple and ordinary machine' (47; my trans.).

Bissessur-Asgarally's observation related to the profound sentiments of trauma from which Le Clézio's protagonists suffer in an increasingly urbanized global village in which their intrinsic worth is denied explains the ending of "la grande vie." After the authorities finally take Pouce and Poussy into custody effectively ending their short-lived "good(s)-life," the narrator concludes, "Elle (Poussy) regardait le profil entêté de Pouce, et elle ne pensait pas à ce qui allait suivre, aux longues attentes dans des corridors poussiéreux et dans des cellules sans jour. Elle pensait seulement au temps où elles allaient repartir, loin, repartir, cette fois, pour ne plus jamais revenir" / 'She (Poussy) was watching Pouce's stubborn profile and wasn't thinking about what was going to happen next—about the long hours of waiting in dusty hallways and dark cells. She was thinking only about the day they would be off again, off and away, far, far away, and this time, they would never come back again' (191; 144). Similar to numerous Leclézian protagonists, such as Daniel in "Celui qui n'avait jamais vu la mer" / 'The Boy who had never seen the sea,' Pouce and Poussy appear to be resolute in their determination to reject the artifice and sterility of the modern world. As subjects that feel imprisoned in the urban labyrinth, contemporary society appears to have little to offer these two young girls that are seeking a more authentic way of life. The remedy to this anguish will be explored in chapter four in the form of a more intimate relationship with the material universe to which all sentient beings are inextricably linked.

Similar to *Désert* and "la grande vie," Le Clézio's recent novel *Ourania*, published in 2006 by Gallimard, also defends those without a voice who are exploited in the global market. The disconcerting passages that expose inconvenient truths about the persistence of child labor practices despite international efforts to eradicate these crimes against humanity profoundly destabilize the reader. Specifically, *Ourania* depicts the failure of two divergent attempts at creating utopian societies which represent efforts to establish viable alternatives to the ultimate failure of McLuhan's idealistic dream. As Stiglitz and many other economists have noted, the unflattering realities of globalization have compelled discontents across the planet to envision a more equitable and just interconnected world.

In spite of the unsuccessful nature of both *Campos* and *Emporio*, the two aforementioned idyllic societies, these endeavors represent an evident dissatisfaction with the modern world including its neoliberal fallacies and materialistic obsessions that is concretized by the previously mentioned global protests. Confirming how *Ourania* was inspired by disquieting reflections concerning modernity, Le Clézio elucidates, "Les échecs de Campos et de l'Emporio, cependant, ne sont pas pour moi caractéristiques de ce lieu ni de ce pays, mais ils sont la réalité à l'échelle mondiale" / 'The failures of Campos and Emporio, however, for me are not (only) characteristic of this place or this country, but they represent reality on a worldwide scale' (Garcin n.p.; my trans.). Le Clézio underscores that these fictitious communities, loosely based on historical utopias, are inseparable from the larger context of globalization.

Outlining the two authentic societies that the geography professor Daniel Sillitoe stumbles upon during his stay in Mexico as a visiting researcher, Alexander Hertich notes,

> A major part of the reality that he discovers is Campos, founded by a half-Canadian, half-Indian who had a vision of a welcoming place outside the world's laws. Speaking their own invented language, Elmen[9] [...] The traditional family structure has been eliminated. Adults, while still protectors, have no authority over children. It is their peers, their brothers and sisters, who act as parents, teaching them through work and example [...] A second center of learning for Daniel is the Emporio, another potential utopia, where in the Greek tradition, thinkers from various disciplines exchange ideas and share them with the local inhabitants (628).

Although the inhabitants of Campos in particular appear to lead a more fulfilling and meaningful life by rejecting the perceived benefits of the global village despite the inherent flaws of their close-knit community, the menacing presence of the modern world is never far away. Moreover, political entities are often distrustful of those that attempt to remove themselves from the artificial borders of the larger society in which they reside. Indeed, this deep suspicion is one of the reasons that seem to have condemned Campos to failure.

As previously indicated, a compelling subplot decries the exploitation of humanity by international corporations and other unscrupulous individuals that profit from the acute poverty of the region. Upon his arrival at Emporio, Daniel is immediately taken aback by the lack of dialogue concerning deep social inequalities, prostitution, and exploitative hiring practices. As the narrator Daniel explains, "J'ai voulu parler de Lili, de la lagune d'Orandino, des camions qui emmènent chaque matin les enfants des Parachutistes pour les faire travailler aux champs, des femmes qui besognent chaque jour à l'usine de congélation et d'empaquetage, pour enrichir la Mac Cormick, la Strawberry Lake" / 'I wanted to talk about Lili, Orandino lagoon, the trucks that pick up the children of the Parachutistes to make them work in the field, the women that drudge every day in the packing and freezing factory to make Mac Cormick and Strawberry Lake rich' (116–117; my trans.). Like the children that Zora exploits and similar to the unfortunate human robots or zombies that work in the same factory as Pouce and Poussy, Mac Cormick and Strawberry Lake generate colossal profits because of the backbreaking labor of economically disadvantaged individuals simply trying not to die of hunger. It is evident that the inadequate salaries that these employees receive are unethical given that many of these people live in the deplorable, infamous slum known as "La Zone." Furthermore, since the researchers of Emporio need the financial support of corporate entities and other exploiters of the local population to fund their projects, this conflict of interest undermines the original humanistic motivations that encouraged the founder Don Thomas to create this initiative.

In reference to the prostitute and sex slave Lili for whom the protagonist has much compassion and respect, the narrator exposes the transnational businesses that in essence govern the region because of their economic and political influence. In "cette ville de pouvoir et d'argent sur laquelle règnent les rois de la fraise et les propriétaires des usines de congélation" / 'This city of power and money ruled by the strawberry kings and the owners of the freezing plants,' "Ce sont eux qui te dévoraient, chaque jour, chaque nuit, ils mangeaient ta pauvreté, ils rongeaient ton cœur, ils buvaient ton sang, ton souffle […] Ils n'en ont jamais assez, il leur faut toujours du sang neuf, de la chair fraîche" / 'It is them that devours you, every day, every night, they eat your poverty, they gnaw at your heart, they drink your blood, your breath […] They never have enough, they always need new blood and fresh meat' (177; my trans.). In addition to highlighting the insatiable zeal of maximizing profits, the writer observes that the capitalist system thrives because of its propensity to ensnare destitute human commodities. For this reason, when one form of exploitation disappears for whatever reason, it must be replaced with another organized network that procures cheap labor costs.

## THE SINISTER REALITIES OF HUMAN AND SEXUAL TRAFFICKING IN THE MODERN WORLD

The tragic saga of Lili is also emblematic of perhaps the greatest crime against humanity perpetrated for financial reasons, sexual trafficking. This debasement and appropriation of another person is a recurring theme in Le Clézio's *oeuvre*. Moreover, *Ourania* cautions the reader that this practice is much more common in the modern world than people might think. Daniel's deep empathy for the anguish experienced by Lili at the hands of her notorious master *El Terrible* is reminiscent of the sympathy expressed by the narrator John, de Nantucket for Araceli in "Pawana."[10] Whereas most of the other researchers from Emporio are indifferent to her desperate plight and even laugh at her expense, Daniel's harsh criticism of his colleagues' complicity in Lili's exploitation threatens his very presence at this institution. In fact, two fellow professors, Garci Lazaro and Leon Saramago, freely admit to purchasing the young woman's services. To the sardonic delight of those that are listening, Saramago himself recounts the following story: "Moi, je suis venu un peu après, je ne savais pas que Garci était déjà passé, on était dans la chambre, elle commençait à enlever sa jupe, enfin à la remonter, et je lui ai dit que c'était pour poser des questions, elle est restée avec la jupe relevée et elle m'a dit : les questions maintenant ou après, comme avec l'autre Missié le docteur ?" / 'Me, I arrived a little later, I didn't know that Garci had already been by, we were in the bedroom, she started to take off her skirt, then to put it back on, and I told her that I had questions, she left her skirt up and said to me: questions now or after, like with the other Mister, the doctor?' (47; my trans.). The thunderous applause in which his colleagues "riaient aux larmes" / 'laughed until they cried' concretizes the failure of Thomas's humanistic dream despite the purity of his intentions (47; my trans.).

This extreme indifference to the immeasurable suffering of Lili and their willful complicity in a system that debases the indigenous population is clearly antithetical to Thomas's vision. However, Daniel reacts aggressively to Saramago's anecdote that he does not consider to be comical. Indicting the "law-abiding citizens" without whose active participation this human trafficking network would not be possible, Daniel emphatically declares,

> Il s'agit d'un être humain, une fille qui mène une vie horrible, une vie qu'on ne voudrait pas souhaiter à ses pires ennemis, l'esclave de ce *Terrible,* dans son cloaque, une fille sur laquelle est passée la moitié de la population masculine de la vallée, tous les fraisiers, les avocatiers, les notables, les banquiers, et même les professeurs et les chercheurs de l'Emporio, et tu appelles ça du "terrain."
>
> You are talking about a human being, a girl who lives a horrible life, a life that you wouldn't wish upon your worst enemies, a slave of this *Terrible,* in his cesspit, a girl that half of the male portion of the population has slept with, all of the people from the strawberry and avocado plants, the local bigwigs, bankers, and even all of the professors and researchers from Emporio, and you refer to her as property (50; my trans.).

The revelation that Emporio is not a veritable utopia given that its members represent the top of the social ladder which renders the exploitation of victims like Lili possible triggers this heated exchange. Instead of trying to maximize their contribution to society, the scholars from this institution constantly vie for power and prestige in an effort to secure limited resources. Noting Le Clézio's scathing critique of personal agendas in academia and his disdain for those that are complicit in the debasement of the Other, Hertich remarks, "Yet all of these places and people also possess a darker side: forced into prostitution in part because of global economics, Lili is the victim of abusive hustlers; the Emporio does not offer an open forum to all researchers, but is filled with backbiting and political intrigue" (629). Given the researchers' lack of respect and compassion for the struggles of the indigenous population, the authentic dialogue that Don Thomas aspired to establish with the entire community appears to be beyond reach.

In addition to the unsettling passages concerning the persistence of sexual exploitation in the modern world in *Ourania*, it is perhaps in the somber collection of short stories entitled *Cœur brûle et autres romances* that the author most clearly articulates his profound concerns related to this ultimate form of debasement. Similar to *La ronde et autres faits divers*, *Cœur brûle et autres romances* has a solemn tone that reflects the anguish of those that suffer from the current socioeconomic paradigm. As this exploration has already established, Le Clézio is a writer whose worldview and astute observations allow him to depict both intense moments of euphoria and equally rending instants of pain that destabilize the reader. However, as Allen Thiher notes, *Cœur brûle et autres romances* is "vintage Le Clézio, powerful and disturbing" (138). These seven macabre vignettes paint vivid portraits of sheer horror which clearly negate universal logic associated with the concept of the global village.

The first narrative that comprises this collection, "Cœur brûle," recounts the story of two sisters that in spite of their common childhood experiences will lead very different lives. Whereas Clémence becomes a judge that sentences juvenile delinquents, Pervenche ironically surrounds herself with the same element of society that Clémence punishes on a daily basis. For this reason, Clémence often thinks about her sister to whom she has progressively become detached. Although Pervenche refuses her sister's help and becomes furious whenever Clémence expresses any sort of pity, the protagonist will fall prey to the very same urban traps that ensnare many other Leclézian protagonists. The cautionary epigraph that precedes the novel *Poisson d'or*, derived from a Nahuan proverb, is also applicable to "Cœur brûle." Like Laïla, Pervenche will discover that "il y a tant de lassos et de filets tendus pour toi dans ce monde" / 'there are so many ropes and nets outstretched for you in this world' (Le Clézio *Poisson d'or* 10; my trans.). In the destitute ghettos in which she spends most of her time, Pervenche makes herself vulnerable to those who are willing to exploit her at market value. The protagonist is literally sold and enslaved as a financial and sexual commodity. Summarizing the sinister pitfalls that victimize Pervenche, Thiher affirms, "Le Clézio narrates the tale of a young woman's degradation as she lives on the margins of society, in southern France, where she falls in with drug dealers, hoodlums, and others willing to exploit her. Her boyfriend, in fact, sells her to dealers who then imprison her for sexual exploitation" (138). Clémence watches helplessly as her sister plunges deeper into the abyss with each passing day.

It should be noted, however, that Pervenche's sexual victimization follows a certain progression. In the beginning, the intense erotic ecstasy that she experiences with Laurent helps her to escape quotidian reality for a few fleeting instants. Underscoring Pervenche's sexual awakening triggered by these euphoric moments of sensorial pleasure, the narrator explains, "Elle aimait bien sentir le cœur de Laurent [...] C'était des instants brillants. Elle pouvait oublier les heures d'ennui au lycée, les éternelles disputes avec sa mère, le regard hostile de Jean-Luc, le dédain silencieux de Clémence" / 'She liked feeling Laurent's heart [...] These were brillant moments. She could forget about the countless hours of boredom at high school, the neverending disputes with her mother, Jean-Luc's hostile gaze, and Clémence's silent disdain' (22; my trans.). Although the protagonist's discovery of her sexuality initially has the potential to lead to positive, transformative experiences that outlast the ephemeral nature of the erotic act itself, Pervenche soon realizes that these ecstatic moments do not facilitate a deeper emotional bond that transcends the purely physical nature of this union.

Even before Laurent sells Pervenche to Dax to support his drug addiction, an earlier incident concretizes his emotional indifference. After an unscrupulous photographer named Stern confesses his desire to exploit Pervenche's physical attributes by taking nude pictures of her, Laurent's reaction as he is waiting in the studio lobby reading fashion magazines is quite revealing. When Pervenche expresses her degust and mistrust of Stern given his dubious intentions, the narrator indicates, "Laurent semblait indifférent. 'Et en attendant, il ne t'a rien payé.' Et bien qu'elle perçut parfaitement le ridicule de la situation, Pervenche se sentit tout d'un coup envahie par la solitude" / 'Laurent seemed to be indifferent. 'While we wait, he didn't pay you anything.' Although she perfectly perceived the absurdity of the situation, Pervenche all of sudden felt invaded by solitude' (26; my trans.). After this traumatic event, Pervenche realizes that she is utterly alone because her only value to Laurent is defined by her utility as an object of desire and pleasure. Laurent has already reduced Pervenche's intrinsic worth and dignity as a human being to the amount of money that her beauty could bring both of them, especially himself. For this reason, it should not come as a surprise to the reader that Laurent will coldly and narcissistically sell his own girlfriend Pervenche in exchange for the fleeting moments of escape and euphoria induced by mind altering substances. Since happiness is the private affair of the individual in Western society, Laurent is easily able to divorce himself from any considerations of ethical responsibility for another person.

Although in an altered state of mind and desperately craving a fix, Laurent appears to be cognizant of the certain fate that awaits Pervenche after the deal is complete. Yet, he knowingly condemns the protagonist to be viciously raped and enslaved by Dax and his friends. Graphically depicting the physical and emotional trauma of this experience, the narrator elucidates,

> elle sent le corps de Dax qui s'appuie sur elle, qui force en elle, comme s'il traversait ses habits, sa peau, jusqu'au plus profond d'elle-même. Elle serre les dents pour ne pas crier. Elle pense : 'si je crie, il va me tuer

> [...] Laurent [...] l'a trahie, vendue. Il s'est servi d'elle comme un animal. Elle pense cela sans horreur, parce qu'elle est maintenant tout à fait au fond du gouffre, seule dans un endroit où personne ne viendra jamais la trouver.
>
> She feels Dax's body on top of her, that forces itself inside of her, as if he passed through her clothes, skin, all the way to her very core. She gritted her teeth to keep from yelling. She thought to herself: "If I scream, he will kill me [...]" Laurent betrayed and sold her. He used her like an animal. This thought didn't horrify her because now she is completely at the bottom of the abyss, alone in a place where no one will ever find her (49; my trans.).

This alarming passage reflects the dire realities of many ghettos across the globe controlled by gangs, drug traffickers, and other criminals that catch vulnerable prey like Pervenche in their nets. Moreover, for those forced by acute poverty to reside in these urban jungles marred by frustration, violence, desperation, and destitution, no easy path to integration into the global village dream exists for these disenfranchised individuals. The end of this tragic narrative of exploitation and extreme suffering offers little consolation to the reader. The denouement is cyclical as Clemence once again clings to this childhood image of her sister forever engraved in her memory before Pervenche is deprived of her humanity and forever engulfed by the void of urban malaise.[11]

The unsettling realism of "Cœur brûle" related to sexual exploitation haunts the reader while providing no solace, but the anguish of the protagonist in "Kalima" is perhaps even more poignant. "Kalima" is a short narrative comprised of thirteen pages that has been relatively neglected by the academic community. This disconcerting and graphic text is also part of the *Cœur brûle* collection. "Kalima" recounts the tragic saga of a prostitute, forced into the profession by dreadful pimps, whose life is violently and abruptly ended by an unidentified potential client that stabs her to death.

The story begins after this Moroccan immigrant's abused body is already lying in the morgue. In a compassionate effort to give Kalima back her dignity that was taken away by criminals that represent the disquieting face of urban ghettos, the narrator actively imagines the unbearable pain that must have been emblematic of her quotidian reality. As the narrator speculates, "Ô Kalima, quel chemin as-tu suivi jusqu'à cette journée du mois de janvier 1986, où tu gis étendue nue sur le marbre froid de la morgue [...] Qui se souvenait de toi, quand tu es arrivée sur le bateau, dans le port de Marseille" / 'O Kalima, what path did you take to end up here on this day in the month of January 1986 where you are lying naked on the cold marble slab of the morgue [...] Who remembers you, when you arrived on the boat, in the port of Marseille' (119; my trans.). Even if Kalima's untimely demise by the hand of those that appropriated her very humanity remains unnoticed by mainstream society that devotes little time to such issues, the narrator attempts to give the protagonist a voice that transcends this indifference.

Similar to Lalla in *Désert*, Kalima's aspirations of integrating herself into a welcoming global village where she can discover both prosperity and happiness are soon negated by harsh realities that often await "non-citizens" in affluent countries. Summarizing the narrative's plot and underscoring its connection to the six other stories of *Cœur brûle*, Thiher asserts,

> Le Clézio shows in his romance the lower depths of Marseilles and other southern French cities, where women from all countries of the world come and end up selling drugs or themselves. Often they wind up in the morgue, like the young prostitute described in "Kalima," a text addressed to a young girl who came up from the tropics to the "white city" in France, where she could never been warm enough in winter (139).

As Thiher and many other Leclézian critics have noted, immigrants from all corners of the globe arrive in developed countries such as the United States and France full of hope that reflects the universal logic of neoliberal ideology. However, Kalima's aspirations, like that of innumerable other victims of modernity, immediately decrystallize and disintegrate given the limited employment opportunities, unsanitary living conditions, and violence that await her. After her sister abandons her without even leaving a forwarding address, Kalima can visualize the unfolding nets that capture her yet she is powerless to avoid these snares. As the narrator explains, "Puis ta sœur est partie, elle a disparu un jour, sans laisser un mot [...] tu es devenue seule au monde, mais déjà tu ne pouvais plus retourner, tu ne pouvais plus t'échapper" / 'Then your sister left, she disappeared one day, without leaving a note [...] you were alone in this world, but you were already unable to return, you could no longer escape' (124; my trans.). With no one left to defend her, Kalima becomes an easy prey for the sexual traffickers that enslave her. Moreover, although the protagonist now realizes that Marseille is far from a promised land of opportunity, she is a prisoner of this vile place that does not possess the means to return to her homeland.

Developing a similar analogy of the mortal trap that will swallow Kalima as in *Poisson d'or* and "Cœur brûle," the narrator elucidates, "Les macs t'ont prise, ils t'ont battue, ils t'ont violée et battue dans une chambre d'hôtel, ils ont écrasé leurs bouts de cigarettes sur ton ventre et sur tes seins, cela a fait les marques indélébiles, comme des fleurs brûlées sur ta peau d'ambre, des marques indélébiles dans ton cœur" / 'The pimps took you, they beat you, they raped and beat you in a hotel room, they put out their cigarette butts on your stomach and breasts, this made water-resistant marks, liked burned flowers on your amber skin, water-resistant marks on your heart' (124–125; my trans.). This passage underscores that of all the traumatized protagonists in this somber collection, Kalima's dreams are the most singed or destroyed. Nothing will ever be able to remove the physical and mental scars from which the young Moroccan woman suffers. No cleaning agent is powerful enough to purify Kalima from the taint of the urban nightmare that she experiences daily.

In spite of Kalima's immeasurable anguish as a sex slave, however, her male aggressors are never able to take away her dignity or appropriate her alterity. As the narrator affirms, "Des hommes venaient, sans parler, ils montaient derrière toi, ils s'enfonçaient en toi comme dans une chair morte, puis ils repartaient sans rien dire, et l'argent restait. Combien d'hommes t'ont connue, ô Kalima? Mais ces milliers de fois, tu n'étais pas là, tu étais ailleurs, tu ne rêvais pas, tu étais dans un autre corps" / 'Men came and went, in silence, they took you from behind, they penetrated you as if you were dead flesh, then they left without saying anything and left the money. How many men slept with you, o Kalima? But these thousands of times, you were not there, you were elsewhere, you were not dreaming, you were in another body' (126; my trans.). The narrator describes an out of body experience that allows the protagonist to transcend debasing acts that she is incessantly forced to repeat with strangers. The men that pay Kalima's pimp might momentarily possess her lifeless body, but the young woman's essence will forever elude them.

During a momentary reprieve from this vicious cycle of prostitution, Kalima experiences one last vestige of hope that will soon vanish. Given that the latest man to whom she is enslaved named Bruno does not force her to sell her body, albeit he is authoritative and abusive, the protagonist briefly imagines a better life. Since Bruno is not as dreadful as the previous individuals that imprison her, Kalima fantasizes that they will leave this dreary ghetto together. Destroying this naïve illusion, one of Bruno's friend's scoffs, "Qu'est-ce qui te prend? Tu es folle? Jamais tu n'aurais pu dire que tu voulais partir avec lui [...] Les filles des rues n'ont pas d'avenir" / 'What is wrong with you ? Are you crazy? You should have never thought that you could leave with him [...] Street girls have no future' (131; my trans.). Bruno's inability to appreciate what Kalima has to offer as a human being and not a mere possession drives the final nail in her coffin. Similar to a long string of men that have appropriated her body for sexual gratification, Bruno does not want a meaningful relationship with a young woman that he cynically considers to be used goods.

Clearly aware that Bruno will not deliver her from this urban prison in which there appears to be no escape, Kalima visualizes an atemporal voyage that would allow her to go back in time thereby never encountering Marseille. Although the protagonist is cognizant that this journey is impossible, this inaccessible fantasy is all she has left. As the narrator explains, "tu as voulu aller vers la mer, comme si tu pensais que ce bateau qui t'avait amenée de Tanger à Marseille allait revenir, exactement le même, et tu pourrais faire le voyage à l'envers, remonter le temps presque à l'horizon et retrouver ce que tu avais perdu" / 'you wanted to go toward the sea, as if you thought that this boat that took you from Tanger to Marseille was going to return, this same boat, and you could do this trip in reverse, go back in time almost to the horizon and rediscover what you had lost' (127–128; my trans.). Without access to a better life in France, the exploited Kalima longs to return not only to her native soil, but also to a time before her physical and emotional wounds concretized her very existence.

The only comfort offered by the end of the narrative is that Kalima's intense anguish has finally come to a close. Imagining Kalima's ultimate flight from this earth and all of the searing pain that her existence entailed, the narrator concludes,

> Maintenant, cette ville, et ces avenues, et ce monde tout entier n'ont plus besoin de toi, ô Kalima. Tu t'es éloignée, et tu laisses tout ce monde dans son ordre, dans sa machination, ce monde où les places continuent à bruire, avec les fontaines et les filles, et les cris des coqs et les aboiements des chiens, et la poussière qui sans cesse monte et retombe, monte et se repose. Mais toi tu n'y es plus.
>
> Now this city, its avenues, and this entire world, they no longer need you, o Kalima. You have gone away, and you are leaving this whole world in its order, in its mechanical frame, this world where the public spaces continue to bustle, with fountains and girls, roosters crowing, dogs barking, and the dust which is always rising and descending and resting. But you are no longer here (132; my trans.).

The nuanced ending of this text underscores several important considerations. First, given that Kalima no longer belongs to the realm of the living, no one will ever be able to harm her again. The final images which conjure both Marseille and rural Morocco also articulate that the protagonist's ultimate destination is neither one of these countries. Although the chaos of human civilization will continue without Kalima since her ephemeral time on this earth is now complete, she is emblematic of the cycle of life and death itself. All life forms, human and otherwise, momentarily surge from the cosmic whole only to return one day to this same resting place that creates and sustains all of existence.

## THE IMMIGRANT AS THE FACE OF CONTEMPORARY HUMAN EXPLOITATION

As Bruno Thibault and other scholars have noted, the dire realities that are antithetical to the neoliberal dream that compels many immigrants and migrants such as Kalima to seek a more abundant life in the developed world are characteristic of a larger humanistic concern often expressed by Le Clézio. In his analysis of the novel *Poisson d'or,* Thibault affirms, "In *Poisson d'or,* he makes heard the voice of ethnic minorities, and describes the difficult working conditions of immigrants in first-world countries […] The immigrant, for Le Clézio, is without doubt the emblematic figure of modernity" ("J.M.G. Le Clézio" 366–367). Indeed, well-known narratives such as *Désert* and *Poisson d'or,* in addition to poignant novellas like "Le passeur" and "Fantômes dans la rue" confirm Thibault's assertion that the immigrant is the face of contemporary human exploitation in both the global village and in the author's works. Moreover, underscoring the aforementioned vulnerability and anguish of those who reside in "Le panier" with Lalla in *Désert,* Donna Seaman notes, "Lalla […] is forced to flee Morocco for Marseilles, where she witnesses the misery of other despised immigrants" (30). In an essay entitled "'Nomad Novelist' J.M.G. Le Clézio: The Integrative Voice," SS Prabhakar Rao reaches a similar conclusion, "*Désert* (1980) deals with the experiences of a young woman, Lalla, from the Sahara and the clash between her native culture and the European culture. The novel is replete with magnificent images of the lost North African culture and the depiction of Europe as seen through the eyes of unwanted immigrants" (55). Thibault, Seaman, and Rao all correctly assert that the traumatic and sometimes deadly struggles of Le Clézio's numerous immigrant protagonists transcend their personal suffering itself. These intense portraits of pure anguish represent the universal deception of millions of immigrants whose ill-founded aspirations of a better life are repeatedly crushed upon their arrival in the host country.

Similar to other recent texts written by Le Clézio, "Le passeur" / 'The Runner' recounts the story of an impoverished individual that leaves his homeland in an attempt to access the neoliberal dream. However, given the exploitation that awaits him after illegally crossing the Italian border into France, the protagonist Miloz realizes that his original vision is illusory and thus begins the arduous journey on foot to return to his country of origin. Specifically, Miloz spends approximately one year as a clandestine immigrant in France before his return voyage. Clearly uncertain of what he will discover after he successfully crosses the mountains, Miloz's motivations are selfless. Miloz does not visualize an existence full of glamour and glitz so often advertised by the media. The protagonist of "le passeur" just wants to procure enough money to marry his fiancée Lena and to ensure their financial security for the future. Similar to Kalima, Miloz's quotidian reveries are soon fueled by an intense desire to return to his place of origin given the harsh living and working conditions that ensnare him upon his arrival.

The first character that the reader encounters Tartamella is emblematic of the underground networks of exploiters, underscored by Stephen Castles in chapter one, which identify easy prey like Miloz in order to generate income. In fact, it is Tartamella that will take money from these destitute individuals that represent many different nationalities before introducing them to "le passeur" or the guide that will lead them into what they hope will be a promised land. In spite of the linguistic and cultural barriers that divide them, this international group is united by the universal language of suffering. As the narrator explains, "Ils sont nombreux [...] De toutes les nationalités, Grec, Turc, Egyptien, Yougoslave, Tunisien [...] Ils sont habillés de toutes les façons [...] et ils parlent toutes sortes de langues. Mais quand Tartamella les regarde, ils les reconnaît bien, parce qu'ils sont tous semblables par la pauvreté, l'inquiétude, la faim" / 'There are quite a few of them [...] Of every nationality—Greek, Turkish, Egyptian, Yougoslavian, Tunisian [...] They're dressed in all different ways [...] and they speak all sorts of languages. But Tartamella can easily pick them out at a glance, for they all look alike because of their poverty, their anxious faces, their hunger' (195–196; 147). Although Tartamella recognizes the destitution and desperation that is written on the face of those that he victimizes, he continues to be complicit in this system of human trafficking.

The narrator also reminds the reader that these diverse individuals are willing to confront tremendous uncertainty to break the chains of poverty. As the narrator states, "Il (Miloz) a un peu peur aussi. Qu'y a-t-il de l'autre côté? [...] Où va-t-il maintenant ? Quel profit va-t-il tirer de cette aventure ? Quand reverra-t-il Lena, Lena aux yeux de topaze? " / 'He's a little afraid too. What awaits him on the other side? [...] Where is he going now? What will he gain from this adventure? When will he see Lena again, Lena and her topaz eyes?' (198; 149). Miloz has more questions than answers concerning what he will eventually find in France, but this journey is worth the risk because of his desperate economic plight. This attitude on the part of Miloz and his international companions reflects the ever growing divide between the rich and poor which has perhaps reached its zenith, at least on a global scale. This fateful decision highlights Pauline Barber's[12] astute observation that globalization is not truly global given the uneven benefits that its processes generate.

Taking advantage of the financial situation that forces people like Miloz to resort to drastic measures, Tartamella and his colleagues have created an elaborate network that transports immigrants to France where they will have little choice but to sign exploitative contracts that make them quasi-slaves. In exchange for long hours of debilitating manual labor, they receive miniscule salaries, reside in precarious, unsanitary accommodations, and are exposed to a dangerous and authoritative working environment. Describing both the deplorable living and working conditions of these disenfranchised people with whom Miloz resides, the narrator elucidates,

> un marteau-piqueur à la main, et ils creusaient tout le jour la pierre blanche éblouissante. La nuit ils dormaient dans une roulette de tôle posée sur des pierres, à l'entrée de la carrière. La carrière était fermée par une clôture de fil de fer barbelé, dont le portail était condamné la nuit par un cadenas. Il y avait aussi un grand chien-loup enchaîné, qui courait attaché à la clôture par un mousqueton passé dans un fil de fer.
>
> A pneumatic drill and put at the foot of a cliff with some other men, and they spend the whole day chipping away at the blinding white rock. At night, they sleep in a metal trailer set up on stones at the entrance to the quarry. The quarry is surrounded by a barbed wire fence with a gate that is padlocked at night. There is also a big German shepherd that runs around the fence on a chain hooked to the metal wire (213; 161).

Under the guise of protecting this group of immigrants from suspicious authorities, Tartamella and his associates quite literally imprison their victims. Given that these immigrants with fake identification papers fear deportation, arrest, or other forms of retribution by the French government, they are forced to accept this prison-like atmosphere which is imposed upon them. As Wickramasekara and Taran from chapter one affirm, irregular immigrants represent a cheap labor force that reduces operational costs, eliminates competitors, and generates colossal profits for those at the top of the ladder.

In stark contrast to Kalima's vision of turning back the hands of time and returning to her homeland, Miloz's dream of being reunited with his fiancée appears to be feasible at the end of the narrative. After demanding the wages that he was owed despite not fulfilling the two year contract that he was coerced to sign, Miloz begins the treacherous reverse voyage, once again by foot, to his country of origin. Although the protagonist worries that the authorities will derail his plan given that he must momentarily rest to eat, the profound indifference of the people that he encounters renders Miloz virtually invisible. As the narrator affirms, "Il n'ose plus aller dans les bars pour boire de la bière, parce que les gens regardent son visage hirsute, brûlé de soleil et de froid, et ses habits usés et pleins de poussière de ciment […] Il y a des jeunes filles si belles […] Mais elles ne le voient pas, elles passent devant lui sans le regarder, leurs beaux yeux cachés par des lunettes de soleil, ou bien fixés au loin à travers lui" / 'He doesn't dare go into the bars anymore to drink a beer because people look at his unshaven face, burnt from so much sun and cold, and his worn clothing, covered with cement dust […] There are young women who are so beautiful […] But they don't see him; they go right past without looking at him, their handsome eyes hidden behind sunglasses or else gazing through him into the distance' (219; 165–166). Miloz takes precautions to protect himself, but these considerations do not seem to be necessary given that those around him appear to be indifferent to his suffering. Since everyone else is too busy trying to actualize his or her own consumerist fantasies based on narcissistic neoliberal ideology and an egocentric view of happiness, Miloz's presence remains essentially unperceived by those around him. In Western society, as long as one's own pockets are full, little motivation exists to reflect upon the anguish of those whose humanity has been reduced to a mere commodity.

In addition to this lack of compassion that denigrates Miloz and makes his phantasmal existence resemble that of a ghost which ironically protects him from danger, the end of the narrative offers additional solace to the reader. Despite his immeasurable fatigue, the image of his beloved Lena sustains the protagonist as he continues to walk. Underscoring Miloz's inner drive that compels him to keep pushing his frail and abused body, the narrator concludes, "La fatigue pèse sur lui, l'air manque, et chaque fois qu'il sent qu'il va tomber, il dit à haute voix, comme le passeur: 'Marche! Marche!' [...] Malgré le vent glacé qui vient des cimes enneigées, il se couche sur le bord de la falaise, et les yeux agrandis par la fatigue, il regarde au loin, comme si son regard pouvait éveiller quelque part, malgré le temps, malgré le silence, les yeux de Lena" / 'His body is heavy with exhaustion; there is not enough air, and every time he feels as if he were going to stumble, he says in a loud voice, just like the runner, 'Get a move on! Get a move on!' [...] Despite the icy wind coming from the snowy peaks, he lies down on the edge of the cliff, eyes wide with fatigue, and stares off into the distance, as if somewhere out there, despite the time, despite the silence, Lena's eyes would suddenly blink open under his steady gaze' (221; 167). Although he was forbidden to write to his fiancée because the foreman indicated that these types of correspondences often alert authorities, Miloz hopes that Lena has been patiently awaiting his return and that her amorous feelings have not changed. For this reason, the tone of the denouement is that of cautious optimism. Perhaps, Miloz and Lena will be reunited if the protagonist is able to reach his final destination. It is probable that Miloz will remain destitute, but it is also possible that he will be content and once again free from the tyranny of human exploitation.

The metaphor of disenfranchised and marginalized immigrants as specters, which concretizes mainstream society's indifference to their suffering, is quite poignant in the narrative "Le passeur." It should also be noted that many Leclézian characters with no fixed origin possess phantasmal properties given that they often appear, disappear, and reappear.[13] However, it is perhaps in the little-known and unedited novella entitled "Fantômes dans la rue" / 'Ghosts in the street' in which Le Clézio develops this disconcerting comparison to its fullest. This realistic and destabilizing short story has been largely ignored by the literary community due to the fact that it appeared in the July 10, 2000, edition of the French magazine *Elle* as a special supplement. Given that a more commercialized and easily accessible form of this novella has yet to be published for the general public, many people are even unaware that this work exists. Yet, "Fantômes dans la rue" is crucial to this exploration of the evaporated dream of the global village because Le Clézio's deep concerns related to the plight of the immigrant are evident.

The cinematic and *mise-en-abîme* techniques that Le Clézio employs in this text allow the elderly female narrator to inhabit the inner circuitry of surveillance cameras all across Paris that record the precarious situation in which many unwanted immigrants in France find themselves. Similar to Lalla in *Désert,* the "ghosts" of "Fantômes dans la rue" suffer from exploitative hiring practices, ethnic discrimination, indifference, ignorance, and xenophobia. Underscoring his former complicity in a systematic network of exploitation as a human resources employee, the aptly named Renault confesses,[14]

> En ce temps-là, quand je travaillais à l'usine, le gouvernement incitait à l'embauche des ouvriers d'Afrique du Nord, Algériens, Tunisiens, Marocains, et aussi des Africains du Sénégal, du Mali, de la Côte d'Ivoire. C'était moi qui étais chargé de les engager, on appelait ça exploiter les ressources humaines [...] C'était mon boulot à l'usine, j'étais bien payé pour ça, pour faire le tri, pour dire à celui-ci, toi, et toi, et à celui-là, non, pas toi.

> During this time, when I used to work at the factory, the government encouraged hiring workers from North Africa, Algerians, Tunisians, and Moroccans in addition to Africans from Senegal, Mali, and Ivory Coast. I was in charge of hiring them, we called this exploiting human resources [...] This was my job at the factory, I got paid well for this, to choose, to say to this person, you, and you, and to this person over there, no, not you (9–10; my trans.).

This former director of human resources who resigns for ethical reasons clearly articulates that many powerful corporations dehumanize both undocumented and legal immigrants as an expendable labor force that ensures massive profits for shareholders. Given the limited opportunities that are available to immigrants, they have no recourse but to accept the slave wages that they receive in addition to harsh working conditions that they often encounter. It should also be noted that Renault's fateful decision to leave Renault has severe repercussions for this protagonist. Indeed, Renault will become a phantom himself that haunts the ugly underbelly of the global village as he loses everything including his wife and children.

Further reiterating his scathing critique of the transnational company for which he used to work, Renault states, "Moi je savais leurs noms, c'était moi qui avais rempli leurs dossiers [...] Mais chez Renault, à la direction, ils ne cherchaient pas à savoir leurs vrais noms, tous les hommes c'était Mohamed, toutes les femmes c'était Fatima. Pour les gens haut placés, même pour les chefs d'atelier, ces gens-là n'existaient pas, ils étaient tous pareils" / 'As for me, I knew their names, I am the one who completed their forms [...] But at Renault, for the management, they did not try to learn their real names, all of the men were Mohamed and all of the women were Fatima. For people at the top, even for the leaders of the factory, these people did not exist, they were all the same' (10–11; my trans.). The now homeless protagonist highlights that Renault actively recruits destitute immigrants that are interchangeable and easily replaced because of their dire situation in a hostile host country. Renault's upper management deprives these individuals of their humanity given that their value is purely defined in terms of their utility to keep the assembly lines running and to not ask questions.

Although Pouce and Poussy also describe the authoritative and debasing atmosphere of modern factories as a "bagne" or prison, immigrants that work in these conditions face additional obstacles that render their successful integration into society difficult. Negative cultural stereotypes, predicated upon ignorance, fear, and ethnocentrism, also reinforce the glass ceiling that prevents many immigrants from climbing the social ladder and truly discovering a better life. In reference to these preconceived notions that adversely affect many different ethnicities and communities, Renault explains, "Jamais, jamais, ils ne pensaient jamais à elles, sauf quand ils avaient besoin d'une cuisinière, pour une réunion, un comité d'entreprise, alors ils disaient au mari 'N'oublie pas, tu dis à Fatima de nous préparer un bon couscous [...] Tu n'oublies pas, hein' [...] Tu vois, c'était comme ça, ceux qui partaient au bled rapportaient des tapis pour les chefs, et ceux qui restaient, leurs femmes préparaient le couscous pour les comités " / 'Never, never, did they think about them, unless they needed a cook, for a business or other committee meeting, then they said to the husband 'Don't foget to tell Fatima to make us some good couscous [...] Don't forget, hey' [...] You see, this is how it was, those who left the slums brought back rugs for the managers, and those who stayed, their wives made couscous for the committees' (14–15; my trans.). This passage concretizes the sardonic attitude of Renault's governing elite. Instead of valorizing the unique cultural contributions of North African men and women to French society and how some of these individuals could perhaps make Renault a better company, it is evident that the limited roles of immigrants are clearly delineated. Convinced of their cultural and intellectual superiority, Renault's management does not provide any professional development opportunities that would allow their disenfranchised and deliberately exploited African employees to gain access to greater prosperity. For this reason, these ghosts incessantly appear and reappear in slightly different forms in the somber corridors of this factory.

Despite the disconcerting realism related to the precarious situation that many immigrants confront daily upon their arrival in the host country, the bittersweet yet also cautiously optimistic tone is similar to that of "le passeur." After the elderly lady indicates that her demise is imminent, she also expresses the following dream for all of humanity: "Je vais quitter mon poste maintenant [...] Je suis bientôt prête. Je vais descendre rejoindre Vincent [...] Peut-être qu'un jour les êtres humains deviendront complètement, magnifiquement visibles [...] Peut-être qu'un jour l'amour sera partout, recouvrira chaque instant de la vie d'une poudre de diamant" / 'I am going to leave my post now [...] I will soon be ready. I am going to come down to rejoin Vincent [...] Perhaps one day human beings will become entirely and magnificently visible [...] Perhaps one day love will be everywhere and it will cover every instant of life with a diamond powder' (46–48; my trans.). This passage reveals the humanistic motivations that compelled the narrator to spend years compiling her obsessive observations. Although she is uncertain if anyone will ever view her project or decide to continue to give a voice to those that are unable to defend themselves in the modern world, she hopes that mainstream Western society will one day remove its myopic lens and acknowledge the immense anguish of those human objects of disdain that are being exploited at market value. Whether anyone else is sensitive to the plight of these frail apparitions that haunt modernity, the narrator can at least bear witness to the wrenching pain that is characteristic of their quotidian reality.

## CONCLUSION

The stark realism of Le Clézio's narratives, such as "David," "Ô voleur, voleur, quelle vie est la tienne?," *Désert*, "la grande vie," *Ourania*, "Kalima," "le passeur," and "Fantômes dans la rue" dismisses the naïve euphoria associated with global village idealism. Not only are billions of people across the planet failing to enjoy the fruits of unprecedented prosperity, but it should also be noted that the forces of modernity deliberately trap many unsuspecting and vulnerable prey into their nets. Although multinational corporations like Renault are generating profits that would have seemed impossible only a few decades ago, poverty is on the rise in both developed and emerging economies. Exploitative hiring practices, or what the economic researcher Gerald Houseman refers to as a "race to the bottom" have exacerbated this growing problem (59). The alleged universal benefits of neoliberal globalization only seem to be applicable to the dwindling social elite. In addition to reminding the reader that the sinister practice of human trafficking, including sexual exploitation, is alive and well, Le Clézio notes that immigrant and migrant populations are the most vulnerable of all. Perhaps the beginning of a solution to complex issues related to globalization is to remove the myopic barriers that prevent us from acknowledging unpleasant realities. Similar to the narrators of "Fantômes dans la rue," human civilization must finally confess that certain fundamental truths related to the current state of the global village are antithetical to romantic illusions that serve to maintain power and privilege at the expense of the Other.

## NOTES

1. (e.g.) Dormoy, Nadine, and Liliane Lazar, eds. *A Chacun sa France.* New York: P. Lang, 1990, 121–133. Seaman, Donna. Rev. of *Désert,* by J.M.G. Le Clézio. *Booklist* Jul. 2009: 30. Lazar, Liliane. Rev. of *Révolutions,* by J.M.G. Le Clézio. *French Review* 78 (3): 622–623.
2. See introduction.
3. In *Le Chercheur d'or,* The Manafs are a traditional, marginalized society with no legal recognition that resides in mountain villages. Moreover, the members of this disenfranchised portion of the population are descended from runaway slaves that still suffer from exploitation and discrimination.
4. Alexis's consumerist obsessions will be further investigated in chapter three.
5. The plight of the immigrant in Le Clézio's narratives will be systematically explored in a later section of this chapter.
6. This poignant narrative will be briefly analyzed in a later section of this chapter.
7. This decision will be analyzed in the context of consumerism in chapter three.
8. In an interview with Tirthankar Chanda from *Label France,* Le Clézio clarifies in reference to the word *romances,* "C'était un mot un peu ironique pour décrire des situations qui sont tragiques. Le livre est composé de sept nouvelles, des récits sombres" / 'This was a slightly ironic word to describe tragic situations. The book is composed of seven novellas, somber narratives' (n.p.; my trans.).
9. A young hydrocephalic prodigy also attempts to create his own language in Le Clézio's short story "Martin."
10. It should be noted that the name of the protagonist John, de Nantucket contains a comma.
11. It is also worth noting that in addition to the polyphony that is indicative of Le Clézio's second literary cycle that begins with texts such as *Voyages de l'autre côté* and *Mondo et autres histoires* highlighted by critics like Claude Cavallero, Le Clézio often creates "autotextual" links between various works. The autotextual relationship between *Ourania* and "Cœur brûle" is quite evident and it reinforces the writer's denunciation of sexual exploitation. The sinister character "le *Terrible*" in *Ourania* appears to represent a rewriting and expansion of the protagonist 'Nacho le terrible' in "Cœur brûle" that victimizes and terrorizes the indigenous population of Mexico while Pervenche's mother Hélène lives there with another dubious character "Edouard" who closely resembles the sadistic Haitian psychiatrist with whom Simone resides in *Le Poisson d'or.*
12. See chapter one.
13. For a more comprehensive discussion of the complex and ambivalent phenomenon of invisibility in Le Clézio's narratives, see Moser, Keith. "J.M.G. Le Clézio's Urban Phantoms and the Paradox of Invisibility." *Modern Language Review* 106 (3): 724–744.
14. The *oeuvre* "Fantômes dans la rue" is a complex work that contains multiple narrative voices including that of the aforementioned elderly lady and "Renault."

# THREE

# Consumerism, the Media, and the Anonymous Forces that Sustain the Modern World in Le Clézio's Narratives

Given the grave realities of the global village, as outlined in the preceding chapters, which clearly negate simplistic neoliberal ideology intentionally propagated to control the increasingly impoverished masses, how is it possible that such a world order can continue to justify its own existence? Inspired by researchers from the field of social justice, such as Jared Diamond, Jean Ziegler, and Hannah Arendt,[1] Claudia von Werlhof poses a similar question, "How else can we understand the fact that in times when civilization has reached its alleged zenith, a human being starves every second?" (100). In Western society, popular culture constantly reinforces the notion that we are living more fulfilling and prosperous lives than ever in comparison to any other period of human history. Yet, on a global level, anguish and systematic exploitation appear to have reached unprecedented levels with no end in sight. For this reason, von Werlhof and numerous other scholars have attempted to elucidate these apparent paradoxes or even blatant contradictions that undermine the universalist ideology associated with McLuhan's euphoric vision. In an attempt to answer von Werlhof's disconcerting question, this chapter will delve into consumerism, popular culture, corporate control of the media, advertising, and marketing in the context of Le Clézio's narratives.

In a recent interview with Andrew Mullen, Edward Herman and Noam Chomsky note, "As long as highly unequal and unfair economic and social orders persist, their dominant elites will have to justify themselves and they will continue to need supportive propaganda"[2] (20). Herman and Chomsky assert that powerful and deeply entrenched hegemonic and ideological structures serve to maintain privileges and the current system of gross inequality. Moreover, the privileged few or those that benefit the most from the current socioeconomic paradigm carefully and selectively disseminate information to prevent those at the bottom of the ladder from revolting. The transnational entities that dominate the global economic landscape incessantly promote and laud consumerist virtues while explaining the exceptions to the rule or those that are living a nightmare and not a dream. Similar to the absurd doctrine of "benevolent colonialism" that justified human trafficking and debasement creating an ethnocentric moral minority that controlled the majority of planetary resources, neoliberalism's fallacy that "everyone is a winner" ensures that the global populace will remain submissive even in the midst of tremendous suffering that places their very existence and that of the earth itself in peril (Dean 56).

## CONSUMERISM, THE NEW OPIATE OF THE MASSES: DOES THE GOODS LIFE = "THE GOOD LIFE"?

As Grant Duncan and others explain in the context of happiness research in chapter one, the myth that the incessant acquisition of materialistic goods automatically equates to a greater appreciation of life itself has permeated all facets of Western society. Indeed, this misguided belief is the "new opiate of the people" (Langman and Morris n.p.). The unhealthy obsession to obtain as many luxury items as possible is now conceived as the ideal model that should guide all of our actions. As Bissessur-Asgarally explains in chapter two concerning the profound anguish and alienation of early Leclézian protagonists, the unequivocal messages of mainstream society encourage the modern subject to enjoy life through consumption while they reduce the intrinsic worth of each individual to mere machines whose only value is defined by their capacity to contribute to and sustain an economic system. Many Leclézian characters, such as Alexis in *Le Chercheur d'or,* strive to live a more authentic and meaningful existence by healing themselves from these destructive compulsions that often prevent one from actualizing a true state of happiness.

Several critics have examined the difficulties that Leclézian protagonists experience because of neoliberal ideology's inability to fulfill deep emotional and spiritual needs that cannot be replaced by monetary possessions. For this reason, *Le Chercheur d'or* is often accurately described as a novel of apprenticeship in which the protagonist blindly pursues narcissistic riches only to discover eventually that human treasures are far more important than those lauded by the supporters of globalization. In fact, it should be noted that the literary scholars Marianne Froye, Claire-Neige Jaunet, Luce Mondor, and Isabelle Roussel-Gillet[3] all analyzed this

Mauritian saga, published in 1985 by Gallimard, from this perspective in a special volume. In the beginning of the novel, Alexis appears to have internalized the dominant ideology of Western society to such an extent that financial affluence and prestige are all that matters.

However, Alexis's literal search will give way to a more symbolic, philosophical quest that represents the possibility of a profound inner transformation. Summarizing the work's plot, Nadine Dormoy affirms, "Le narrateur du *Chercheur d'or* est évidemment un héros quêteur. On peut, dans un premier temps, lui trouver des ressemblances avec le chevalier médiéval Perceval, ou Parsifal, à la recherche du Graal. De même que la quête de Dieu renvoie à la quête de soi, la recherche du trésor aboutira à la découverte de soi" / 'The narrator of *The Prospector* is obviously a hero on a quest. We can at first find resemblances between Alexis and the medieval knight Perceval, or Parsifal, in search of the Grail. As the search for God reflects the search for oneself, the treasure hunt will lead to a greater discovery of oneself' (88; my trans.). Specifically, Alexis will rediscover the sacred grandeur of the elements from which he had become alienated given the countless years of his life that he wasted in pursuit of the unknown Corsaire's chimerical buried riches. Underscoring the fundamental role of the young indigenous man Denis in terms of re-awakening certain dormant cosmic sensibilities inside of the protagonist, Lotte Garsdal explains, "Alexis, le personnage principal, est très lié avec Denis, un jeune indigène, en compagnie de qui il est initié à la vie dans la nature" / 'Alexis, the main character, is very much linked to Denis, a young indigenous boy, in whose company he is initiated to life in nature' (21; my trans.). This existential remedy to the anguish experienced by Le Clézio's traumatized subjects that are utterly disconnected from primordial elemental forces will be discussed in the following chapter. Moreover, it should be noted that *Le Chercheur d'or* is a much more complex work than it originally seems. The ambivalent nature of the end of the novel including Alexis's moral epiphanies themselves disquiets the reader.

Although Alexis is raised in a family that loses nearly everything that they own because of the chimerical fantasies of his father related to buried treasure and other projects such as the "projet d'aérostat" / 'airplane transportation (plan)' and "le projet de la centrale électrique" / 'power station project,' the protagonist will inexplicably appropriate these unrealistic paternal dreams for himself (43; 33). Specifically, Alexis convinces himself that the Corsaire's treasure is the key to restoring his family's fortune, glory, and social reputation. Justifying his decision to abandon his mother and sister Laure during their time of need to search for gold, the narrator explains, "je partirais sur le *Zeta,* ce serait mon navire Argo, celui qui me conduirait à travers la mer jusqu'au lieu dont j'avais rêvé, à Rodrigues, pour ma quête d'un trésor sans fin" / 'I would leave on the Zeta; it would be my Argo, the ship that would take me across the sea to the place of my dreams, to Rodrigues and my quest for the boundless treasure' (119; 103). Clearly espousing a neoliberal view of happiness, the protagonist fantasizes about the seductive image of success and inner satisfaction that the realization of this pipe dream will bring. For all of the problems that ail his family, Alexis envisions that financial prosperity and the increased consumption that such a life of luxury entails represent the only remedy.

Blatantly admitting that his intentions are narcissistic rather than altruistic before his imminent departure, the narrator confesses, "Je ne voulais penser à personne. Seule Laure a su mon départ, mais elle n'a rien dit à Mam [...] Là-bas, à Rodrigues, nous pourrons commencer une vie nouvelle, nous aurons une grande maison, des chevaux, des arbres. Est-ce qu'elle pouvait me croire?" / 'I did not want to think of anyone. Only Laure knew that I was leaving, and she hadn't told Mam [...] We'll start a new life on Rodrigues. We'll have a big house with horses and trees. Did she believe me?' (124; 107–108). Although Alexis pretends that he has embarked on this arduous and uncertain journey to ensure the collective happiness and economic security of the entire filial unit, it is evident that the protagonist has a difficult time thinking of anyone but himself. Alexis only reflects upon the repercussions of his actions for others in an attempt to free himself of any feelings of remorse or guilt. For this reason, the narrator's incessant quest to unlock the enigma surrounding the legendary Corsaire's hidden treasure should be interpreted as a self-centered act that Alexis hopes will one day fulfill all of his personal consumerist aspirations. Unlike certain Leclézian characters such as the narrator of "Ô voleur, voleur, quelle vie est la tienne?" which embody the image of sacrifice, Alexis's veritable motivations are indicative of the profound avarice that has wreaked havoc on Western society.

The narrator of *Le Chercheur d'or* has embraced the empty virtues of consumerism so deeply that it almost prematurely costs him his life. After Alexis spends countless hours of physically debilitating manual labor attempting to unearth the Corsaire's buried riches, Ouma and her brother Sri will help the protagonist recuperate from heat stroke and exhaustion. In a response to Ouma's interrogation "Vous aimez vraiment l'or?" / 'Do you really love gold so much?,' the narrator asserts, "Je lui parle de la cachette que j'ai trouvée sous les pierres de basalte, des signes qui indiquent ces pierres et ce ravin, mais je suis véhément et confus, et elle doit croire que je suis fou. Pour elle, le trésor ne compte pas, elle méprise l'or comme tous les manafs" / 'I tell her about the hiding place I found under the basalt stones and the signs indicating these stones, this ravine, but I am confused and too vehement and she must think that I am mad. The treasure means nothing to her; like all Manafs she holds gold in contempt' (252; 224). Alexis is undoubtedly in a state of delirium, but the true illness from which he suffers is the materialistic obsessions that now concretize his entire existence. The endless pursuit of economic wealth and the neoliberal dream of unbridled consumption prevent Alexis from living a meaningful and fulfilling life. The narrator himself has been consumed by simplistic ideology and compelling fantasies. Therefore, Alexis is blind to all of the real treasures, such as an intimate relationship with the Other (Ouma), that might actually be able to facilitate a deeper appreciation of his ephemeral existence on this earth.

In the context of the global village which continues to spread its shallow values across the planet destroying traditional virtues, Anne Cunningham notes, "advertising,[4] as the defining institution of capitalist systems, imparts hollow ideals and thus tears at the very fabric of society" (229). Indoctrinated at birth with unequivocal messages which urge the modern subject to consume his or her way to happiness, Alexis's superficial identity becomes inseparable from his compulsion to possess as much as possible. Although consumerist propaganda insists that human beings were always supposed to live the neoliberal dream and that the current era therefore represents the pinnacle of civilization, it is evident that for many of Le Clézio's protagonists like Alexis the realization of McLuhan's vision is a tragic saga of broken promises, exploitation, and seductive illusions. Moreover, in reference to both consumerism and ecological sustainability, Margee Hume explains, "There is some evidence of those opting for a simple lifestyle, rejecting the excesses of the modern consumer economy" (386). Even though the supporters of globalization adamantly maintain that no viable alternative to the current system exists nor is one needed, Le Clézio often depicts traditional civilizations that have resisted integration into the global village. Given that Alexis is tirelessly pursuing neoliberal fallacies that are unattainable for most people, his existence is inauthentic and void of any real meaning. The author's representations of indigenous cultures in numerous works remind the reader that consumerist virtues in and of themselves cannot fulfill basic human needs such as a sense of belonging and emotional connections to other people. Furthermore, ethnocentric attitudes related to cultural superiority have convinced us to devalorize the marginal voices of traditional communities that have much to contribute to humanity if we are willing to listen.[5]

Alexis's example in *Le Chercheur d'or* illustrates that the quality of an individual's life is not defined by how much a person is able to consume. In this Mauritian saga, Le Clézio also deconstructs the simplistic notion that everyone is benefiting from the manner in which globalization is currently being managed. In her discussion of the "fantasy structure" of neoliberal ideology, Jodi Dean underscores, "as neoliberalism emphasizes competition, it holds onto the notion that everyone is a winner, a notion clearly at odds with competition because in competition there are winners and losers" (55–56). In addition to the elusive treasure hunt that is the focus of the narrative, Alexis's father also unsuccessfully attempts several capitalistic endeavors as previously noted. It is perhaps the failure of these ill-fated ventures that compels him to delve deeper into even more illusory fantasies. The financial destitution and eventual bankruptcy of Alexis's family is emblematic of the unpleasant reality that neoliberal economic policies have generated both unparalleled prosperity for a slim minority and unprecedented poverty for others. Alexis's father takes the necessary risks that he hopes will create a better life for his family, but the gamble backfires as he plunges them into greater desperation.

In a typical *Bildungsroman* fashion, the progressive unfolding of the narrative initially appears to suggest that the protagonist's quest will ultimately culminate in a radical inner transformation that transcends the literal search itself. While with Ouma in the enigmatic Mananava forest, Alexis discovers another way of life that differs drastically from that of mainstream Western society. Describing the profound state of contentment that he experiences with Ouma in this privileged site far removed from the modern world, the narrator declares, "Nous avons rêvé des jours de bonheur, à Mananava, sans rien savoir des hommes. Nous avons vécu une vie sauvage, occupés seulement des arbres, des baies, des herbes [...] nous pêchons des écrevisses [...] Ici, tout est simple" / 'Our life on Mananava, far from other people, is like an exquisite dream. We live like primitives, concerned only with the trees, coves, grass, and water [...] we hunt for crayfish [...] Nothing is complicated here' (364; 328). The reader ponders whether Alexis has defeated his materialistic obsessions and is finally capable of once again appreciating nature outside of its utilitarian value as a financial commodity. In other words, has the narrator re-established an intimate relationship with the cosmic whole from which he realizes that he is linked?

A strong declaration by the protagonist himself confirms why numerous critics have categorized *Le Chercheur d'or* as a coming of age novel. As the narrator states, "je ne pense guère à l'or, je n'en ai plus envie" / 'I hardly ever think about the gold; I don't desire it anymore' (365; 329). Given the direct nature of this confession, the reader wonders if Alexis has been able to free himself from the shackles of consumerist ideology that literally caused him to squander years of his life searching for buried treasure. It briefly seems as if the protagonist has re-awoken to realize that an authentic existence in harmony with the elements and a meaningful, committed relationship with Ouma represent the ultimate form of wealth.

Yet, the reader soon begins to question the depth of Alexis's moral development during the Manaf rebellion.[6] The stifling atmosphere of carnage and uncertainty created by these revolts clearly destabilizes Ouma. Describing Ouma's profound concern for her family and people, the narrator explains, "Elle parle du malheur et de la guerre qui doivent revenir, encore une fois, de la mort de sa mère, des manafs que l'on chasse de partout, qui doivent repartir maintenant. J'essaie de la calmer" / 'She talks about the war's horrors, which she says will return, about the death of her mother and the plight of the Manafs, who have always been chased from their homes, and who are now being forced to leave Mauritius. I try to calm her down' (367; 331). Alexis comforts his distraught lover, but he fails to take any concrete action to keep Ouma out of harm's way. Even during moments of tremendous tragedy that place his companion's very life at stake, Alexis's deep narcissism prevents him from doing anything. After it becomes painfully evident that she cannot count on Alexis during times of distress, Ouma reunites with her brother and the rest of her marginalized community in a British refugee camp. Similar to his earlier decision to abandon his mother and sister when they needed him the most in search of monetary riches in a distant land, Alexis will impotently watch as Ouma faces deportation from her ancestral homeland. For this reason, Alexis's dramatic declaration that "J'ai le cœur serré en pensant à Ouma dans la prison du camp, où elle a choisi de rejoindre son frère" / 'My heart aches as I think about Ouma, put in the prison camp because she chose to rejoin her brother' should not necessarily be taken at face value (370; 334).

In addition to Alexis's indecision and continued self-absorption that cast doubts upon his alleged inner transformation, numerous critics have discussed the symbolism of one of the protagonist's final gestures. Once again alluding to what he insists represents a type of moral re-awakening, Alexis reveals, "J'ai sorti de mon sac les papiers du trésor qui me restent encore, les cartes, les croquis, les cahiers de notes que j'ai écrits ici et à Rodrigues, et je les ai brûlés sur la plage [..] Maintenant, je sais que c'est ainsi qu'a fait le Corsaire après avoir retiré son trésor des cachettes [. . .] Il a tout détruit, tout jeté à la mer [. . .] pour être enfin libre" / 'I get what papers I still have relating to the treasure out of my bag—the maps, sketches, and books of notes that I made here and on Rodrigues—and I burn them on the beach [. . .] I now know that this is what the Corsair did after taking his treasure out of the hiding places [. . .] He destroyed everything and threw it into the sea [. . .] so that he could be free at last' (373; 336–337). Although the protagonist appears to have finally taken the first step in terms of liberating himself from the selfish consumerist aspirations that have defined his existence and prevented him from enjoying true happiness, should the reader still remain skeptical given that this episode is not the first time that Alexis has announced such ethical epiphanies?

The final paragraph of the novel adds even more ambivalence to this complex *roman d'initation*. Expressing his future hopes of a life full of contentment with Ouma, Alexis daydreams, "Alors Ouma est avec moi de nouveau, je sens la chaleur de son corps, son souffle, j'entends battre son cœur [. . .] Jusqu'où irons-nous ensemble? [. . .] De l'autre côté du monde, dans un lieu où l'on ne craint plus les signes du ciel, ni la guerre des hommes" / 'Ouma is with me again, I can feel her breath, the warmth of her body, her heartbeats [...] Where will we go together? [...] We'll go to the other side of the earth, to a place where we need fear neither signs in the sky nor the wars of men' (375; 338). First of all, it should be noted that this ecstatic dream of reuniting with his eternal amorous flame is at best tenuous because Ouma has already been deported. Alexis squandered an earlier chance to help his lover and to build a lasting relationship. Moreover, the specific aspirations about which Alexis muses seem to be more indicative of his own personal fantasies. The maritime voyages that the protagonist evokes represent his vision alone of what a meaningful existence might entail. Ouma's voice is entirely absent from this disconcerting, albeit on the surface romantic, reverie.

In reference to this Mauritian saga, Bruno Thibault also similarly underscores this disquieting ambiguity. Affirming the blatant contradiction between Alexis's dramatic verbal gestures and his actions, Thibault notes,

> *Le Chercheur d'or* annonce ce nouveau cycle, mais il n'y pénètre pas. Au contraire, la conclusion du roman apparaît confuse et bloquée. Alexis a atteint un point-limite de son développement: il est incapable d'aller au-delà […] il retrouve Ouma parmi les coupeurs de canne […] Mais Ouma est bientôt déportée avec d'autres travailleurs immigrés […] La conclusion du *Chercheur d'Or* débouche par conséquent sur la solitude et sur l'incertitude du héros.
>
> *The Prospector* announces this new cycle, but it does not probe it. On the contrary, the end of the novel appears to be confusing and obscure. Alexis has reached an impasse in his development, he is incapable of going any further [...] he rediscovers Ouma amongst the cane cutters [...] But Ouma is deported soon with the other immigrant workers [...] The ending of *The Prospector* consequently reveals the hero's solitude and uncertainty ("La Métaphore Exotique" 853; my trans.).

As Thibault outlines, despite his affirmations to the contrary, Alexis appears to have reached an impasse in terms of his moral development. The reader is left to speculate concerning whether the protagonist is in fact capable of truly embracing non-monetary treasures and valorizing what the Other has to offer. Is Alexis again attempting to convince himself that he has conquered his materialistic and narcissistic demons with grand yet empty gestures?

Other researchers, such as Karen Levy, have also probed the ambiguous nature of Alexis's inner quest to rid himself of the consumerist ideology that has blinded him for most of his life. Taking advantage of basic Levinisian concepts which affirm a given subject's responsibility to the Other, Levy explains, "The originality of Le Clézio's work stems from the double inscription of the alterity of both eros and ethics in an Other who is gendered female […] And he exposes the crisis of subjectivity that develops when the appeal of an Other invades an individual's sovereignty and puts her/him in positions where ethical choices must be made"

(257). Although it is evident that Alexis appreciates Ouma on a physical level because of the intense moments of ecstasy that they share together, the ambivalent ending of *Le Chercheur d'or* provides more questions than answers. The reader wonders if Alexis will forever remain stuck at a certain stage of progression or if future revelations will lead to greater transformation. It is unclear if the protagonist will one day shed his Western cloak in order to defeat the cancerous impulses that are emblematic of those that continue to undermine the universal logic of the global village notion.

Unlike Alexis whose family is part of the colonial governing elite of Mauritius,[7] Lalla in *Désert* grows up in a traditional society in the Western Sahara in which fundamental values have not yet been entirely eradicated by the powerful forces of modernity. However, the menacing presence of globalization is quite visible even for these modern-day descendants of the legendary Tuaregs as evidenced by the aforementioned sweatshop from the preceding chapter. Furthermore, Lalla's immigration to France is not motivated by a narcissistic quest to live the life of opulence so often promoted by the mainstream media. The young female protagonist of *Désert* is appalled with the materialistic excess that seems to dictate all facets of the Western world upon her arrival in Marseille.

After a fortuitous encounter with a photographer that convinces her to pose for pictures, Lalla will unwittingly become one of the most influential and coveted models on the entire planet. As the narrator elucidates, her photographs are "partout, sur les pages des magazines, sur les planches de contact, sur les murs de l'appartement" / 'everywhere, on the pages of magazines, on the contact sheets, on the walls of the apartment' (345; 280). The young female celebrity will soon discover, however, that her fans and the rest of the public are not truly interested in getting to know her as an individual. It is the neoliberal image of success that she represents which intoxicates the masses. Although Lalla's story is indeed improbable, as noted by William Thompson in his analysis of the novel, a public with an insatiable appetite for anecdotes that reinforce consumerist ideology devours every morsel of these illusory exceptions to the rule. In the context of Antonio Skarmeta's narrative *Match Ball* which deconstructs idealistic humanistic notions associated with neoliberalism, Ricardo Mouat affirms, "in *De la séduction* Baudrillard links seduction with the image and, specifically, with the cinematic image and the cult of the movie star" (139). The protagonist of *Désert* is not a film icon, but because of her physical attributes she briefly becomes a pop culture phenomenon. Similar to Hollywood fixtures such as Angelina Jolie, an adoring populace obsessively wants to know everything about Lalla.

Despite the undeniable enthusiasm of her many admirers, the protagonist quickly realizes that the public's appreciation is indicative of superficial, empty virtues. Lalla is soon inundated with fan mail because of the aggressive efforts of her publicist to ensure that her image is everywhere.

Instead of being flattered by these correspondences from complete strangers, the young woman scoffs at the artifice and naïve ideology that these letters represent. Explaining Lalla's strong reaction, the narrator elucidates,

> Le plus extraordinaire de tout cela, ce sont les lettres: elles arrivent de tous les côtés, qui portent le nom de Hawa sur l'enveloppe. Ce sont les journaux de mode, les magazines qui les font suivre, en ajoutant le nom du photographe et son adresse […] Les lettres disent quelquefois des choses extraordinaires, des choses très bêtes qu'écrivent des jeunes filles qui ont vu la photo de Hawa quelque part et qui lui parle comme si elles la connaissaient depuis toujours. Ou bien des lettres des jeunes garçons qui sont tombés amoureux d'elle, et qui disent qu'elle est belle […] Lalla se met à rire: "Quels menteurs!"
>
> The most extraordinary thing about it is all the letters: they come from all over, with Hawa's name on all the envelopes. They're from magazines, fashion reviews that forward them after adding the photographer's name and address […] Sometimes the letters say extraordinary things, or really dumb things written by young girls who have seen Hawa's picture somewhere and who talk to her as if they had always known her. Or else letters from young boys who have fallen in love with her […] and say she's beautiful […] Lalla starts laughing. "What liars!" (347; 281–282).

Lalla appears to be quite troubled once she realizes that her publicist, advertisers, publishers, and others are profiting economically from selling a lie to other young females. First of all, only a tiny fraction of the population will ever have the opportunity to reach this status. Moreover, for women that are born with physical characteristics that do not correspond to the ideal image of Western femininity, this unrealistic dream of being like Lalla is impossible to obtain. For this reason, the appealing image to which Baudrillard refers in mainstream society is not only counterproductive but it is also detrimental to true humanistic values. Although Lalla is emblematic of the glorious vision of success incessantly touted by the media, most people that compulsively attempt to satisfy these materialistic urges fall prey to the same chimerical traps that snared Alexis in *Le Chercheur d'or*.

Yet, perhaps the most disconcerting aspect of these letters for Lalla is that these provocative images do not reflect who she truly is as a human being. The protagonist wonders how it is possible that so many people want to emulate her example without knowing anything at all about her. In other words, why are utter strangers, as opposed to family members and friends with whom one actually has intimate contact, considered to be appropriate role models for anyone? The unpleasant answer to this question lies in the undeniable fact that neoliberal institutions including the media, radio, newspapers, and television itself[8] generate billions of dollars in revenue by selling this idealized portrait of happiness and success.

Giving the masses an uplifting, albeit rare, success story of an illiterate woman from humble beginnings in the Sahara desert that was able to access an existence of fame and fortune serves to conceal gross socioeconomic inequalities and keep those at the bottom of the social ladder in check. It should also be noted that the captivating image that Lalla represents is merely skin deep. The unequivocal message promoted by such depictions is that the protagonist is both beautiful and rich, thus she must be satisfied with her life. This type of superficial ideology in addition to the promotion of materialistic excess that erodes the quality of Alexis's life in *Le Chercheur d'or* has destroyed traditional values in the Western world. Given the plethora of such information that bombards our senses on a quotidian basis, it should come as no surprise that people are willing to starve themselves or purchase certain beauty products in a desperate attempt to conform to a shallow standard because they are convinced that this behavior is the most efficient path to happiness.

Underscoring the consumerist logic that dominates the contemporary landscape of popular culture, Nicki Cole notes, "scholars like Adorno, Horkheimer, and Barthes [...] turned their lens to the everyday and offered a close analysis of the cultural products people interact with, and theorized the connection between these and the forces of capitalist domination. They claim that popular culture, as ideological force, serves to rearticulate the relations of production and consumption in everyday life—it reproduces the status quo, and in doing so, supports hegemonic domination of the capitalist system" (n.p.). The theories of researchers like Adorno, Horkheimer, and Barthes are quite useful for interpreting the image of which Lalla is indicative. First of all, capitalist marketing of consumer goods skillfully manufactures not only desires for specific items themselves, but advertisers have also found a way to sell the neoliberal dream itself! Fashion magazines, such as the ones in which the protagonist appears, articulate and promote a materialistic vision of glamour and luxury that few of their readers will ever experience for a single day. For this reason, Lalla is not solely an unrealistic and simplistic image of happiness, but even worse she has been reduced to a mere product to be consumed by the general populace.

For the media, Lalla's improbable saga is a useful tool to reinforce narcissistic, neoliberal fantasies that sustain the titans of industry. Therefore, it is perhaps not the protagonist's story itself that interests the litany of journalists and paparazzi that badger her while in Paris, but the capacity of Lalla's journey to deceive others into believing that the global village has no losers. Furthermore, the protagonist represents a lucrative product of which many individuals would like to take advantage. Underscoring Lalla's newly-discovered celebrity status as a worldwide sex symbol and image of an ideology that affirms that all citizens of the global village have equal access to unprecedented prosperity, the narrator explains, "Maintenant, partout on parle de Hawa. A Paris, les journalistes viennent la voir, et il y a une femme qui lui pose des questions, un soir, dans le hall de l'hôtel" / 'Now, Hawa is being mentioned everywhere. In Paris, reporters come to see her, and one evening in the lobby of the hotel, a woman asks her questions' (352; 286). Not only does Lalla derive little if any pleasure from her fame, but she is also distrustful of those that have promoted her to such an extent. The protagonist realizes that she is a pawn in a larger hegemonic system of exploitation that reinforces the current socioeconomic paradigm in which she herself represents "This package of a new and better life [...] linked to the ultimate expression of one's consumer aspirations" (Leichenko and Solecki 246).

Once Lalla discovers that her value in Western society is purely utilitarian in terms of generating profit for corporate entities and solidifying exploitative ideology that solely benefits the "happy few," she decides to end her promising modeling career abruptly almost as soon as it began. Similar to Alexis in *Le Chercheur d'or* and other Leclézian characters, the female protagonist of *Désert* experiences no fulfillment whatsoever in the quest to acquire material wealth. However, in stark contrast to Alexis, Lalla's journey that culminates in fame and fortune before her eventual return to the Sahara is entirely accidental. Through no calculated decision of her own, social notoriety and affluence find Lalla.

In fact, the protagonist's attitude concerning monetary treasures resembles that of Ouma. As the narrator emphatically declares, "Elle ne veut pas d'argent, cela ne l'intéresse pas. Chaque fois que le photographe lui donne de l'argent [...] Lalla prend les billets de banque, en choisit un ou deux, et elle lui rend le reste [...] ou bien elle parcourt les rues de la ville, à la recherche des mendiants aux coins des murs, et elle leur donne l'argent" / 'She doesn't want money, it doesn't interest her. Every time the photographer gives her some money [...] Hawa takes the bills, picks out one or two, and hands him back the rest [...] Or sometimes she wanders the streets of the city looking for beggars at the corners of buildings, and she gives them money' (352; 285–286). Although the exclusive lifestyle of opulence which eludes the vast majority offers itself to Lalla, the protagonist is out of place in Western society which only valorizes consumer goods and services. Lalla's realization that she was poor but happy in the Sahara desert reinforces Crawford's assertion from chapter one that unbridled consumption is not always the most logical path that leads to true inner contentment. Allowing her photographer to keep most of the revenue that her provocative photographs generate and giving much of the rest away to those in need, Lalla only uses monetary currency to fulfill her basic necessities. The protagonist rejects the euphoric and glamorous life of consumerist excess that is placed at her fingertips.

Describing the inner turmoil that pervades the protagonist during her brief stint as a cover girl, the narrator poses the following questions:

"Que cherche-t-elle? Que veut-elle de la vie?" / 'What is she looking for? What does she want from life?' (351; 285). Not only have the empty materialistic virtues of Western society failed to provide Lalla with a sense of accomplishment, tranquility, or satisfaction, but they have also rendered her profoundly unhappy. For Lalla, the incessant quest to acquire as much money and possessions as possible creates an inner void that only more meaningful experiences and relationships can fill. The intensity of the protagonist's existential crisis will compel her to return to her homeland and to turn her back on the global village.[9]

Life is harsh for the Sahrawi in the unforgiving desert sands where one mistake could be one's last, but this quotidian struggle for survival is preferable to profound alienation from which Lalla suffers in the ghettos of Marseille. At the end of the narrative, the protagonist will give birth in the same way that her ancestors have done for centuries. She will also reestablish an intimate rapport with the rest of the universe to which all living substances are linked including human beings. As Elena Real notes in her analysis of the text, the protagonist will heal herself from "l'angoisse de l'homme séparé de la terre-mère" / 'the anguish of humanity separated from Mother Earth' (184; my trans.). In the context of Le Clézio's fiction, the following chapter will further explore the traumatic cosmic disconnect that drives the author's divergent protagonists to seek a more meaningful existence in harmony with the elements. For Le Clézio's characters, the neoliberal view of contentment is sometimes an enticing illusion, but smoke and mirrors cannot help one consume his or her way to happiness.[10]

## THE "LIBERAL" OR NEOLIBERAL MEDIA?

Given that the significant body of growing research from many divergent fields, such as "happiness research," unequivocally suggests that the dominant ideology of unfettered consumption is a malevolent force which is antithetical to humanistic virtues, why do universalist notions related to the concept of the global village continue to persist as the driving political, social, and ideological forces of modernity? Although Alexis, Lalla, and Laïla are fictitious characters from the hand of one of the most gifted writers of his generation, the inability of consumerist values to satisfy their fundamental psychological and emotional needs is emblematic of the failure of McLuhan's misplaced faith in globalization. Moreover, for Le Clézio's protagonists and indeed for millions of people around the planet, the irresistible images of consumerist fantasies are empty sardonic caricatures that often prevent the modern subject from actualizing a more authentic state of personal fulfillment in addition to creating a sense of place and belonging. Many contemporary media researchers, echoing the concerns of astute artists such as Le Clézio, have explored the hegemonic structures that systematically promote and maintain the current system of inequality and injustice.

It is hardly surprising that the greatest champion of globalization which continues to derive unprecedented economic benefits from the neoliberal financial paradigm, the mainstream media, is still selling pipe dreams to the masses. Deconstructing the laughable conservative view of the media as a "liberal" institution that protects people from capitalist excess and rampant corporate greed, numerous scholars have denounced its complicity and even active role in silencing and subjugating the majority of the world's population. Building upon the ideas of Noam Chomsky and the diverse field of social justice, Aaron Cooley notes, "One key aspect to this situation is the media's inability to present viewpoints and facts, which is at odds with the idealized mission of being the fourth estate [...] The most damning and representative example was the study for the Program on International Policy Attitudes [...] that found that Fox News had the highest percentage of viewers that believed that weapons of mass destruction were found in Iraq" (580–581). The fear of alienating its conservative base of viewers in addition to its ultimate goal of generating revenue for the titans of industry that own the network prevented what is perhaps the most influential news medium in the United States from telling the truth concerning the political justification for a bloody conflict for which American families continue to pay the price. Given that the former president himself revealed his supposed disgust with the fact that WMDs were never discovered in his recent book *Decision Points*, it seems unfathomable that many individuals in the extremely misinformed American populace still believe that weapons were found in Iraq. However, this tragic reality underscores the carefully managed campaign of misinformation and superficial coverage of the most serious issues by high paid spin doctors that prevent citizens from questioning deliberate deception that reinforces the domination of the political and social elite.

After reminding the reader that "Today's corporate conglomerate-driven commercial media [...] was constructed as a result of a concerted effort of business interests," Andrew Kennis adamantly declares, "The news media needs to be constituted in such a manner that would foster a responsibility to the public, not to powerful corporate and governmental interests" (4; 8). Given that the primary goal of any corporation is to maximize profits above all other considerations, Cooley, Kennis, and other researchers wonder how the myth of the liberal media still lingers despite evidence that major news outlets have failed to hold their government accountable for blatant transgressions in recent years. Since taking a stand on a controversial issue could result in public retribution and a substantial loss of income, global conglomerate media entities have a much greater incentive to conceal unpleasant realities as opposed to exposing them. As evidenced in the neoliberal ideology that they incessantly laud, mainstream news networks behave more like Alexis in *Le Cher-*

*cheur d'or* than defenders of the common good. By suppressing any real dialogue concerning the alleged benefits of globalization and by selectively filtering all information that is disseminated, the neoliberal media has ensured that its shareholders are numbered among the "happy few" that continue to reap colossal benefits as millions of others fall prey to acute poverty that jeopardizes their existence itself.

In a recent essay entitled "Noam Chomsky and the Manufacture of Consent for American Foreign Policy," Kurt Lang and Gladys Lang reexamine Chomky's so-called propaganda model in the context of globalization. Before reaching the disconcerting conclusion that "present media practice falls short of the ideal" of the fourth estate notion, Lang and Lang explain, "The propaganda model assigns to the media system just one major function to which everything else is subordinate. That function is the 'manufacture of consent' for government policies that advance the goals of corporations and preserve the capitalist system" (99; 94). Given that contemporary mainstream media outlets are owned and managed by the corporate elite, news entities themselves serve to maintain privileges and the economic supremacy of those at the top of the social ladder. As Lang and Lang reiterate, "Far from being autonomous creations, media systems inevitably reflect [...] the distribution of economic, political, and symbolic power in the society" (94). Dismissing the naïve misconception that a deregulated and conglomerate media could valorize basic principles of justice and equality above the primary aim of any capitalistic venture (i.e., profit), Lang and Lang note that the ultimate mission of profit-driven news networks is to glorify the system and to promote consumption. For this reason, it would be more accurate to assert that the media cares more about creating consumer citizens than it does an informed populace that might actually be capable of defending itself against exploitative practices and ideology.

Instead of perceiving the media as a vital part of a system of checks and balances that ensures the proper functioning of the democratic process itself, "Herman and Chomsky see something standing in the way of the people's best democratic tendencies, which they term the propaganda system that affects the media and the messages received by the American people" (Cooley 588). Given that Chomsky's ideas have often been marginalized because they are deemed to be too "polemical" for even the academic community (Edgley 24), Cooley reiterates, "much more mainstream thinkers have argued along parallel lines about the destructiveness of a monolithic media system" (589). Although Herman and Chomsky's propaganda model (PM) initially received a rather lukewarm reception in intellectual circles, the dire inequalities that are indicative of the global village nightmare have encouraged contemporary thinkers to reexamine the PM paradigm (Mullen and Klaehn). Many critics originally dismissed Herman and Chomsky's ideas as exaggerated, but the ongoing processes of globalization which have exacerbated the problems that they pinpointed in works such as *Manufacturing Consent* have made it more difficult to ignore their concerns related to the consolidation of power and the propagation of consumerist ideology.

Before briefly explaining the five filters[11] of the Propaganda Model which explain how the media systematically and carefully controls what information is disseminated to the general public, David Model asserts that the "global commercial media system dominated by a small number of super-powerful, mostly US-based transnational media corporations [...] works as a system to advance the cause of the global market and promote commercial values" (1). Similar to Lang and Lang, Model underscores that instead of being a fourth estate or a "liberal" institution that strives to protect the average citizen, the major news outlets reflect the consumerist values of the powerful entities that own them. In other words, it is illogical and idealistic to believe that those who are deriving the most benefits from the current financial system are also those that are sworn to defend the integrity of humanity against capitalistic abuses that undermine democracy itself.

In a short piece entitled "Ideological Conformity in America," published in 1979, Noam Chomsky outlines the crisis of democracy and the corporate takeover of the media system which had already begun during this time period. Chomsky declares,

> To my knowledge, in the American mass media you cannot find a single socialist journalist, not a single syndicated political commentator who is a socialist [...] Basically, there are two reasons for this. First, there is the remarkable ideological homogeneity of the American intelligentsia in general, who rarely depart from one of the variants of state capitalist ideology [...] The second reason is that the mass media are capitalist institutions [...] The fact that these institutions reflect the ideology of dominant economic interests is hardly surprising (77–78).

Given that primary news outlets are indeed capitalistic entities driven by the profit motive as Chomsky properly notes, they have a vested interest in ensuring that no real dialogue will ever take place concerning the advantages and pitfalls of the system itself. Instead of exposing the imperfections of each socioeconomic paradigm, the giants of industry have little incentive whatsoever but to promote the neoliberal virtues of McLuhan's evaporated dream which affirm that the present situation of historic global inequality somehow represents the peak of human civilization. By brainwashing the masses with propaganda that supports their continued social and economic domination, the transnational neoliberal media has convinced many of the inhabitants of the global village that no alternatives are possible or even warranted given their concerted efforts to marginalize all voices of dissent that could potentially end the narcissistic aspirations of the "happy few."

Approximately thirty years after Chomsky's short article and two decades after the inception of the Propaganda Model, in an interview with Andrew Mullen, Chomsky and Herman highlight the unmitigated failure of the media to place public interests before corporate values. After citing numerous concrete examples, including the blatantly erroneous justification for the Iraq war, the theorists state, "Globalization and cross-border integration, and the spread and increased importance of commercial media and advertising as a funding source, have made the Propaganda Model ever more widely applicable" (18). Indeed, it is because of the powerful forces of globalization that scholars have rediscovered the PM paradigm. Recent events that concretize the inability of news outlets to constitute a fourth estate have urged many researchers to delve deeper into the ideas of Herman and Chomsky. In reference to the evolving reception of *Manufacturing Consent,* Andrew Mullen and Jeffery Klaehn elucidate, "The first wave of criticism—in the late 1980s, following the book's publication and in the 1990s—was marked by hostility, indifference and/or an outright dismissal of the PM and its findings. The second wave of criticism, from the early 2000s witnessed a greater engagement with the PM that resulted in a number of important debates" (219). Given that the current, dire social inequalities are antithetical to both basic principles of social justice and the initial enthusiasm for the neoliberal concept of the global village, the official line promulgated by the media is becoming more difficult to justify. Echoing the sentiments of Herman and Chomsky themselves, Mullen and Klaehn conclude, "Given the globalizing economy and the ever-increasing (global) power, reach and influence of large, transnational corporate and financial institutions—in the face of growing poverty and powerlessness amongst the vast majority of the world's population—we would suggest that the PM is even more relevant today than when it was initially advanced" (225).

Although Chomsky's assertion that the political and financial elite are two sides of the same coin originally sparked controversy, this disconcerting reality is also becoming more evident in today's interconnected and interdependent world. As Alison Edgley explains, "For Chomsky, the state's role is to protect and expand the interests of the rich and powerful while at the same time controlling the 'rascal multitude' (a term employed by and representative of the elite's view of ordinary people)" (25). By framing and skewing public perception of important issues, the corporate media has effectively removed the checks and balances designed to protect those at the bottom of the social ladder from exploitation in the capitalist system. This manipulative form of communicating with the masses has generated catastrophic policies, such as trickle-down economics, intentionally designed to increase the elite's stranglehold of wealth in addition to social capital.

Antonio Gramsci's theory of cultural hegemony provides further evidence in support of Chomsky's claim that "the existing media and political systems are mutually supportive" (Mullen 21). Defining the concept of hegemony and revealing the media's specific role in a larger framework of subjugation, Andrew Kennis asserts,

> Hegemony is comprised by a complex layering of social structures, each with its own logic and mission; however, each mission coalesces and produces a larger structure that has an encompassing overall mission that assumes and subsumes smaller missions. A relevant example of this are the different parts of the news media which may have differing individual agendas, but coalesce to support state-corporate interests by being ultimately subservient to the state-corporate apparatus with which they are intimately linked (10).

Given that the ultimate goal of any capitalist enterprise is the maximization of profit, the role of the mainstream corporate media in creating, sustaining, and justifying the gross inequalities that abound should not be underestimated. As poverty continues to rise on a global scale to epic proportions, the media continues to sell, in fact quite literally, outdated and disproven neoliberal fantasies to the general public. In order for prosperity to rain down upon the privileged few, the masses must be ignorant and subservient second-class citizens that only have access to filtered information.

Building upon the ideas of both Gramsci and the international relations researcher Owen Worth, Kennis further elucidates, "today's form of hegemony is evidenced when multinational corporations combine neoliberal ideology with international trade and are able to exploit this powerful combination using their own news media in order to realize unprecedented profits" (13). The media has justified its euphoria for globalization, which is starting to wane in many divergent circles, for decades by claiming that its uneven processes will eventually benefit all of humanity. However, Chomsky and Herman's Propaganda Model and Gramsci's theory of cultural hegemony in addition to the research of numerous contemporary scholars suggest that the media's motivations for promoting the global village concept are entirely self-serving. Given that news outlets are controlled by the same conglomerates that dominate the contemporary socioeconomic landscape, the media's unwavering enthusiasm for neoliberal globalization is a creative, humanistic mask that conceals a materialistic desire to accumulate more wealth and to keep the monetary cycle flowing.

## SUSTAINING THE CONSUMER REPUBLIC THROUGH ADVERTISEMENT AND MARKETING

Identified as an essential filter of the PM that reinforces a system of hegemonic control, advertising plays a crucial role in promoting the shallow virtues of consumerism and the pervasive neoliberal view of happiness. As a later section of this chapter will explore, Le Clézio's early narratives, such as *Les Géants* and *Haï*, concretize his concerns related to the dubious role of advertising in sustaining modern consumer republics. Although the unequivocal message of nearly every single advertisement is that the acquisition of a certain good or service will automatically improve the quality of one's life, the veritable motivations are maximizing profits for transnational corporations whose influence is felt all around the world. Similar to the media's self-promotion of its role as the fourth estate or the protector of public interests, advertisers also pretend that their intentions are humanistic as well. As Herman and Chomsky underscore, advertising is an essential hegemonic tool for maintaining an exploitative system that serves the interests of the "happy few." It should also be noted that advertising revenue is perhaps the most important financial foundation that generates colossal profits for the multinational entities that own the information superhighway.

As the recent film *The Joneses* explored in chapter one illustrates, advertisers are not just selling a specific good, but they are also promoting an idealized image of happiness that corresponds to neoliberal fantasies. Inspired by Plato's ideas concerning the predictable consequences of compulsive and uncontrolled consumption which have come to fruition, Ian Boyd and Deweese Boyd assert, "Those who live in the luxurious city indulge desires that overstep the limits of what is necessary for their flourishing, either because they cannot control their excessive desires [...] or because these desires have led them to hold false beliefs regarding their need and their good [...] their desires have enabled them to deceive themselves regarding their own good, believing that the unnecessary is necessary" (118). After informing potential clients that a new product exists, advertisers attempt to convince the consumer that living a fulfilling life without this item is not an option. In other words, advertising intentionally fabricates false needs that are in reality luxuries not necessities. However, the alluring images of success and contentment which inundate the modern subject blur the distinction between basic fundamental needs and materialistic excess. If the consumer believes that a certain product is vital to his or her happiness, then it is no longer a luxury item.

The integrated political and social elite of the global village have also painstakingly attempted to meld the notion of civic duty with consumption itself. As Sue-Im Lee notes in the context of a specific Karen Yamashita protagonist, "Bobby's only way to keep terror at bay is to purchase appliances, gadgets, and furniture, affirming to himself that a good American is a consuming American" (509). Given the rather infamous post–9/11 calls for consumption investigated in chapter one, contemporary notions of responsible citizenship are inseparable from self-centered neoliberal virtues that have obliterated any meaningful kind of ethical social underpinning which valorizes anything except money. By equating frivolous consumption with patriotic duty, advertisers have created purchaser citizens[12] whose only way to express their identity or sense of belonging to a given society is to acquire goods incessantly. The modern subject is bombarded with ideological arguments that such excessive spending not only results in personal satisfaction, but that it also strengthens the system allowing others to derive benefits as well. In a world of finite resources that are dwindling every day, the inhabitants of the neoliberal global village are always urged to increase their consumption. The ecological ramifications of this destructive logic will be probed in the following chapter.

Similar to Lee, Dannagal Young explains that advertisers have been exploiting historical periods of adversity for at least half a century. During times of tribulation, citizen consumers must be indoctrinated with the notion that the most logical course of action is to consume our way out of tragedy. As Young notes in her analysis of American advertisements from World War II, "the advertisements [...] illustrate an America in which citizens were fighting to defend an economic system and the right to acquire goods and services" (41). Young reiterates, "By contrasting the heavily regulated economies of Germany and Japan to America's free enterprise system, advertisers could invoke patriotic themes while reminding readers of goods and services that enhanced their quality of life" (30). Moreover, even if consumers had very little money to spend during this tumultuous period, advertisers realized the future necessity of linking political and economic notions. In order to maintain their supremacy, the major corporations of this age needed the economy to restart immediately after the end of this tragic conflict. In a clear affirmation of the impact of this propaganda, Americans would euphorically celebrate their military victory by excessive spending in the years that followed World War II. Advertisers had successfully convinced the American populace that material comfort and happiness itself were at stake in the outcome of the war.

In her essay entitled "Patriotic Acts of Consumption: Lucile (Lady Duff Gordon) and the Vaudeville Fashion Show Craze," Marlis Schweitzer asserts that advertisers have been profiting from tragedy since World War I. Summarizing the ideas of both Lizabeth Cohen and Charles McGovern, Schweitzer affirms, "Although, as historian Lizabeth Cohen has shown, it wasn't until the post–World War II era that the concept of the 'citizen consumer' was fully realized, McGovern demonstrates that the lines between consumption and citizenship were already beginning to blur during World War I" (586). In reference to Gordon's controversial vaudeville performance, Schweitzer reiterates,

> In framing Fleurette's *Dream at Peronne* as a war drama and insisting that the majority of the money made by the act was going to support

> displaced French citizens, Lucile aligned theatrical spectatorship and fashion consumption with the ideals of philanthropy, humanitarianism, and patriotism. Although critics were skeptical about Lucile's motives and questioned whether a million-dollar spectacle was really the most appropriate way to assist war refugees, Lucile remained adamant about the connections among fantasy, consumption, and altruism (585).

Similar to Young's astute observations related to World War II advertisements, Schweitzer clearly establishes that corporations were already beginning to connect tragedy and consumption in the public imagination in order to record lucrative profits as early as World War I. The concerted effort by advertisers to rationalize how the incessant pursuit of one's own narcissistic aspirations is a civic duty that epitomizes the collective good has been exacerbated by the effects of globalization which is constantly seeking to expand its far-reaching influence.

Undoubtedly the greatest factor that has led to the creation of a metaphorically smaller, interconnected, and interdependent world is modern technology. It is easier to communicate with people at the opposite end of the globe than ever before given the utility of the Internet, social media networks, VoIP software such as Skype, and recent logistical advances. However, although McLuhan originally thought that technological inventions would serve public interests, the titans of industry have exploited these powerful tools to expand their global domination. In the context of this sinister reality and referring to the contemporary writer Brian Fawcett's novels, Richard Pickard states, "Media technology, like franchise capitalism, leads not to greater local involvement but to greater corporate domination. Postmodernism, in its techno-evil economic incarnation as the Global Village, threatens the whole idea of meaningful community [...] Postmodernism itself is not the evil [...] the evil is the world of monopoly capitalism" (111–112). Similar to other contemporary theorists such as Dean Barnlund examined in chapter one, Pickard affirms that the global village dream has spiraled into a nightmare. Given that the most powerful transnational companies in the world now own the means of disseminating information to the public, it is not surprising that their products fill the shelves of stores all across the globe. Moreover, controlling major global news outlets ensures that exploitative practices, injustice, and inequality can easily be concealed and that seductive advertisements are continually transmitted to eager consumer citizens.

In addition to taking advantage of the fact that they own the entire media system, advertisers deliberately attempt to overload the viewer with more information than he or she is capable of processing efficiently. As Aaron Cooley explains, "As technology has created more and more ways of bombarding our senses with information, the propagandists have been there, sucking all the meaning from news" (591). Echoing the sentiments of Cooley, Robert Sack underscores the "hybrid language" of media advertisements, comprised of many different types of sounds and images, which attack the sensorial sensibilities of consumers urging them to fulfill their desires and social responsibility (658). According to Cooley and Sack, marketing is intentionally designed to ensure that the subject is not capable of reflecting and making a rational decision. Given the sophisticated and relentless nature of the sensorial overload to which the individual is exposed, one only has enough time to obey the orders that he or she receives. Moreover, as Cooley notes, this sensorial overload prevents those that are not living the neoliberal dream from questioning why so many exceptions to the rule exist. Furthermore, corporate control of the media has allowed conglomerates to shape the news itself into a sensational product that is easy for the masses to consume, thereby increasing their control of the global marketplace.

Although most contemporary media theorists agree that advertisements play a crucial role in sustaining the modern capitalist state, researchers often express divergent viewpoints concerning the amount of autonomy that a consumer citizen possesses. In order to justify their blatant attempts to manipulate subjects intentionally and thereby expanding their social and financial control of society, advertisers insist that they provide a wealth of useful products from which the consumer can choose. For this reason, if the acquisition of a specific good or service fails to improve the quality of one's life, then consumers will stop purchasing this item. This lucid decision forces transnational corporations to create new products that more accurately represent the needs and desires of their global client base. Moreover, the deliberate refusal to acquire merchandise that does not deliver on its promise to maximize comfort or provide inner satisfaction holds corporate entities accountable for the materials that they manufacture. This view of the contemporary citizen, predicated upon the ideology that the modern subject has an active role in shaping and maintaining the market, corresponds to Georges Bataille's notion of the "sovereign spender" (Bennett 2). In everyday language, this financial theory is referred to as the "power of the purse string(s)."

Affirming his skepticism of this image of a powerful consumer that possesses the ability to dictate a global free market economy, Robert Crawford states, "Envisaging the consumer as a rational, middle-class individual proved comforting for advertisers" (123). Similar to the myth of benevolent colonialism which provided an ethical framework for systematic human exploitation, the idea of the "sovereign spender" has ensured advertisers that they are rendering a philanthropic service to humanity. It is the responsibility of the consumer to decide the specific corporate giant that he or she wishes to enrich based on which products contribute the most to society and which items help him or her actualize narcissistic neoliberal fantasies of the good life. This pervasive mentality is emblematic of both the neoliberal view of happiness and the worldwide consumerist culture that defines the current state of the global village. As Kevin Blackburn explains in the context of advertising, the "consumers ethic [...] told the individual that the path to happiness was to keep buying the products of mass consumption" (qtd. in Crawford 138). According to this "ethic," the freedom to choose what type of merchandise or services are the most pragmatic and fulfilling is what protects the consumer from abusive practices.

The idealistic view of the empowered citizen purchaser is quite compelling, however, it should be noted that no possibilities exist outside of the system itself. For as Langmann and Morris note, "Capitalism's consumer culture [...] renders people powerless without recognition of their humanity/dignity [...] Consumerism created artificial realms of pseudo-agency as choices between mass-produced advertised brands and styles limits human potential for self-fulfillment" (n.p.). Does it really matter if an individual opts to drink Pepsi or Coca-Cola? Given that both of these choices are inseparable from the hegemonic forces that reinforce the domination of the "happy few," does the modern subject that is condemned to live in a consumer republic really possess any freedom at all? If no alternatives outside of the market itself are valorized or even recognized, then personal autonomy ceases to exist. In other words, all "choices" are carefully manufactured by the titans of industry and their media outlets which disseminate this information to the public. For this reason, "In *La société de consommation* (1970), Baudrillard dismissed the economists' notion of rationally, calculating, self-aware, self-interested *homo oeconomicus* as a purely mythic creature" (qtd. in Bennett 23). As Jean Baudrillard elucidates in an affirmation similar to that of Herman and Chomsky, certain artificial ideological constructions are appealing illusions that serve to rationalize the current situation of gross inequality. Like the naïve conception of the media as a protective fourth estate, a sinister reality lurks beneath the alluring consumerist ideology that is indicative of advertising. Both the notion of the mainstream media as a social watchdog and the idea of the sovereign spender clearly serve entrenched corporate interests as opposed to liberating the masses.[13]

## THE EFFORTS OF THE "HAPPY FEW" TO SILENCE THE MAJORITY AND TO IMPOSE A MONOLITHIC CULTURE IN LE CLÉZIO'S NARRATIVES

In Le Clézio's enigmatic early novel *Les Géants*, originally published in 1973, he denounces the powerful invisible forces that the narrator terms "les maîtres" / 'the masters.' Although the identity of these exploitative entities that subjugate and destabilize the protagonists is initially nebulous, certain passages will later reveal the author's profound concerns related to the profit-driven media and the aggressive, incessant advertisements that bombard the modern subject. Finally identifying the malevolent forces to which the entire narrative alludes, the narrator states, "Je connais son nom, un nom étrange et maléfique, inscrit au-dessus de ma tête, brillant comme une enseigne. Il s'appellera ainsi: VARIOUM BROADCASTING PROPERTIES [...] La pensée de Varioum est pareille à un couvercle d'étain sur la terre" / 'I know his name, a strange baleful name, it is inscribed above my head, and shines as brightly as an electric sign. Its name will be: VARIOOM BROADCASTING PROPERTIES [...] his thinking is like a tin lid covering the earth' (264; 243). Instead of providing an invaluable service to humanity as the ideology of the sovereign spender affirms, Varioum appears to be a far-reaching media consortium that oppresses the inhabitants of the global village.[14]

Additionally, Varioum is inseparable from the corporate "giants" to which the title alludes. Before the narrator directly exposes this media outlet as a propaganda tool that indoctrinates the populace, it is not by chance that the author lists the most powerful multinational conglomerates of this time period. Moreover, many of these companies, such as Alcoa, Siemens, Shell, Texaco, and Kodak still exist today (262; 240). Affirming the dubious intentions of these real-life corporations and the fictitious entity Varioum that transmits their neoliberal agenda to all corners of the globe, the narrator muses, "Polaroid, R.C.A., Procter & Gamble, quelles sont vos pensées? Où êtes-vous cachés? Qu'y a-t-il derrière vos noms terribles et beaux? Mais vous n'entendez pas la voix des hommes, vous êtes de l'autre côté de la vie, du côté qui détient la connaissance. Vous êtes sans visage, sans voix, sans désir, et c'est pour cela que les visages, les voix et les désirs vous appartiennent" / 'Polaroid, R.C.A., Procter & Gamble, ... what are your thoughts? Where are you hidden? What is behind your beautiful and terrifying names? But you do not hear the voices of mankind, you are on the far side of life, on the side that holds knowledge to ransom. You are faceless, voiceless, without desire, and that is why all faces and voices and desires belong to you' (262–263; 240–242). Given that no meaningful dialogue is taking place between those that control the means of disseminating information and the disenfranchised members of society that have no voice, the Leclézian narrator realizes that Varioum's true goal is not to communicate but rather to expand its financial and social domination. Varioum is not a fourth estate that protects the protagonists of *Les Géants* from corruption, but instead it is a powerful weapon of the integrated social and political elite that frames public perception, prevents the masses from asking disconcerting questions related to inequality and injustice, and most importantly eliminates any viable alternatives to the current system.

Revealing the veritable message of advertisers hidden beneath the surface of humanistic and neoliberal propaganda, the narrator explains, "Obéissez! Obéissez! Marchez, achetez, mangez! [...] Buvez Pils! Le Drink des gens raffinés" / 'Obey! Obey! Walk, buy, eat! [...] Drink Pils! The drink for people of good taste' (56; 49). This passage highlights the fact that the content of every single advertisement is in essence the same.

After informing the viewer or listener that a new product exists, advertisers attempt to convince the consumer that the acquisition of this item will result in greater material comfort and happiness. The ideology of consumption or the naïve notion that a direct correlation exists between amassing consumer goods and personal fulfillment is inseparable from the intentions of the marketing industry. For this reason, advertisers must constantly reinforce the dominant ideology of the consumerist global village in order to maintain and to expand their control. By aggressively reminding the potential client that the good life equals the "goods life," the moral of the Pils advertisement is that this product is indispensable if the purchaser citizen wishes to maximize his or her happiness. Furthermore, as the narrator notes, this specific commercial reflects the seductive image of success and luxury lauded by the champions of globalization. A "refined" existence that is worth living entails consuming Pils and all of the other readily available consumer items on the shelf. Yet, many of Le Clézio's protagonists, such as Alexis, Lalla, and Laïla, discover that meaning and contentment are not commodities that can be sold to the highest bidder. Additionally, the obsessive quest to satisfy materialistic desires often prevents the modern subject from attaining a deep state of happiness.

The true linguistic intention of advertisers is not to foster a meaningful dialogue concerning what products most benefit society, but to impose a "skillfully managed reality" that is emblematic of the larger social values that sustain the system (Horkheimer and Adorno 59). By carefully framing the linguistic content of their messages, the corporate elite's form of communicating with the masses represents a concerted effort to enlarge their domination. In an interview with Pierre Boncenne, Le Clézio reveals that this deliberate attempt to seek even greater financial and social control by manipulating language itself and selectively filtering the information that is available to the public inspired early works such as *Les Géants*. As the author affirms, "Dans tous les livres que j'ai écrits, jusqu'à *La Guerre* et *Les Géants*, j'ai ressenti comme une nécessité d'écrire le monde de la ville, le monde mécanique, l'agression du langage et celle des formes [...] la publicité ou le grand commerce visent à ce déséquilibre, à cette impression d'insécurité, pour que les gens produisent et achètent davantage" / 'In all of the books that I wrote up until *War* and *The Giants*, I felt compelled to write about the inner world of the city, this mechanical world, and the aggression of language and its forms [...] advertising and commerce aim for this imbalance, for this impression of insecurity, in order for people to consume and to buy more' (34–35; my trans.). In addition to expressing his unsettling concerns related to the nature of the modern urbanized world itself, Le Clézio notes that advertising represents a summons to the purchaser citizen that everyone has a moral obligation to consume. Given that the neoliberal economic paradigm is based on the unending zeal to acquire more possessions, advertisers and the social elite that they represent must remind the consumer that frivolous spending strengthens the economic system allowing more people to access the dream. Refusing to purchase the latest fads or brands is not only detrimental to one's own happiness, but this behavior is also selfish and irresponsible according to neoliberal virtues given that thriftiness is antithetical to consumerist ideology.

Deconstructing the notion of the sovereign spender that exercises considerable control over the global market, the narrator of *Les Géants* asserts, "Le langage des Maîtres ne veut pas communiquer. Il n'est pas fait pour être parlé, ni entendu. C'est un langage qui dévore des informations et donne des ordres" / 'the language of the Masters has no desire to communicate. It is not designed to be spoken or heard. It is a language that devours information and gives orders' (173; 159). The corporate giants and the media outlets that they own are not motivated by an intrinsic desire to improve the quality of life for billions of people across this planet by means of useful inventions, but instead their intentions are much more sinister. The financial elite systematically filter their primary forms of communication and the knowledge that is disseminated to marginalize any dissent that would jeopardize their goal of expanding their sphere of influence. The role of the consumer citizen is not to reflect carefully before making a purchase, but to obey impulses and manufactured desires without question. Le Clézio astutely noted as early as the 1970s that the duty of the model citizen in a consumer republic is simply to obey.

Given that nothing appears to exist outside of the system for the protagonists of *Les Géants*, Bogo le Muet, Machines, and Tranquilité, they are not autonomous individuals that possess the power to decide how they want to live their lives. Expressing his frustration concerning the growing influence of transnational entities across the planet, the narrator declares, "leurs machines invisibles sont reliées à tous les points de la terre, à tous les points du corps" / 'its (their) invisible machines are linked to all the points of the earth, to all the points of the body' (265; 244). Reiterating this concern that it seems impossible to escape the ever expanding forces of globalization while inside of Hyperpolis, Tranquilité confesses, "Il n'y a pas d'endroit où se cacher. Les regards de la lumière indécente viennent vous trouver, où que vous soyez" / 'there is no place to hide. The immodest light's long glances will seek you out and find you, wherever you may be' (115; 107). Although Hyperpolis is literally a sort of convenient superstore where a client can purchase nearly any of the consumer products that are part of our daily lives, this disconcerting place represents both a metaphor and an indictment of consumer society. First of all, the author's decision to name this character Tranquilité is intentionally ironic given that she is profoundly traumatized by what she experiences in this store.[15]

Bombarded by the sights, sounds, and odors that entice her to fulfill her materialistic desires, Tranquilité attempts to free herself from these chains but her senses are unable to process this assault. This sensorial overload, investigated by researchers such as the aforementioned Aaron Cooley and Robert Sack, renders Tranquilité powerless to the seductive messages that continue to attack her sensibilities. Specifically, Sack highlights the "hybrid language" of the media that utilizes a plethora of visual and auditory stimuli in order to promote consumption. Clearly cognizant of the veritable intentions of advertising and the role that it plays in a consumer republic, it should be noted that the structure of the novel itself reflects this hybrid form of communication. Moreover, the work begins and ends with the strong declaration "il faut brûler Hyperpolis" / 'Hyperpolis must be burnt down.' In addition, the incorporation of graphic designs and other media artifacts is indicative of the contemporary marketing industry. In his analysis of *Les Géants*, David Walker notes the author's "vision cauchemardesque du commerce tout-puissant" / 'nightmarish vision of all-powerful commerce' (119; my trans.). Moreover, describing Tranquilité's anguish and feelings of entrapment in this sinister space, Walker asserts, "Dès le moment où elle entre dans le magasin, les sens de l'héroïne sont sollicités et assaillis: Le Clézio dépeint chez elle une forme d'hyperésthésie dont sont coutumiers les personnages d'autres romans lecléziens" / 'From the moment that she enters into the store, the heroine's senses are targeted and assailed: Le Clézio depicts inside of her a form of hyperesthesia with which characters from other LeClézian novels are familiar' (119; my trans.). As Walker also underscores, Tranquilité is visibly destabilized and frightened by this calculated sensorial onslaught, but she cannot entirely avoid the alluring traps that have been set for her all over the store. These captivating yet empty images which represent consumerist fantasies spellbind and mesmerize the protagonist, as she desperately seeks refuge in a serene space that is nowhere to be found. Moreover, given that Hyperpolis and the symbolic, narcissistic dream that it sells are synonymous with the propagation of the neoliberal global village across the world, it is evident that Le Clézio articulates his concerns related to the powerful forces of globalization and the "happy few's" deliberate efforts to exploit others at market value.

Both Bruno Thibault and Sevket Kadioglu confirm Walker's hypotheses concerning the media and the question of autonomy in Le Clézio's narratives. In reference to *La Guerre* and *Les Géants*, Thibault elucidates, "Dans ces deux romans, les machines ont remplacé le corps des hommes et les mass media ont remplacé leur pensée" / 'In these two novels, machines have replaced men's bodies and the mass media has replaced their thought' (2; my trans.). Instead of being a faithful watchdog that protects the average citizen from systemic abuses, the mainstream media appears to be merely a propaganda outlet in Le Clézio's fiction that reinforces the hegemonic power structures of the elite. With limited access to information that is not filtered or distorted by the titans of industry for their benefit, the majority of the populace has been reduced to a robotic, brainwashed homogenous mass that is incapable of critical thought or deconstructing exploitative ideology. As Sevket Kadioglu explains, "Dans une telle société technocratique de consommation, l'individu s'efface et perd la volonté d'agir et de penser [...] Dans ce monde du règne tyrannique des objets, de la marchandise, l'homme est bien loin de se sentir comme un être humain mais il s'y sent un produit programmé à consommer et à acheter" / 'In such a technocratic consumer society, the individual is erased and loses the will to act and to think [...] In this world of the tyrannical reign of objects, of merchandise, man is far from feeling like a human being but he feels like a product programmed to consume and to buy' (129,135; my trans.). Similar to Lalla and Laïla, Bogo le Muet, Machines, and Tranquilité seek to flee the bureaucratic and sterile atmosphere of the modern consumer republic. Given that the protagonists of *Les Géants* cannot discover an easy path to escape the far-reaching influence of Hyperpolis, the only solution is to find a way to uproot this firmly entrenched system if this is even possible. Although consumerist ideology claims that the simple act of purchasing the right goods will lead to happiness, Le Clézio's diverse characters concretize the failure of neoliberal virtues to fulfill fundamental human needs, such as companionship, a sense of collective belonging to a social or ethnic group, and existential meaning.

Kadioglu notes that overloading the purchaser citizen's senses with more information than he or she can process efficiently renders the subject vulnerable to the consumerist propaganda that is embedded in each advertisement. After removing a client's natural defense mechanisms thereby manufacturing consent, the robot consumer becomes the ideal neoliberal citizen programmed for materialistic excess. As Kadioglu affirms,

> Le monde moderne vise ainsi à multiplier les besoins artificiels et à transformer tout en une marchandise. Il doit toujours créer plus de besoins pour survivre, car une fois qu'on s'est engagé dans cette voie, il est bien difficile de s'arrêter. Et maintenant les entreprises qui déchiffrent les codes génétiques et qui en possèdent les patentes, veulent transformer, dans le système de marché, la vie en une marchandise et maîtriser nos destins biologiques.
>
> The modern world aims in this way to multiply artificial needs and to transform everything into a product. It always has to create more needs to survive, because once we have started on this path it is very difficult to stop. And now businesses are deciphering genetic codes and they possess the patents; they want to transform, as part of the free market system, life into a product and master our biological destinies (135; my trans.).

Kadioglu explains that an economic system which necessitates constant growth and expansion must eventually attempt to possess everything around it if it wishes to sustain itself. Ultimate domination is only possible after successfully conquering the empire of the human mind with powerful weapons of mass deception and reducing human beings themselves to a mere commodity. Although the shallow values of consumerism are not capable of fulfilling basic human needs, as evidenced in *Le Chercheur d'or*, *Désert*, and *Poisson d'or*, the hegemonic power structures that benefit from the current system continually fabricate false desires which claim to be able to fill the inner void that the previous consumer good(s) failed to satisfy. The message of the neoliberal elite or "happy few" is quite simple. If an individual is unhappy, then he or she is not buying enough consumer products. The ideology of consumption exploits the victim with pervasive indoctrination transmitted through neoliberal media outlets, and then blames the discontented client when products fail to deliver on their promises of "la grande vie."

In reference to the expanding economic and social grip of transnational corporations and their religion of consumption throughout the global village, the narrator of *Les Géants* grumbles in disgust, "La pensée des Maîtres est si puissante qu'on n'en voit pas la fin [...] Elle invente tout. Tout vient d'elle, va vers elle. Les passions, les désirs, les douleurs, les plaisirs, les goûts et les dégoûts, les images, les mots, les émotions, les obsessions, tout cela est d'elle, en elle" / 'The Master's thought is so powerful that it seems limitless [...] It invents everything. Everything derives from it, and moves in its direction. Passions, desires, pains, pleasures, likes and dislikes, images, words, emotions, obsessions: all these derive from the Masters' thinking, exist within it' (259–260; 239). Although the anguish and fear expressed by the protagonists of *Les Géants* at times seem to border on paranoia, recent events which concretize the failure of the media to have any consideration whatsoever for public interests that are outside of its own goal of generating revue for its shareholders in addition to numerous financial crises and government bailouts on a global scale affirm that this deep apprehension is justifiable. Decades before it was popular to broach such topics, Le Clézio was astutely cognizant that the consolidation of power in society was already perhaps greater than at any point in the history of human civilization. Moreover, as Langman and Morris assert from chapter one, consumerist ideology has replaced traditional social and spiritual paradigms to such an extent that it has become a religion of its own with billions of faithful believers across the planet. Even if Bogo le Muet, Machines, and Tranquilité are somehow able to remove their ideological shackles, they are uncertain if an uncontaminated space exists in the globalized world where they can heal themselves from this cancer.

Reminiscent of the conscious decisions made by Lalla and Laïla to reject an empty life of luxury and to seek alternatives to universalist global village logic, Bogo le Muet, Machines, and Tranquilité realize that their existence is inauthentic in their sterile consumer republic in which all choices are dictated by market forces. This frustration explains why "L'homme qui ne s'appelle plus Machines" / 'the man who is still called Machines'[16] walks into Hyperpolis with several containers of kerosene to burn down this supercenter at the end of the narrative (327; 300). Although this act of aggression is certainly naïve given that Hyperpolis is emblematic of forces that are much larger than this one store itself, it is nonetheless an important gesture in terms of understanding the fragmented plot similar to that of a *nouveau roman*.[17] This experimental, cautionary tale urges the reader to no longer be complacent in an exploitative system that is spiraling out of control despite its seductive propaganda. The somewhat aggressive and apocalyptic tone of this text which commands the reader to "Libérez-vous" / 'Free yourself' should be understood as a scathing indictment of consumerism and the irreparable destruction that it has already inflicted throughout the global village.

In an aforementioned interview with Boncenne, Le Clézio decries "le langage publicitaire, le langage des slogans, de la politique, de la sociologie, de tout ce qui tourne autour de l'homme et qui a l'air de le servir, mais, en réalité, se sert de lui" / 'advertising language, the language of slogans, politics, sociology, of everything that beats around man and which appears to serve him, but in reality, which uses him' (44; my trans.). Affirming similar sentiments to those of Herman and Chomsky related to the integrated sociopolitical elite and their hegemonic institutions whose humanistic ideology justifies their domination, Le Clézio is skeptical of any artificial capitalistic creation that claims to improve the quality of our lives or to defend public interests. In this context, it should be noted that the media's euphoria for the global village is inseparable from its enthusiasm for the technological advances that have rendered a more interconnected and interdependent world possible. Both John Brown[18] and David Walker note that technology is not presented in a favorable light in *Les Géants*

Contrasting Le Clézio's unsettling concerns to the rather ecstatic sentiments of the earlier French writer Pierre Mac Orlan, Walker asserts, "Or, alors que Mac Orlan célèbre les 'graphismes nouveaux' qui pour lui inaugurent une 'poésie du haut commerce,' Le Clézio se montre soucieux d'une évolution plutôt sinistre dans la prolifération de la technologie 'graphique' car, parmi ses expériences typographiques, il dresse le catalogue d'une série de termes à résonances troublantes" / 'And yet while Mac Orlan celebrated these new graphemes that for him inaugurated a 'poetry of high commerce,' Le Clézio shows himself to be concerned about the rather sinister evolution in the proliferation of 'graphic' technology, (from) among its typographical experiments he draws up a list of terms that have troubling resonances' (113; my trans.). After underscoring both the allure and the apprehension that graphic art triggers for the protagonists of *Les Géants*, Walker concludes, "En fait le roman tout entier vise à dévoiler la nature des techniques de surveillance et de contrôle qui vont de pair avec les méthodes du marketing de masse dans la société moderne" / 'In fact, the entire novel aims to reveal the nature of surveillance and control that go hand in hand with mass marketing methods in modern society' (113; my trans.). Indeed, it is because of technology that Tranquilité in particular feels as if her every move is being recorded, watched, and analyzed by the "Masters." Given that their cameras seem to be everywhere in addition to the sophistication of their other inventions designed to read her mind, Tranquilité feels incarcerated in Hyperpolis with no means of escape. Not only do the "Masters" attempt to control her body, but they also endeavor to appropriate her every thought transforming her into a helpless robot conditioned to obey the summons to consume without question. Similar to Pickard, Le Clézio seems to wonder if certain inventions were intentionally manufactured by the corporate elite as an exploitative, malevolent hand that feeds the "happy few" at the expense of expendable others.

Undermining the simplicity and dogmatism of neoliberal ideology which asserts that the current state of the global village represents the most monumental achievement of human civilization in reference to *Les Géants*, Walker summarizes, "Ce récit est donc fondé sur une vision anti-utopique de la société où les individus sont assujettis, contrôlés et manipulés par les agents tyranniques de l'hypermarché, avatar totalitaire du grand magasin" / 'This narrative is founded upon an anti-utopian vision of society in which individuals are subjugated, controlled and manipulated by the tyrannical agents of the hypermarket, totalitarian avatar of the supercenter store' (114; my trans.). Given that all desires are carefully controlled and manufactured in the modern consumer republic, the characters of *Les Géants* are not autonomous agents that help construct the system through the power of the purse string(s) but rather conditioned automates that impulsively obey the hybrid messages transmitted by the integrated social and political elite. In a specifically literary context but posing the same disquieting questions as Joseph Stiglitz and other renowned economists, Le Clézio portrays the anguish of the modern subject for whom globalization has indeed failed to deliver on its fundamental ideological promises of greater prosperity and happiness for humankind. Although advertisers and the latest technological advances that they incessantly market pretend to serve human interests, they correspond to a neoliberal view of contentment that fosters and justifies corporate domination of the brainwashed masses.

At first glance, Le Clézio's text *Haï*, published in 1971 by Éditions Albert Skira, differs drastically from *Les Géants* in terms of both content and especially style. Given that this essay was directly inspired by Le Clézio's extensive contacts with indigenous civilizations in both Mexico and Central America including extended stays with the Emberas and

Waunanas of Panama, it has been correctly identified by numerous Le Clézio scholars as one of the "Indian texts" (Waelti-Walters 107). However, *Haï* is not merely a "volume on art," but it is also a valorization of an alternative worldview that the writer discovered from living with divergent Amerindian societies (Waelti-Walters 107). Moreover, it should be noted that recent works such as *Raga* reinforce the writer's predilection to give a voice to minority civilizations that continue to resist integration into the global village. Rejecting the ideology of consumption and the neoliberal definition of happiness, Le Clézio often explores in his diverse writings what other philosophical and socioeconomic models might have to offer the modern world.

Although *Haï* appeared two years before *Les Géants,* the author's choice to alternate between traditional images of Amerindian art and Western advertisements in *Haï* is best understood after reading *Les Géants*. Given that the author never explicitly indicts corporate titans and the destructive values that they represent in *Haï,* the incorporation of urban images mingled with advertisements from familiar transnational entities such as Coca-Cola, BP, Marlboro, and Hennessy is generally much more subtle with the exception of a few direct passages in this early Indian text as opposed to the overtly antagonistic tone of *Les Géants*. After the writer himself develops a deep appreciation of the many positive aspects of the Amerindian civilizations with which he resided, he is able to articulate his disdain for the consumerist virtues of Western society more clearly because he is now familiar with other opposing worldviews. For this reason, both *Haï* and *Les Géants* contain art forms that are the most indicative of their respective societies.

In stark contrast to the cult of the Hollywood film star or pop singer which is an expression of a narcissistic dream of fortune and fame, Amerindian artistic works are more pragmatic in nature and community-oriented. Whereas the manipulative graphic art that urges the purchaser citizen to fulfill his civic duty saturates Western media outlets, Le Clézio notes that the act of aesthetic creation is not designed to glorify or to enrich the individual or conglomerates in many Amerindian cultures. Describing Native American painting in *Haï,* the writer elucidates, "Peinture héréditaire, qui ne cherche pas à affirmer la supériorité d'un individu sur tout le reste de la tribu. Hommes, femmes, enfants, tous sont peintres, tous 'artistes' " / 'Hereditary painting, which does not strive to affirm the superiority of the individual over the rest of the tribe. Men, women, children, all are painters, all 'artists' (116; my trans.). This frank assessment of the materialistic and individualistic nature of Western art explains why Lalla and Laïla reject the empty virtues of consumerism. Although both of these female protagonists are offered a life of luxury, they do not want to be reduced to an artificial product ready to be consumed by purchaser citizens. Given that their improbable journey is inaccessible for the vast majority of the inhabitants of the global village, Lalla and Laïla also do not wish to be complicit in an exploitative system that markets an idealized image of success which not only is incapable of providing true happiness but that is also unattainable for most people.

Further juxtaposing the collective aspirations of Amerindian "artists" to the egocentric impulses that define mainstream art in Western society, Le Clézio adamantly underscores his "Haine de la peinture! Ces effigies glacées [...] Que veulent-ils? Il ne sont là pour que témoigner de l'impuissance de l'individu, de son désir de dominer [...] Ils répètent avec acharnement, avec haine, ce mot odieux et ridicule, le génie" / 'Hate of painting! These cold effigies [...] What do they want? They are only there in order to bear witness to the powerlessness of the individual, of his desire to dominate [...] They repeat with ferocious determination, with hate, this odious and ridiculous word, genius' (107; my trans.). Le Clézio notes that all forms of art in Western society including popular music and the hybrid advertisements of the mainstream media are inseparable from the ideology of consumerism. Instead of reinforcing traditional virtues that emphasize the common good and a sense of belonging to a certain community and its set of values, Western art places the artist on a pedestal as a "genius" that has earned the right to live a life of opulence while millions of people around the globe confront famine on a daily basis. Although carefully calculated advertisements designed to create false desires and artificial needs are perhaps the greatest manipulative tools manufactured by the corporate elite to sustain their dominance, the pervasive ideology of consumption has tainted everything in the modern world including popular culture and its forms of artistic expression.

## CONCLUSION

Similar to numerous other Leclézian protagonists, Alexis, Lalla, and Laïla find no lasting meaning or sense of fulfillment in the insatiable quest to consume one's way to happiness. In fact, Lalla and Laïla will both forgo careers that promise to be quite lucrative affording them all of the material comforts that modern society valorizes. Cognizant that the seductive images of success lauded by the media are alluring albeit chimerical visions of contentment and existential purpose, the young female characters of *Désert* and *Poisson d'or* will abandon the global village in an effort to satisfy profound, inner needs that cannot be purchased. However, as Thibault and Levy underscore in their analyses of *Le Chercheur d'or*, Alexis appears to reach an ethical impasse in terms of his capacity to appreciate the Other.

Indoctrinated with messages from birth that are emblematic of the neoliberal view of happiness which unequivocally encourage each individual to think only about which consumer products will actualize one's own self-centered, manufactured fantasies, the modern subject has no reason to reflect upon the repercussions of his or her own actions for other people. Moreover, since neoliberal ideology professes that the endless acquisition of material goods benefits everyone, narcissistic consumption has been distorted into a humanistic, civic duty. In a closely connected global community in which social and economic inequality are at unparalleled levels, *Les Géants* explores the hegemonic structures that justify and promote an economic program that benefits the "happy few." Although the author's deep concerns related to the consolidation of power and influence by the corporate elite through far-reaching ideological propaganda might have seemed exaggerated to some readers when the text first appeared in 1973 similar to the initial critical reception of Herman and Chomsky's Propaganda Model, the unmitigated failure of the media to reflect the fourth estate ideal in recent years has made this specific narrative more relevant than ever. Le Clézio's astute observations concerning Amerindian and Western art in *Haï* affirm that despite the concerted efforts of the supporters of neoliberal globalization to eliminate any alternatives to the current socioeconomic paradigm, other possibilities exist which could potentially create a more just and egalitarian society in the wake of the collapse of McLuhan's original vision for humanity.[19]

## NOTES

1. For precise references related to these researchers, see page 100 of Claudia von Werlhof's aforementioned essay "The Globalization of Neoliberalism, its Consequences, and Some of its Basic Alternatives."
2. Herman and Chomsky's "Propaganda Model" (PM) will be briefly analyzed later in this chapter.
3. Rochefort-Guillouet, Sophie. *Dissertations sur la recherche du bonheur*. Paris: Ellipses, 2005.
4. The role of advertising in terms of reinforcing and propagating the ideology of consumerism will be discussed in a later section of this chapter.
5. The efforts of indigenous societies to resist the powerful forces of globalization will be further investigated in chapter five.
6. I first explored this disquieting moral ambivalence in my book entitled *"Privileged Moments" in the Novels and Short Stories of J.M.G. Le Clézio: His Contemporary Development of a Traditional French Literary Device* (New York: The Edwin Mellen Press, 2008). However, my initial interpretations have been adapted to fit the parameters of this given study. Specifically, instead of focusing on eroticism, this section probes ethical questions related to consumerism and the ideology of consumption.
7. It should be noted that several critics, such as Robert Alvin Miller, Dauda Yillah, and Geoff Woollen have explored the semi-autobiographical filial guilt that is omnipresent in all of the so-called Mauritian texts in addition to other narratives such as *Onitsha*. See the references section for all of the pertinent details concerning these studies. Moreover, the author himself has also directly broached this topic in numerous interviews.

8. The media researcher Paul Adams asserts that "Television is itself a product of late capitalism and, as such, has to be seen in the context of the promotion of a culture of consumerism" (122).

9. Numerous critics have also highlighted the crucial role that Lalla's enigmatic and mystical experience in the nightclub (p. 354–357) plays concerning her decision to resist integration into the global village. See Moser, Keith, *"Privileged Moments" in the Novels and Short Stories of J.M.G. Le Clézio: His Contemporary Development of a Traditional French Literary Device*. (New York: The Edwin Mellen Press, 2008.)

10. Given that Laïla's journey in *Poisson d'or*, published by Gallimard in 1997, is similar to that of Lalla in *Désert*, it is no coincidence that their names also closely resemble each other. *Poisson d'or*, like the texts examined in the previous chapter, is also a disquieting and realistic novel that depicts the struggles of immigrants desperately longing for a more prosperous life in the modern world. Elucidating the author's motivations for writing this work, Bruno Thibault affirms, "In *Poisson d'or*, he makes heard the voice of ethnic minorities, and describes the difficult conditions of immigrants in first-world countries" ("J.M.G. Le Clézio" 366). Moreover, Laïla will also reject the possibility of fame and fortune at the end of this narrative as well.

11. The five filters of the PM are: ownership, advertising, official sources, flak, and marginalizing dissent. For a more comprehensive discussion, see David Model and Lang and Lang.

12. The term "Purchaser Citizen" has been in common usage since the 1950s. See Steigerwald, David. "All Hail the Republic of Choice: Consumer History as Contemporary Thought." *The Journal of American History*, September 2006: 385–403. Additionally, Dannagal Young notes the following synonyms that Lizabeth Cohen coined in *A Consumers' Republic*: Citizen Consumer, Purchaser Consumer, and Purchaser as Citizen (27).

13. For another point of view concerning the complex question of autonomy and the media that underscores both the power of consumer choice and deliberate exploitation, see Cunningham, Anne. "Autonomous Consumption: Buying into the Ideology of Capitalism." *Journal of Business Ethics* 48: 229–236. Specifically, Cunningham reaches the following conclusion: "By the very fact that capitalist values are so fundamental to our way of life, advertising is unlikely to condition consumers to act in ways that contradict our belief systems. As such, advertising, though it may in other ways detrimentally affect society and consumers' well-being, does not violate our autonomy" (236).

14. For a discussion of *Les Géants* in the larger context of the author's nuanced views concerning language itself, see Moser, Keith. "Le paradoxe du langage ou le 'terrible privilège' de l'humanité selon J.M.G. Le Clézio" *J.M.G. Le Clézio dans la forêt des paradoxes*. Eds. Bruno Thibault and Keith Moser. Paris: L'Harmattan, Collection Études transnationales, francophones et comparés, 2012: 211–220.

15. Despite the intentional misspelling of this French word, Le Clézio unequivocally underscores that no tranquility is to be found in Hyperpolis.

16. The official English translation, although excellent overall, in this specific passage is rather problematic, as evidenced by the original French version of the text.

17. As Jennifer Waelti-Walters and other scholars have noted, Le Clézio's early texts bear the influence of both existentialism and the so-called French "new novel." However, Le Clézio was always in the margins of both of these important literary movements.

18. "A New Book of Flights: Immigration and Displacement in J.M.G. Le Clézio's *Poisson d'or*." *World Literature Today* 71: 731–735.

19. Chapter five will probe the efforts of Le Clézio's protagonists to resist integration into the global village and to seek alternatives to the ideology of consumption.

# FOUR

# Deconstructing the "Genesis Myth"[1] and Simulating Cosmic Empathy for the Entire Material Universe

In addition to Le Clézio's concerns related to human exploitation in all of its forms and the ideological, hegemonic structures that justify and maintain the current situation of inequality in the neoliberal global village, numerous critics have noted the deep ecological consciousness that permeates all facets of his diverse literary repertoire. Moreover, researchers such as Robert Alvin Miller assert that Le Clézio's profound anxiety concerning the fragility of the cosmic forces that render life possible on this planet is inseparable from his disquieting questions related to the nefarious effects of globalization. In the context of the short story "Pawana," which has been accurately described by the French poet Bruno Doucey as "l'œuvre d'un écrivain engagé dans une lutte pour la défense des grands mammifères marins" / 'the work of an engaged writer fighting to defend large marine mammals,[2] ' Miller affirms, "Chez Le Clézio, les injustices et les destructions que la mondialisation cherche en vain à effacer de notre mémoire affleurent mystérieusement à la surface" / 'In Le Clézio's fiction, the injustice and destruction that globalization seeks in vain to erase from our memory mysteriously rise to the surface' (32; my trans.).

In what is perhaps the only critical work that attempts to explore Le Clézio's fiction from an ecocritical perspective,[3] Maria José Sueza Espejo also examines the ecological commitment to which both Doucey and Miller refer. Reflecting upon traditional literary studies and the emerging field of ecocriticism, Sueza Espejo underscores, "*Pour lire Le Clézio*, étude profonde de la production littéraire leclézienne, écrite par Jean Onimus [...] souligne l'engagement de cet écrivain en qualité de défenseur de la Nature et de l'Univers, étant donné que son œuvre entière peut être considérée un chant poétique à la Nature, exaltation d'un désir de communion entre les hommes et les femmes avec l'Univers" / '*Pour lire Le Clézio* (Reading Le Clézio), an in-depth study of Le Clézio's literary production, written by Jean Onimus [...] underlines the writer's engagement as a defender of Nature and the Universe given that his entire work could be considered a poetic song to nature, (an) exaltation of a desire of men and women to commune with the Universe' (329–330; my trans.). Although many researchers divide Le Clézio's nuanced and vast corpus into at least two distinct time periods, the author's concern for the toll inflicted upon the environment by the modern, industrialized world is a recurring thread that is omnipresent throughout his work. For this reason, Pierre Kyria describes Le Clézio's first protagonist Adam Pollo from *Le Procès-Verbal* as a(n) "homme (qui) cherche sa place dans le chaos des choses et des gens" / 'man (who) is looking for his place in the chaos of things and people' (9; my trans.). Indeed, much of Le Clézio's fiction is emblematic of a philosophical and spiritual quest to re-conceptualize the appropriate relationship between humanity and the rest of the material universe.

This chapter will also elucidate that the writer's texts deconstruct the superiority complex, inherited from Renaissance humanism, which places human beings upon a pedestal as members of a privileged species that have the inalienable right to exercise complete dominion over the remainder of the planet. As Germaine Brée explains, "Du *Procès-verbal* au *Déluge*, il s'était attaqué avec rage ou sarcasme à une représentation de la vie privilégiant uniquement le groupe humain, ses conflits et les lignes de son destin, individuel, ou social" / 'From *The Interrogation* to *The Flood*, he attacked with considerable rage or sarcasm any representation of life that uniquely privileges the human group, its conflicts and the trajectory of its individual or social destiny' (51; my trans.). Brée reiterates, "C'est aux frontières de l'humain, cerné par l'inconnu, que Le Clézio installe son monde" / 'It's at the boundaries of the human being, surrounded by the unknown, that Le Clézio sets up his world' (52; my trans.). Not only do the author's works transgress traditional anthropocentric borders in Western society deliberately created to justify human exploitation of the biosphere, but they are also indicative of Le Clézio's predilection to protect the defenseless Cosmic Other from the destructive impulses of consumerism and greed.

Thus, Le Clézio's literary project gives a voice not only to the marginalized and disenfranchised individuals that are living the neoliberal nightmare, but his compassion also extends to the entire biotic community which has suffered greatly from the actualization of the global village. In reference to J.M. Coetzee's *Life & Times of Michael K,* Anthony Vital explains the importance of literature that expresses an ecocentric worldview which articulates the cosmic trauma that has scarred much of the planet as follows: "nonhuman nature, lacking an equivalent to human linguistic codes, does not speak. It has to be spoken for by the same humans who are de-centered as speaking subjects" (89). As this study will elucidate, perhaps more than any other contemporary author, Le Clézio is astutely cognizant of the gravity of the ecological calamity. Furthermore, both the author's fiction and public discourses underscore the urgency for both action and a radical paradigm shift that summons human beings to take responsibility for their role as planetary stewards in the face of stern environmental warnings.

## COMBATING THE PERVASIVE NATURE OF THE GENESIS MYTH: RE-CONCEPTUALIZING A POST-MATERIALIST WORLD THROUGH THE LENS OF PHILOSOPHICAL MATERIALISM

By combating what he terms the "genesis myth," Le Clézio's narratives allow the reader to re-envision a *post-materialist* world through the lens of philosophical materialism and cosmic humility. Le Clézio first coined the expression "genesis myth" during a speech at Mississippi State University on March 30, 2009. Although this event represents perhaps the only time that he uses this given phrase, this notion is indicative of deep cosmic sensibilities that are omnipresent in both his narratives and public discourses. Offering an operational definition of what the genesis myth means to him and what it could encompass, Le Clézio explains, "nature is given to man so he can use it" ("What Is Literature?" n.p.). The author further elucidates,

> If we think of the economy of nature, the new world had given the wrong image to the rest of the world. The new world gave, through the conquistadors and the new commerce the image of an indefinitely rich nature that would be used without limits. This is very wrong. Nature has its limits and we are finding this out today. So this is also one of the necessities for writers, to find the limits of the use of the cities of the urban world ("What Is Literature?" n.p.).

Echoing recent scientific discoveries outlined in chapter one that have revived the metaphor of the planet as an economy or a web that is a self-regulating but delicate entity, the writer criticizes modern society for its incessant zeal to appropriate and transform the entire cosmos. Similar to other contemporary artists from all corners of the globe, Le Clézio poses disconcerting questions concerning the present and future repercussions of nature being reduced to a mere commodity whose only value is purely instrumental in terms of maximizing human satisfaction and prosperity.

The egocentric and anthropocentric mentality that the remainder of the cosmos, including other living creatures, only exists to help us live more abundantly threatens to destroy the ecological equilibrium that sustains life itself. Le Clézio deconstructs this ecocidal[4] worldview by highlighting that human beings are inseparable from the cosmic forces which conceived all life forms. His notion of the genesis myth closely corresponds to Estok's definition of ecophobia which posits that human beings possess "the biblical imperative to control everything that lives" (208). However, the Christian theological perspective of the relationship between humanity and the cosmos is much more nuanced than it at first appears. The deep ecological sensibilities of Saint Francis and the literary contributions of Christian mystics, such as Teilhard de Chardin, underscore the often ambivalent ideological positions of the religious institution itself. Moreover, Noah's decision to save two members of every single species unequivocally implies that each life form exists for a reason in the Christian cosmogonic myth that attempts to explain the origins of the universe.[5] Yet, in spite of these apparent paradoxes, the mainstream interpretation of the proper relationship between humankind and the universe, at least in the general public, tends to favor absolute dominion as opposed to responsible stewardship. It is this anthropocentric mentality that Le Clézio exposes as naïve and fundamentally unsustainable.[6]

The author's efforts to reveal simplistic, erroneous, anthropocentric ideology are similar to the mission of ecocritics like Lance Newman. In a contention reminiscent of the genesis myth, Newman affirms, "The problem is bad ideas—such as that people were meant to exercise dominion over nature […] or that limitless growth is the essence of human social destiny" (2). As evidenced in his speech at Mississippi State University, Le Clézio is aware that debunking the outdated scientific model of species adaptation alone will not prevent an even greater ecological crisis from transpiring. Literature and the humanities in general have an important role to play in terms of articulating how recent discoveries, such as Grand Unified Theory and Quantum Contextualism examined in chapter one, should impact both public consciousness and decision making. Although the doctrine of human exceptionalism is entirely incompatible with modern ecology, obsolete notions still continue to linger and to dictate global governance of nonrenewable environmental resources. For this reason, perhaps the battle to save the earth will ultimately be decided by those who support unfounded and misguided ideology and those who attempt only to conquer the empire of the human mind.

Given the environmental consciousness of the writer from the beginning of his career to the present, the journalist Adam Gopnik notes that Le Clézio has been described as a de-centered humanist.[7] Summarizing the portion of the public conversation between Gopnik and Le Clézio that took place as part of the 2010 PEN World Voices Festival in which they discuss these characterizations, an unidentified author from the magazine *La Newyorkaise* explains,

> Gopnik brought up the fact that one of Le Clézio's students or a follower of his work once said his ambition was to obtain "a humanism with-

> out human beings at the center," asking if this was true. "I wish I could do that, but I am a human being; everything I write is from a human being's point of view," Le Clézio lamented. He said that he feels the closest to this state of "humanism without humans" when he reads ancient Indian spiritual texts or the poems of Rimbaud: "When I read this, it makes me shiver," he said ("Every Word Contains the World" n.p.).

Despite his evident concerns related to the ecological calamity of epic proportions unleashed upon the rest of the universe in the name of "progress," Le Clézio is cognizant of his limitations as a writer. In a similar vein as the ecocritic John Gatta who astutely asserts that "our sense of the nonhuman world is always inevitably mediated through human imagination," Le Clézio realizes that a complete fusion with the cosmos is impossible (619). Yet, in spite of this unpleasant reality, Le Clézio's protagonists strive to eliminate the affective and physical barriers that prevent them from having a close, primordial relationship with the universe to the greatest extent possible. Re-establishing a direct sensorial contact with the biosphere, the author's complex characters embrace post-materialist ethical values that transcend hollow consumerist virtues which conceptualize the natural world purely as an ends to a mean.

However, perhaps the term "re-centered humanism" would more accurately depict Le Clézio's environmental awareness. As Bruno Thibault asserts in his analysis of *La Quarantaine*, "le héros leclézien poursuit une quête: il cherche le lieu où renaître et se recentrer" / 'the Leclézian hero pursues a quest: he searches a place to become born again and to re-center himself' (845; my trans.). Given that the modern subject could easily spend the majority of his existence in complete separation from the other organic particles of matter to which he is linked behind walls of brick, wood, and cement, this disconnection is the source of profound alienation for numerous Leclézian protagonists as Thibault outlines. This desperate attempt to re-center themselves or to understand their small place in the greater scheme of life itself explains why Le Clézio's characters often flee the sterility and artifice of the modified urban landscape that are indicative of the neoliberal global village.

In *L'Extase Matérielle*, *Terra Amata*, and *La Fièvre*, the author highlights basic principles of philosophical materialism that also correspond to modern ecology which transgress species boundaries, eliminate false and misleading dualities, and undermine anthropocentrism. Published in 1967 by Gallimard, *L'Extase Matérielle* could be described as a work of pure philosophy, espousing a monistic worldview, which attempts to articulate the physical reality that everything is comprised of matter. Although Le Clézio was clearly disappointed with the final product given that he considers this text to be "une tentative vaine d'écrire un essai philosophique" / 'a vain attempt at writing a philosophical essay,' not everyone shares the writer's point of view concerning this essay (Roussel-Gillet "Ecrivain de l'incertitude" 30; my trans.). In fact, Stephen Smith declares that *L'Extase Matérielle* is "possibly the single most important tract in his entire oeuvre" (58). Indeed, it is perhaps in this early seminal essay in which Le Clézio most clearly expresses his ideas concerning the relationship between humanity and the cosmos.

The novel *Terra Amata,* also published in 1967, is an experimental text[8] that recounts the universal story of a human being thrown into the chaos of existence. The aptly named *Terra Amata,* whose title means "beloved earth," examines both the grandeur of life and the anguish from which an ephemeral being suffers during its fleeting existence upon this planet. The reader follows the enigmatic protagonist Chancelade from birth to his demise. As Fredrik Westerlund explains, "*Terra Amata* [...] raconte les étapes de la vie à travers des scènes quotidiennes exposant le destin du personnage Chancelade, de sa prime enfance jusqu'à sa vieillesse et sa mort" / '*Terra Amata* [...] recounts the stages of life through daily scenes exposing the destiny of the character Chancelade, from the moment of his birth to old age and death' ("*Les Fleuves dans l'œuvre Romanesque*"61; my trans.). Affirming that Chancelade's story is really *our* unending collective saga, the narrator speaks directly to the reader, "Ce que vous avez lu, ce n'est pas moi qui l'ai écrit vraiment" / 'I didn't really write what you've just read' (243; 217). In an even more explicit passage related to the universal nature of *Terra Amata,* the narrator confesses, "Mais assez inventé, maintenant. Il n'y a pas de Chancelade, il n'y a jamais eu de Chancelade. Il n'y a eu que moi, en train d'écrire ces mots, et sachant qu'ils ne cachent rien" / 'But that's enough of inventing. There is no Chancelade, there never was any Chancelade. All there ever was, was me, writing these words and knowing they hid nothing' (230; 205).

Explaining the difference between these two texts which appeared in the same year, Jennifer Waelti-Walters asserts, "*The Ecstasy of Matter* offers a philosophy of life, in the sense of giving a description of what it is like to be alive, a living particle in a material universe [...] *The Ecstasy of Matter* was the search for a theory behind life. *Terra Amata* is the practice" (69). The theoretical and intellectually stimulating *L'Extase Matérielle* blends well with the more accessible text *Terra Amata* which could be interpreted as a pragmatic representation or reenactment of what existence and the human condition entail. In his essay entitled "J.M.G. Le Clézio's *Terra Amata*: A Micro-Fictional Affection for the Real," Roland Racevskis offers the following description of *Terra Amata*: "In 1967 [...] Le Clézio posed a venerable literary question—that of how to live—in a new way. As the title suggests, this novel is about the earth and more specifically about a certain way of approaching the world's concrete realities" (409). As Racevskis notes, not only does *Terra Amata* explore the timeless philosophical question of the relationship between humanity and the cosmos, but it also re-examines the physical realities of the universe at a time in which the sense of displacement from the cosmic whole has never been greater for the human inhabitants of the global village.

*La Fièvre* is a collection of short stories, comprised of nine varied narratives, which appeared in 1965. Despite the diverse nature of these texts, several thematic threads link the divergent novellas together. In addition to highlighting the influence of both existentialism and the *Nouveau Roman* upon the young author, all of the protagonists experience a sort of cerebral "fever" that transcends the physical ailment, resulting in painful, ecstatic, or bittersweet epiphanies concerning the human condition itself. As Waelti-Walters explains, "A fever is something which can happen to anyone [...] it has one main effect: it attacks our normal means of perception [...] During the course of a fever we see our world move, distort, metamorphose around us, offering wider possibilities, flashes of apparent and deeper understanding, different awareness" (32). For the purposes of this specific investigation, the three most relevant narratives from this early collection are "Arrière" / 'Backwards,' "L'homme qui marche" / 'The Walking Man,' and "Le monde est vivant" / 'The World Is Alive.' These particular texts in addition to *L'Extase Matérielle* and *Terra Amata* illustrate that Le Clézio's fascination with ecology and his attempts to redefine the boundaries between the human and nonhuman world are salient features of his entire literary repertoire.

Instead of conceptualizing the human race as the center of the universe and one's given culture as the model *par excellence* to be emulated, the writer exposes the inherent flaws of any type of ideology that creates a superiority complex. In all of the aforementioned works, the author reminds the reader that we are merely particles of matter outside of which no other reality exists. As the ecocritic Anthony Vital expresses, "separation from other species, from elemental matter is impossible" (92). As minute elements of this interconnected, interdependent universe, human beings have the same intrinsic right to exist as everything else. For this reason, the narrator of *L'Extase Matérielle* underscores the "petitesse" (smallness) of humanity in an intertwined cosmos in this early seminal essay.

In the texts "Arrière"[9] and "L'homme qui marche," the narrator employs a similar metaphor describing himself as a "nain" / 'dwarf' which realizes that his microcosmic existence is part of a larger force that transcends the human species. Near the end of "Arrière," the narrator is struck by the following existential realization: "Je suis un nain [...] je ne suis pas digne qu'on se souvienne de moi, qu'on se penche vers moi, qu'on me regarde. Oubliez-moi" / 'I am a dwarf [...] I am no longer worthy to be remembered, to be approached, to be looked at. Forget me' (104; 103). The narrator's epiphany concerning his miniscule role in both society and in the universe should be understood in the greater context of life itself. Given that the cosmos existed billions of years before the first human beings appeared on this planet and that abundant life on earth could very likely continue even if our race were to disappear entirely, Le Clézio reveals that the genesis myth is an illusory, albeit compelling, delusion of narcissistic grandeur. The narrator realizes that not only will other humans inhabit the same space as him long after his fleeting existence, but the indifferent trajectory of the biosphere will also continue with or without his species. Moreover, the pervasive myth that human beings were destined to control the universe is an equally chimerical product of our fragmented planetary consciousness.

Emphatically declaring that no escape exists from the ontological prison of matter itself, the narrator of "L'homme qui marche" muses, "Et au-delà? Et plus loin? Il n'y a pas de plus loin" / 'And beyond? And further on? There is no further on' (126; 125). The end of the narrative reinforces this monistic conception of reality. After the narrator experiences brief moments of euphoria triggered by a sensorial contact with other forms of matter and by the innate musicality of the cosmos,[10] J.F. Paoli or the "walking man" highlights "la réalité universelle" / 'universal reality' and the "gigantesque concert de bruits et de couleurs [...] la symphonie éternellement calme, éternellement vivante, de la vérité posée à plat sur le monde, comme s'ils n'avaient été qu'une parcelle mouvante, comme lui, comme les autres, qu'une poussière minuscule flottant dans le corps infiniment exquis, infiniment divin de la matière" / 'gigantic concert of sounds and colours [...] the eternally calm, eternally living symphony of the truth laid down flat upon the world; as though they had been only a moving fragment, like himself, like other people, only a minute speck of dust floating within the infinitely exquisite, infinitely divine body of matter' (131; 132). Similar to Spinoza's conception of a universe comprised of one sacred substance, Le Clézio explains the existential paradox of an ephemeral being that is inextricably linked to eternal forces that never die but only incessantly change forms. Like dust in the wind, the traces of each distinct sentient being that has ever roamed this planet will eventually be effaced and recycled to create new life. Given that these natural processes, which correspond to rudimentary scientific principles such as the first law of thermodynamics, dictate the fleeting existence of every creature, Le Clézio once again deconstructs the genesis myth. He reveals that all existential hierarchies are artificial and arbitrary reflections of wishful thinking that justify unbridled environmental exploitation.

In "Le monde est vivant," the writer further develops his understanding of the philosophical implications that derive from a basic comprehension of cosmic cycles. Articulating the physical realities of the natural world and explaining the origins of the universe, Le Clézio elucidates,

> elles étaient encore là, les traces du cataclysme ancien qui avait modelé la terre [...] On voyait encore la catastrophe telle qu'elle avait été pétrifiée des siècles auparavant ; le chaos reposait là [...] Qu'il (le monde) avait explosé autrefois, qu'il avait éclaté de toutes les forces de ses os

> vivants, bousculant tout autour de lui [...] Toute cette friction est lente, très lente. Mais une force surnaturelle anime le fleuve, et l'eau pousse tout le temps, elle n'a pas de répit, elle arrache la poussière à la terre, elle écrase, elle vide, elle rogne.

> they were still there, the traces of the ancient cataclysm that had moulded the earth [...] One could still see the disaster in the form in which it had petrified centuries before; chaos was at rest there [...] That once upon a time it had exploded, burst out with the full strength of its living bones, knocking over everything around it [...] All this friction goes on slowly, very slowly. But a supernatural strength dwells in the river, and the water is pushing all the time, it has no respite, it is tearing dust from the earth, crushing, emptying, gnawing away (176–177; 181–182).

The author poetically illustrates that the big bang theory is not a scientific phenomenon that should merely be relegated to the past. Although the majority of the earth's miniscule movements are imperceptible to the naked eye or ear, the planet is never static. The same cosmic forces which created all life forms continue to transform the biosphere. Given the epistemological limitations of human knowledge related to the cosmos, who knows what will happen in the future? No one can truly predict what the future holds for humanity. The undeniable fact that the universe is not constrained by self-centered, naïve concepts of human destiny proves that the genesis myth is not only misleading but it is also a false, oversimplified representation of the complex nature of reality.

Le Clézio's reflections upon ecology[11] and what its scientific principles suggest for all material life forms including human beings undermine unsubstantiated dualities whose only support derives from ideology. In fact, this knowledge, based on modern science which rejects the adaptation model, completely eliminates the philosophical separation between the subject and object. In her article entitled "Un Espace pour le vide," the Le Clézio scholar Elena Real explains in the context of the author's narratives, "La séparation de l'homme et du monde est consommée [...] L'écart qui sépare le monde intérieur du monde extérieur disparait" / 'The separation between man and the world is consumed [...] The gap that separates the inside world from the outside world disappears' (183–184; my trans.). Delving into the philosophy of Merleau-Ponty, Fredrik Westerlund reaches a similar conclusion: "en remettant en question l'identité d'un 'moi' cohérent, Le Clézio dissout la frontière qui sépare le moi du monde" / 'by questioning the identity of a coherent 'I,' Le Clézio dissolves the border that separates the I from the world' (*"Les Fleuves dans l'œuvre Romanesque"* 50; my trans.). As Real and Westerlund underscore, not only do Le Clézio's narratives transgress traditional boundaries that place "humans" and "animals" in distinct ontological categories, but they also often eliminate any division whatsoever amongst any material beings. Although the Cartesian notion of the *bêtem-*

*achine* examined in chapter one is an appealing idea that has justified the imposition of the neoliberal global village all around the planet, it is predicated upon the same anthropocentric, faulty logic as the genesis myth. Perhaps the greatest literary device that Le Clézio employs to dismiss destructive binary codes that define "us" and "them" in defense of the Cosmic Other is science itself. Even if many people realize that "everything is linked" as clearly stipulated in the first law of ecology, they may have never reflected upon the philosophical and ethical ramifications of this knowledge. If every sentient creature is comprised of the same sacred substance as the writer poetically elucidates in the aforementioned narratives, then what gives humanity the authority to govern anything or to decide what is in the best interest of the entire universe?

In an attempt to delineate Le Clézio's de-centered humanism, highlighted by numerous other critics such as Real and Westerlund, Isabelle Roussel-Gillet affirms, "Selon la typologie des trois humanismes, proposée par Alain Finkielkraut, Le Clézio serait un humaniste à la fois classique et galiléen: classique puisqu'il 'veille sur le trésor des œuvres admirables' et galiléen puisqu'il condamne la domination de l'erreur de l'anthropocentrisme" / 'According to the typology of the three humanisms, proposed by Alain Finkielkraut, Le Clézio would be both a classical and Galilean humanist at the same time: classical since he 'contemplates the treasure of admirable works' and Galilean since he condemns the domination that stems from the error of anthropocentrism' (136; my trans.). Concretized by his defense of the intrinsic value of every human life, as outlined in chapter two, Le Clézio is indeed a classical humanist. Moreover, the author firmly believes that all human civilizations have achieved tremendous accomplishments that should not be minimized. The same writer that describes himself as a "product of western civilization, which invented extraordinarily beautiful things, and at the same time behaved terribly" is also astutely cognizant that the homocentric, myopic worldview, which is emblematic of the modern world and its values, could very well lead to our own peril in addition to that of other species (Jaggi n.p.). Perhaps embracing a more ecocentric way of thinking could help maximize humanity's potential while simultaneously limiting the auto-destructive, nefarious effects of our seemingly unending greed. Indeed, studying the physical laws of the universe and reflecting upon what they mean in terms of re-envisioning the relationship between humanity and the cosmos is an exercise in humility. This first step forces us to ask disquieting questions about the nature of modernity and compels us to dismiss neoliberal fantasies that have no basis in reality. By exploring basic ecological truths that run contrary to fictitious, ideological constructions, such as the genesis myth, Le Clézio "lève les barrières entre animal et humain" / 'removes the barriers between animal and human' (Roussel-Gillet 159; my trans.). Reminding the reader that the physical realities of the biosphere have always existed independently from our imagination, Le Clézio's fiction obliterates the groundless ideology of human exceptionalism that has induced unprecedented suffering upon an interconnected and interdependent cosmos.

Drawing upon modern quantum theory and the resulting worldview generated by ecophilosophy, Serpil Oppermann asserts, "Postmodern fictions also transcend false dichotomies in a process of writing that self-consciously relates texts and contexts [...] many writers, from J.M. Coetzee to Don DeLillo, explore various environmental issues and contest dichotomies between nature and culture, world and word, and text and context" (243–244). Given his predilection to give a voice to the Cosmic Other by exposing the arbitrary nature of the ontological categories created by human beings in an attempt to explain our existence and to justify our incessant exploitation of the physical environment, many of Le Clézio's texts should be considered to be works of ecophilosophy. Similar to other contemporary authors that also ask disconcerting questions related to modernity and globalization, Le Clézio's literary project reflects the "ecocritical attempt to think beyond conceptual dichotomies that modernity, the Enlightenment, and science were thought to have imposed on Western culture—the separation of subject and object, body and environment, nature and culture [...]" (Heise "The Hitchhiker's Guide" 506–507). Le Clézio's entire *oeuvre* represents a scathing critique of all the illusory products of the Western imagination that have misled and deceived humanity resulting in alienation and alarming environmental degradation. The global village vision and the prevailing religion of consumerism are predicated upon many disproven ideological notions that have not only failed miserably to maximize prosperity and happiness for all, but which also threaten the life of each sentient being on this planet.

## COSMIC HUMILITY AND THE EXISTENTIAL NATURE OF BIOTIC EGALITARIANISM IN LE CLÉZIO'S NARRATIVES

The cosmic humility espoused by Le Clézio in his varied fiction, which is based on a deep understanding of the universe and humanity's place in it, deconstructs the pervasive homocentric paradigm that attempts to explain human existence. He reminds us that we are thrown into the chaos of existence through no choice of our own and for no apparent reason. All life forms endeavor to survive and to thrive in spite of the inherent mortality that is inscribed in the genetic code of each distinct species. Paradoxically, the law of conservation of energy and the first law of thermodynamics posit that energy can never truly be created or destroyed. For this reason, the absolute disappearance of a given being from the biosphere is impossible. Although all creatures must one day succumb to death, immortality is also paradoxically inescapable. Referring to this inevitable and ultimately indecipherable reality, Le Clézio affirms in *L'Extase Matérielle*:

> La vie, la mort sont des modalités sans importance, comme végétal ou minéral. La vie et la mort sont des formes qu'adoptent la matière, parmi tant d'autres [...] C'est ici que se trouve le plus grand espoir des hommes, vraisemblablement: c'est ici que peut commencer leur transfiguration, leur extase matérielle: jamais rien ne disparaîtra [...] il y aura, il y a toujours eu, il y a quelque chose. Mais c'est aussi le désespoir. La souffrance vaine de ce qu'on n'a pas connu, de ce qu'on ne connaîtra jamais [...] Ce vertige de l'inexprimable, de l'insensible, ce vertige du monde terrible de la matière [...] Ce monde où le néant n'est pas possible.
>
> Life and death are modalities with no importance, like vegetative or mineral. Life and death are forms that matter adopts, among many others [...] This is presumably where the greatest hope of mankind is to be found: this is where their transfiguration can begin, their material ecstasy: nothing will ever disappear [...] there will be, there always was, there will always be something. But this is also desperation. The vain suffering of that which we never were able to know, of that which we will never know [....] this vertigo of the inexpressible, of the senseless, this vertigo of the terrible world of matter [...] This world where nothingness is not possible (226–227; my trans.).

After once again articulating the epistemological limitations of humankind whose consciousness of the universe is destined to be fragmented, Le Clézio reveals that it is merely by chance that we temporarily inhabit our current ontological shell of being. Not only is each of us inseparable from the cosmic whole that created everything that exists, but we also could have easily appeared as a different form of matter. Furthermore, it is impossible to know how our energy might one day resurface to generate new life. This knowledge, derived from a basic understanding of deep ecology, rejects all notions of human superiority and the genesis myth.

The first chapter of *Terra Amata* appropriately entitled "Sur la terre au hasard" / 'On the earth by chance' articulates the same existential realities as in *L'Extase Matérielle*, albeit in a more accessible form for the lay reader. In fact, *Terra Amata* does not only represent the universal story of humanity as numerous critics have noted, but it is also an artistic expression of what it means for every sentient being to inhabit this shared planet. As the narrator explains, "Ils sont tous là. Chacun avec son nom, avec sa vie minuscule et grave, avec ses œufs, ses larves, ses choses à manger, ses excréments. Avec son danger de mort qui guette, qui fait frémir le cœur au fond de la carapace hermétique" / 'They are all there. Each one with its name, its tiny solemn life, its eggs, its larvae, the things it eats, its excrement. Each with its lurking danger of death, making the heart tremble deep within the hermetic carapace' (14; 6). By underscoring the physical realities of existence and how each creature comes into being, Le Clézio eliminates any meaningful distinction between "human" and "animal." Moreover, the author asserts that the universe does not really place any species in a privileged position over another given that mortality equals the playing field. Homocentric ideology is defenseless against the only certainty and greatest truth of all.

Reiterating that the greater scheme of life itself transcends the concerns of one species and any notions of manifest human destiny, Le Clézio elucidates,

> Sur cet immense paysage où frappe la chaleur continuelle, tous ces noms sont reliés les uns aux autres par des fils tenus, presque invisibles. Il y a toutes les histoires, toutes les aventures [...] Ce sont les millions de petits drames, les milliards de petites tragi-comédies [...] C'est ici qu'il faudrait s'asseoir, sans doute, sur un rocher, ou bien se coucher sur l'herbe dure, pour écrire toute l'histoire du monde.
>
> All over this huge landscape beaten down on endlessly by the sun, these names are linked with one another by fine, almost invisible threads. They contain every story, every adventure [...] Millions of little dramas, billions of little tragi-comedies [...] Yes, it's here one ought to sit down, on a rock in the middle of the earth, or lie down on the hard grass, and write the whole history of the world (14; 7).

Given that the author confesses that this narrative is an attempt to depict both the anguish and euphoria that each ephemeral organism experiences during its fleeting existence, *Terra Amata* is perhaps Le Clézio's most ambitious and comprehensive project. Furthermore, the metaphor of life as an intricate, interconnected, and interdependent web to which the writer alludes during his speech at Mississippi State University is emblematic of his fascination with deep ecology and his profound cosmic sensibilities. Many critics simply attribute this ecocentric worldview to the author's extensive contacts with various Amerindian civilizations, such as the Embreras and the Waunanas. Although these formative experiences undoubtedly transformed Le Clézio and his writings by his own admission,[12] it would perhaps be more appropriate to hypothesize that the type of knowledge which the author acquired from rich Amerindian cultures refined a preexisting cosmic awareness. It is noteworthy that *Terra Amata* (1967) predates Le Clézio's sustained living experiences (1970–1974) with the Embreras and Waunanas which inspired the author's translation of Chief Seattle's speech "Toutes choses sont liées" / 'Everything is linked' from *La Fête Chantée*. For this reason, it might be more accurate to speculate that Amerindian societies helped Le Clézio hone an ecocentric way of knowing that brought even deeper feelings to the surface.[13] Moreover, is the author unique in this regard, or has the modern world and its inauthentic, destructive lifestyle alienated us all from establishing a necessary relationship with the rest of the material universe?

Returning to the existential epiphanies of Chancelade in *Terra Amata*, these realizations are inseparable from Le Clézio's well-documented curiosity related to cosmogonic theories and myths. As the narrator asserts, "Il y avait eu une étincelle, ainsi, un jour, et depuis, plus rien n'avait été en repos [...] Jamais Chancelade n'avait rien vu d'aussi beau, et d'aussi terrible [...] La terre est comme ça. Elle est une sorte de peau recouverte de tics, une face qui grimace et sursaute sans arrêt [...] Mais à quoi bon ? Le jeu continue, devant, derrière, au-dessus, au-dessous" / 'One day there had been a spark, and since then there had been no rest anywhere [...] Chancelade had never seen anything so beautiful and so terrible [...] That's what the world is like. A sort of skin covered with ticks, a face ceaselessly grimacing and twitching [...] But what's the good? The game still goes on, in front, behind, above, below' (175; 154–155; 196–197; 174–175). Although the author's nuanced, balanced, and well-informed worldview has been dismissed by certain scholars as naïve and even politically correct,[14] such passages negate these types of groundless criticisms. Reminiscent of numerous other Leclézian protagonists, Chancelade possesses an insatiable thirst for life, but he is aware of the human condition from which there is no escape in addition to the physical realities of the universe. Similar to the aforementioned short stories from *La Fièvre*, the narrator of *Terra Amata* realizes that the earth is in a constant state of motion. The same primordial cycles that one day randomly created human life from the infinite material combinations or possibilities still continue to transform the biosphere. Furthermore, these eternal transmutations will always continue with or without humankind. Le Clézio illustrates that the notion of human control or planetary governance is an appealing myth that conceals bittersweet realities.

In addition to his fiction, the author's public interviews, speeches, and his concrete engagement in support of various environmental causes reinforce his ecocentric ethic. In response to an inquiry from the journalist Pierre Boncenne, Le Clézio unequivocally affirms, "je ne crois pas qu'il y ait des animaux inférieurs à d'autres, qu'un cheval ou un lion représentent les rois des animaux, et un mollusque l'étape la plus basse [...] j'aime les insectes [...] la perfection de leurs carapaces [...] Ici, à Albuquerque, il y a heureusement beaucoup de fourmis, et je les trouve très sympathiques" / 'I don't think that there are animals that are inferior to others, that a horse or a lion represent the king of animals, and a mollusk is the lowest (form of life) [...] I like insects [...] the perfection of their shells [...] Here in Albuquerque, there are fortunately a lot of ants and I find them very pleasant' (41; my trans.). This apparent biotic egalitarianism is hardly surprising given the aforementioned texts in addition to the fact that the author volunteered to contribute the preface to the French translation of Aldo Leopold's *L'Almanach d'un comté des sables* or *A Sand County Almanac*. In this preface, Le Clézio declares, "*L'Almanach d'un comté des sables* révèle la permanence du monde, dans tous ses gestes et dans tous ses règnes [...] Le pouvoir de *l'Almanach* est dans la musique des mots qui fait surgir les odeurs, les couleurs, les frissons, dans tous ces noms qui écrivent le poème de la terre" / '*A Sand County Almanac* reveals the permanence of the world, in all of its gestures and rules [...] The power of the *Almanac* is in the music of the words that makes odors, colors, and sensations spring up, in all of these names that compose the poem of the earth' (n.p., my trans.). Le Clézio's passionate description of Leopold's work could easily be applied to his own narratives. In other words, is Le Clézio's "Poème né un jour dans le ventre d'une femme, et qui a grandi, livré à lui-même, dans le poème plus grand que la réalité" / 'a poem born one day in the belly of a woman, which launched on his own had grown up into the greatest poem in existence' the same poetic verse that the reader discovers in *A Sand County Almanac* (*Terra Amata* 206; 184)?

The Mauritian writer Carl de Souza recounts an incident that transpired in Mauritius which further illustrates that Le Clézio's non-anthropocentric humanism which extends to the entire universe is similar to Leopold's notion of a "land ethic." In his Nobel homage to Le Clézio, de Souza explains, "J'ai rencontré Jean-Marie Le Clézio, hors des livres [...] lors de la défense d'un petit jardin devenu, pour certains, insignifiant au cœur d'un Port-Louis qui se développait trop vite-encore faut-il qu'on précise le terme 'développement'" / 'I met Jean-Marie Le Clézio, outside of his books [...] during the defense of a little garden that had become insignificant for some people in the heart of Port-Louis that was developing too fast—once again we need to define the term "development"' (18; my trans.). Given that Le Clézio generally prefers to stay out of the limelight, his active participation in this affair is quite revealing. Although he tends to avoid divisive, polemical conflicts, his recent support of environmental initiatives concretizes his deep sensibilities and concerns related to a globalized world that becomes even more urbanized with each passing day.

Le Clézio's decision to collaborate with the rest of the Mauritian artistic community to save this sacred space from the forces of "progress" in Port-Louis is perhaps surprising given the author's predilection to not become directly involved in political issues. However, the writer's justification for saving this park appears to be more philosophical than political. As de Souza underscores, "Au cours de son intervention pour la défense de cette oasis dans une ville qui se bétonnait, il avait argué en faveur d'un droit à l'existence d'arbres, intrinsèque à toute chose vivante, de son propre chef et non nécessairement pour être au service de l'homme" / 'During his intervention for the defense of this oasis in a city where everything is increasingly covered in concrete, he had argued in favor of the trees' right to exist, intrinsic to each living thing, by its own behest and not necessarily to serve mankind' (18; my trans.). Not only is Le Clézio's logic reminiscent of his efforts to dispel the genesis myth, but it is also emblematic of the non-anthropocentric humanism that pervades his fiction.

For Le Clézio, humanity does not have the right to exercise absolute dominion over the rest of the universe without reflecting upon the greater consequences of our actions for other life forms. Affirming that the worth of these trees in this garden and the species that depend upon these resources for survival is not utilitarian in terms of the value that humans place upon them, Le Clézio's worldview clearly reflects what the sustainability researcher Don Clifton refers to as an "ecocentric approach" (78). Elucidating what it means to dismiss homocentric notions, such as the genesis myth, that create arbitrary and fictitious distinctions between human and nonhuman realms, Clifton asserts, "the ecocentric approach provides a basis for protecting Nature where no human interest is apparent. Nature is seen as having value for its own sake, where protecting Nature is not conditional on it satisfying an instrumental-to-humans condition" (78). Similar to human beings, these living organisms were thrust into the chaos of existence only to appear by mere chance as trees. Therefore, no valid hierarchy exists from a philosophical or scientific standpoint that gives humans the inalienable right to wreak havoc upon everything else around them without a passing thought.

Le Clézio's line of defense to protect these material life forms from anthropocentric aggression corresponds to what is perhaps the most fundamental concept of ecocritical thought, the idea of intrinsic value. As Lars Samuelsson explains, "Ever since environmental ethics (EE) began to take form as an academic discipline in the early 1970s, the notion of intrinsic value has occupied a prominent position within the field, and one of the most frequently debated questions has been that of whether some nonhuman, nonsentient natural entities have intrinsic value" (518). Although most people would agree that trees do not have feelings and are not even aware of their existence, Le Clézio contends that this does not give human beings the right to impose their will upon them thereby taking away their ontological sovereignty. Affirming that the theory of intrinsic value is at the heart of ecocritical concerns, Lawrence Buell notes,

> the Endangered Species Act of 1973 legalized the kind of comprehensive species and habitat protection that Aldo Leopold had in mind […] when he declared that all life-forms hold their existence as a matter of biotic right. But the notion that a sequoia or a river or an ecosystem might be considered the legal equivalent of a person was most influentially set forth by Christopher Stone in his 1972 article (and later book) *Should Trees Have Standing*? (202).

Le Clézio's rending plea resembles Leopold's land ethic and Stone's questions concerning the boundary between the human and the Cosmic Other because it urges us to share this common space that is home to all of the earth's inhabitants, including both sentient and nonsentient beings. Similar to his aforementioned fiction but in a public forum, Le Clézio beckons global human civilization to re-envision the alleged divisions between humanity and the rest of the universe at a time of tremendous ecological calamity and uncertainty. The existential epiphanies of Le Clézio's protagonists force the reader to question whether the inalienable rights of humankind are limited to our species.

These realizations, derived from cosmogonic theories and an intimate knowledge of the physical universe and its laws, compel the author's characters to seek alternatives to "l'univers carcéral et stressant de la ville, voire le village global" / 'the incarcerating and stressful atmosphere of the city, that is to say the global village' (Fanchin 18; my trans.). Given all of the barriers that modern society has put in place that prevent human beings from having a direct, sensorial contact with other material organisms, Le Clézio's protagonists often flee urban spaces in which they have very little if any connection to the rest of the cosmos in an attempt to re-establish a communion with the natural world. Explaining the profound cosmic alienation from which Adam Pollo suffers in *Le Procès-Verbal* given the sterility of modern society that completely separates us from other forms of matter, Bruno Thibault elucidates, "Adam fuit les idées, les concepts, et les systèmes abstraits qui conditionnent la vie moderne pour renouer contact avec le milieu naturel et la réalité matérielle qui nous entoure" / 'Adam flees the ideas, concepts, and the abstract systems that condition modern life in order to renew contact with the natural environment and the material reality that surrounds us' (40; my trans.). As Thibault and numerous other Le Clézio scholars have established, the author's protagonists often have no choice but to abandon a society whose homocentric ideology does not correspond to the physical laws of the universe or the only true reality. The global village appears to have nothing to offer Le Clézio's characters that generally reject modernity entirely or which live on the periphery of a given community. Although the ideology of consumerism and notions of human superiority are appealing illusions, they fail entirely to provide the modern subject with a deeper sense of belonging or any type of meaningful connection to the cosmic forces that are larger than oneself to which everything is linked.

Other critics in addition to Thibault have also highlighted the urban dystopia that epitomizes the existential crisis that afflicts numerous Le Clézian protagonists, especially from the early period of his writings. In this vein, Sevket Kadioglu muses, "Il ne sera pas déconcertant de dire que les protagonistes des romans de la première période de Le Clézio souffrent d'une angoisse due à l'inadaptation au monde auquel ils appartiennent" / 'It would not be inaccurate to say that that the protagonists of Le Clézio's novels from the first period suffer from an anguish that is due to their inability to adapt to the world to which they belong' (125; my trans.). Pinpointing the origin of this diasporic[15] trauma, Kadioglu further elucidates referring to the modern lifestyle, "cette société destructive a rompu le lien de l'homme avec la réalité en séparant le matériel du spirituel et l'esprit, de la nature qui ne peuvent mettre en œuvre la pensée quand ils ne font qu'un [...] Dans *L'Extase Matérielle*, Le Clézio nous invite à savourer la réalité, la grande réalité qui est la vie [...] Chez lui [...] la connaissance de la matière est la conscience de la vie" / 'This destructive society has broken the link between man and reality by separating the material from the spiritual and the mind, from nature that can only put thought into action when they are one [...] In *The Ecstasy of Matter*, Le Clézio invites us to taste reality, the grand reality which is life [...] In his works, knowledge of matter is consciousness of life' (128; my trans.). As Kadioglu affirms, Le Clézio's characters attempt to establish an intimate relationship with the material world in an effort to understand themselves and to comprehend their small place in the larger scheme of existence. Although technologically advanced modern societies have created inventions which advertisers incessantly claim have improved the quality of life for billions of people around the planet, these same consumer products have generated a complete affective disconnect between human beings and the remainder of the biosphere. In an inauthentic, ontological prison behind walls designed to create a barrier that protects us from the wrath of the elements allowing us to live more comfortably, it is easy to forget that nothing reigns supreme from matter itself. The erection of too many physical obstacles[16] that deny any type of meaningful connection with the earth has generated an anthropocentric, fractured state of consciousness in which a vague yet profound sense of loss resonates inside of the modern subject.

Although the existential remedies to dissipate the anguish of the human condition and the cosmic alienation from which Le Clézio's protagonists suffer have remained remarkably consistent throughout his entire *oeuvre*, later characters from the so-called second phase[17] seem to have discovered a way to live the theories expressed in earlier works. A pantheistic fusion with other forms of matter, triggered by the senses, fills the author's characters with a greater sense of purpose and fulfillment that is nowhere to be found in the modern world. As Hervé Lambert explains, "Dans le cosmos rêvé, la fusion devient un principe universel" / 'In the ideal cosmos, fusion becomes a universal principal' (93; my trans.). Given that the neoliberal view of happiness is unable to provide any type of lasting meaning for protagonists such as Alexis, Lalla, and Laïla that reject the excess and artifice of the global village nightmare, Le Clézio's characters pursue a much older dream that predates the industrial age.

In reference to the traditional worldview espoused by many Amerindian societies that has clearly influenced the author, Raymond Cadorel affirms, "Ce qu'il faut, c'est entendre la voix indienne, c'est renoncer à la cacophonie du langage occidental, au logos dévoyé des mass-médias et de la publicité. C'est aussi renoncer à l'anthropomorphisme occidental, revenir à une conception cosmique de l'homme, au mariage du ciel et de la terre" / 'What we need is to listen to the Indian voice, that is to reject the clamor of Western language, logos of the mass-media and advertisements that lead astray. This also means rejecting Western anthropomorphism and returning to a cosmic conception of man, of the marriage between heaven and the earth' (88; my trans.). As Cadorel underscores, the belief systems of many indigenous societies which compel the subject to envision themselves as minute parts of a larger reality represent a point of departure for re-conceptualizing a more sustainable and significant relationship between humanity and the universe. Moreover, redemption from the absurdity of the human condition does not present itself in the form of a celestial paradise that awaits believers after their ephemeral existence on this earth in Le Clézio's fiction, but rather from an acceptance of material reality from which an ontological being cannot escape in addition to a close rapport with the biosphere. For this reason, Jean Onimus offers the following description of Leclézian spirituality: "S'il y a une mystique chez Le Clézio, elle est toute terrestre, ou plutôt cosmique: un déploiement, à perte de soi, dans l'espace et la lumière" / 'If there is a mysticism in Le Clézio's works, it is entirely terrestrial, or rather cosmic: an unfolding, losing oneself in space and light' (520; my trans.). By re-centering themselves as Thibault notes, adopting a more humble, ecocentric existential paradigm, and reuniting with elemental matter from which all life originally surged and which continues to evolve, Le Clézio's protagonists attempt to heal the scars that have been incessantly reopened by centuries of scientifically erroneous, dualistic, Manichean thought.[18]

Affirming the importance of communing with the material world, the narrator of *L'Extase Matérielle* urges the reader to "Chercher au-delà des mots, au-delà de l'intelligence. Chercher avec tous les sens grand ouverts, et avec les autres moyens inconnus, la voie de la communication avec la matière" / 'Search beyond words, beyond intelligence. Search with all of your senses fully opened, and by other unknown means, the path of communication with matter' (185; my trans.). Instead of continually denigrating and transforming matter for financial gain, the author beckons the citizens of the modern world to seek a more intimate union with the One. Yet, Le Clézio is also cognizant that this initiation will not be easy to facilitate because the physical and affective distance that separates us from the rest of the universe has also caused certain sensibilities to become dormant deep inside the human psyche. Moreover, the author also targets another aspect of Cartesian philosophy that elevates the mind as humanity's most defining characteristic that creates a cosmic schism between the "human" and Cosmic Other.

Highlighting the significance of our sensorial faculties for understanding ourselves and the biosphere in which our species one day appeared, the narrator of *L'Extase Matérielle* empathically declares, "Je veux toucher tout ce qui peut être touché. Goûter tout ce qui peut être goûté. Sentir tout ce qui sent. Voir, entendre, recevoir en moi par tous les orifices, toutes les ondes qui partent du monde et le font spectacle" / 'I want to touch that which can be touched. Taste that which can be tasted. Feel that which can be felt. See, hear, receive by all of my orifices, all of the waves that emanate from the world and make it the spectacle of all spectacles' (238; my trans.). As the narrator elucidates, salvation from the gratuitous nature of existence in an absurd universe is not to be found in pretentious exercises of logic designed to illustrate human superiority or the intellectual supremacy of the individual over the group, but rather by revitalizing our senses to their original vigor. Gérard Fanchin explains, "C'est-à-dire que pour Le Clézio aussi bien que pour les personnages, nos facultés sensorielles sont d'abord et avant tout des facultés vitales, que les habitudes du monde moderne ont engourdies, ankylosées" / 'This is to say that for Le Clézio as well as for his protagonists, our sensory faculties are first and foremost vital faculties that the habits of the modern world have numbed, hardened' (22; my trans.).

Perhaps the only existential cure is to experience life "directement en contact avec les éléments" / 'in direct contact with the elements' (Onimus, 520; my trans.). For this reason, the author juxtaposes "the dehumanizing, devitalizing values of a modern society to those values of individuals who follow their authentic stream of life, their path or way" (Kronegger 131). Similar to the solution proposed by numerous ecocritics, Le Clézio expresses the importance of living more authentically. Such an exercise not only involves stripping away the thick layers of homocentric ideology that gives human beings the right to mold and manipulate matter for egocentric reasons, but it also entails at least temporarily removing ourselves from the sterility of our houses and all of the other edifices in which we spend the vast majority of our time. In other words, how can one comprehend the universe in relatively complete isolation from it? Understanding matter and hence ourselves is to breathe, taste, touch, hear, and feel this supreme ontological reality.

Yet, it should be noted that the remedy which the author proposes to fill the existential void that modern civilization has exacerbated with its theories and other creations that have led humanity further from essential truths is both tragic and uplifting. A complete re-integration into the cosmic whole is only possible after a fleeting being returns to the earth before being recycled into another life form. Therefore, although many of Le Clézio's protagonists appear to find meaning by means of a close, primordial relationship with nature, this cosmic matrimony will never be complete until their ultimate demise. In the context of *Le Procès-Verbal*, Nadine Dormoy reveals, "Il (Adam) observe de loin la mort des autres, mort qui aboutit toujours à une fusion, à une absorption dans les éléments [...] Le suicidé, l'homme écrasé par un camion [...] provoquent curiosité et fascination" / 'He (Adam) observes from a distance people that die, a death that always leads to a fusion, an absorption into the elements [...] The man who commits suicide, the man crushed by a truck [...] provoke curiosity and fascination' ("la transcendance de l'instant" 86; my trans.). Adam Pollo's incessant reflections upon mortality should be interpreted as part of the same epistemological search that compels other Leclézian protagonists to delve into cosmogony and ecology.

Expressing his zeal to understand exactly how the organic cycles of the earth work and in an effort to discover what and who we truly are, the narrator of *L'Extase Matérielle* euphorically imagines, "cette route qui part des ténèbres et me conduit au sein du gouffre serein [...] je goûte déjà à l'ivresse de mon épanouissement en lui, sous forme de neige qui fond [...] je viens à toi, je viens à toi, je suis, je suis, je suis" / 'this route which emanates from the darkness and drives me to the heart of the serene abyss [...] I can already taste the intoxication of my disappearance into it, in the form of melting snow [...] I am coming to you, I am coming to you, I am, I am, I am' (66; my trans.). The narrator of *L'Extase Matérielle* is ecstatic concerning his eventual re-integration into the biosphere because he reaches a similar epiphany to that which strikes the reader in "Arrière," "L'homme qui marche," and "Le monde est vivant." All organisms, sentient and otherwise, which temporarily inhabit this planet in their current arbitrary form possess a type of eternal life given the fact that the energy which created and sustained them will never perish. This existential and material reality, confirmed by modern scientific theories, is the greatest equalizer of all for the entire biotic community of life. Moreover, Le Clézio's appreciation and fascination with deep ecology in addition to all of the positive and heartrending connotations that such an understanding entails dissuade critics from simplifying his complex corpus to a mere reflection of the writings of a "nature worshipper." Le Clézio's profound concerns related to how the actualization of the global village affects the larger chain of being are grounded in fundamental ontological realities.

## DEMYSTIFYING THE VALUES OF RENAISSANCE HUMANISM AND ENVISIONING A BIOCENTRIC ETHIC

In addition to exploring the existential implications of the physical laws of the universe in texts, such as "Arrière," "L'homme qui marche," "Le monde est vivant," *L'Extase Matérielle*, and *Terra Amata*, Le Clézio is also a gifted prose writer whose narratives appeal to the imagination of the reader urging him or her to think and perhaps even live otherwise. Given that his environmentally engaged fiction from the latter half of his literary career is undoubtedly inspired by a well-informed ecocentric worldview, predicated upon modern scientific principles, Le Clézio's biocentric ethic is best understood by examining his entire *oeuvre*. Although a considerable amount of debate exists concerning whether the his works should be divided into distinct time periods, characterized by divergent themes and entirely different writing styles, a deep ecological awareness has always permeated his texts, speeches, and interviews. This section will explore how the short stories "Pawana," "Villa Aurore," and "Orlamonde" concretize Le Clézio's commitment to the Cosmic Other during a troubled age in which the exigency of the environmental crisis is no longer in doubt.

The narrative "Pawana," originally published by Gallimard in 1992,[19] is a rewriting of the acclaimed novel *Moby Dick* by Herman Melville. Bruno Thibault describes the text as a "direct homage" to this classic literary work ("Awaité Pawana" 723). Thibault is indeed correct that this short story is a blatant re-adaptation of *Moby Dick,* as evidenced by the aptly named character Charles Melville Scammon. However, it should also be noted that Le Clézio's version contains much less moral ambivalence concerning the appropriate relationship between humanity and the rest of the universe. "Pawana" is a clear indictment of the whaling industry which nearly exterminated an entire species for materialistic and narcissistic reasons.

Placing the text in a historical perspective during a time period in which whales represented the most lucrative natural resource, Alain Le Goff explains in the critical analyses which are part of the 2003 edition, "Nantucket était le plus grand port baleiner de toute la côte est des États-Unis, autrement dit du monde entier. Sur les quais on trouvait des matelots qui venaient de toutes les mers du globe: des Norvégiens, des Anglais, des Bretons, des Portugais […] Nantucket était une Babel où l'huile de baleine coulait à flots" / 'Nantucket was the largest whaling port of all the Eastern coast of the United States, otherwise stated of the entire world. On the docks were sailors who came from all around the globe: Norwegians, English, Bretons, Portuguese [...] Nantucket was a Babel where whale oil flew like a steady stream' (52; my trans.). Given that modern society is still dependent on oil for its energy consumption, albeit a different type, "Pawana" is not merely an account that depicts cosmic crimes perpetrated in the past, but it is also a narrative that cautions human beings to protect the planet and to learn from the costly mistakes of each generation before it is too late. As Thibault elucidates, "Punta Bunda[20] corresponds to an apocalyptic vision: the ruins of the buccaneer village prefigure the world of tomorrow, when men will exhaust natural resources, leaving behind them large vacant cities, dilapidated and barren. In Punta Bunda all is empty and dead because men have devastated everything" ("Awaité Pawana" 725).

In "Pawana," Le Clézio poses disquieting questions related to whether anything will ultimately survive unfettered human greed if the current trajectory of human civilization continues down the same destructive path. The author's recent epitextual plea in support of the Innuit artistic community, which includes the Francophone writer Rita Mestokosho, reinforces the contemporary relevance of Pawana's ecological stance. Urging the reader of a newspaper column to reconsider the potential environmental impact of the powerful company Hydro-Quebec's project to manipulate the Romaine River to produce electricity, Le Clézio passionately declares, "Regardez bien la photo qui accompagne cette tribune, car dans quelques temps, elle ne sera peut-être plus qu'un souvenir. La rivière Romaine est un de ces lieux merveilleux qui ont survécu sur notre planète très maltraitée par la civilisation industrielle" / 'Look at this photo well which accompanies this press forum, because soon it will perhaps only be a memory. The Romaine River is one of those marvelous places that have survived our very poorly treated planet by industrial civilization' ("Quel Avenir" n.p.; my trans.). Given the author's direct intervention into this unresolved political conflict and the ecocentric logic that he employs to defend this privileged space, Le Clézio's "Punta Bunda" represents a longstanding pattern of environmental exploitation and the ramifications of short-sighted, economic ventures such as the Hydro-Quebec project.

The central focus of the narrative "Pawana" is an undiscovered, legendary secret lagoon where female whales congregate in large numbers to give birth to their young. During one specific whaling expedition, Captain Scammon's crew attempts to find this hidden passage, if indeed it even exists. Clearly elucidating their motivations for what many of their fellow sailors might have considered to be a chimerical pipe dream, the narrator Charles Melville Scammon explains to the young John de Nantucket, "Nous allions être les premiers à découvrir l'ancien secret des poissons-diables, l'endroit où les femelles se réunissaient pour mettre au monde leurs petits. Nous allions revenir immensément riches, ce serait peut-être la dernière campagne" / 'We were going to be the first to discover the ancient secret of the devil fish (whale), the place where the females came together to bear their young. We would come back immensely rich, so this would perhaps be the last expedition' (58–59; 7). For the members of the crew, it is evident that the only value of whales and the rest of the cosmos is purely instrumental in terms of human interests. The sailors' intentions correspond to the neoliberal view of happiness, dismissed by researchers such as Grant Duncan, examined in chapter one. To Scammon and his employees, this passage represents the actualization of the consumerist dream. In simple terms, this potential discovery will allow everyone involved to live the "good(s) life" without ever having to worry about money again.

After the carnage begins, the author paints the following vivid portrait of the first victim: "la baleine jaillit à nouveau à la surface de la lagune, en un bond extraordinaire, qui nous laissa tout sans forces, tant étaient grandes la beauté et la force de ce corps dressé vers le ciel. Elle resta immobile quelques fractions de seconde, puis elle retomba [...] et flotta à la surface [...] et on voyait le sang teinter la langue, rougir le soufflé de ses évents" / 'The whale surged back through the surface of the lagoon in an extraordinary leap that weakened us all, so great were the beauty and force of this body up against the sky. She hung immobile for some few fractions of a second and then fell back [...] and floated to the surface [...] and we saw blood tint her tongue, redden the breath of her spouting' (66; 9). Although the crew is visibly destabilized by the natural beauty of the whale, they inexplicably continue their misguided butchery for weeks until nothing remains of this site but a "lac lourd et âcre du sang" / 'heavy, acrid lake of bloodshed' (88; 11). Underscoring the evolution of the affective state of the crew, Thibault asserts, "The sailors rushing in pursuit of the whale embody at the outset all the brutality and ferocity of men without gods. But thereafter they appear to be seized by a mystical horror: they are shown silent and immobile in the lagoon reddened by the blood of their victim" (725). Given that the sailors are clearly distressed by the pain that they have inflicted upon this once peaceful place, the reader ponders why they were unable to end this massacre. The only plausible explanation is that the protagonists of "Pawana," similar to Alexis in *Le Chercheur d'or* explored in the preceding chapter, are blinded by avarice. Materialistic obsessions, a reflection of the ideology of consumerism, have convinced the crew that the riches that they will procure from harvesting the whales and selling them as barrels of oil on the open market will make them forget about the terror for which they are responsible.

In addition to personifying the whales by using terms such as "enfants" / 'children,' "mère" / 'mother,' and "petits" / 'little ones,' perhaps Le Clézio's most poignant literary device in "Pawana" is the ecological metaphor itself of the cosmos as an intertwined and self-regulating entity. Elucidating his emotional reaction after briefly returning to Punta Bunda three years later, John de Nantucket declares, "Le siècle nouveau commence, plus rien ne sera comme avant. Le monde ne retournera plus à son origine. La lagune n'est plus le lieu où la vie pouvait naître [...] La mer devient vide à nouveau, sans un signe, sans un souffle. Comment peut-on oublier, pour que le monde recommence" / 'The new century begun, nothing will be as before. The world will not go back to its origin. The lagoon is no longer the place where life once could be born [...] the sea is empty again, without a signal, without a whisper. How can one forget, so that the world can start anew' (88; 12). This disturbing metaphor of cosmic sterility is emblematic of the grim reality that abundant life will cease to exist if too many links are removed from the chain of existence. In Punta Bunda, the earth has been so irreparably scarred that it is no longer able to recycle its energy to generate new life.

This cautionary tale of consumerist greed possesses what ecocritics refer to as an ecocidal tone. Le Clézio contests the myopic, neoliberal notion of progress that finds much of its roots in Renaissance humanism. Referring to this specific idea of social progress and evoking the environmental devastation that this homocentric mentality justifies, Ursula Heise states, "This domination strips nature of any value other than as a material resource and commodity and leads to a gradual destruction that may in the end deprive humanity of its basis for subsistence" ("Hitchhiker's Guide" 121). In this vein, "Pawana" represents a more accessible version of the worldview, based upon deep ecology, which Le Clézio expresses in his earlier texts, such as *L'Extase Matérielle* and *La Fièvre*. This somber narrative is a testament to what could potentially transpire on this planet because of the "Cartesian view that elevates the perceiving mind and authorizes the denigration of material nature" that he thoroughly debunks in the works examined earlier in this chapter (Miall 77).

The metaphor of nature as an economy or a web to which Le Clézio refers in his speech at Mississippi State University and which he develops in a literary context in "Pawana" also illustrates the undeniable influence of Amerindian cultures upon the author. In the aforementioned translation of "Toutes choses sont liées" / 'everything is linked' from *La Fête Chantée*, the Duwamish leader asserts, "Nous le savons: la terre n'appartient pas à l'homme, c'est l'homme qui appartient à la terre […] toutes choses sont liées comme le sang qui unit une même famille. Toutes choses sont liées. Tout ce qui arrive à la terre arrive aux fils de la terre. L'homme n'a pas tissé la toile de la vie, il n'est qu'un fil de tissu. Tout ce qu'il fait à la toile, il le fait à lui-même" / 'We know this: the earth does not belong to man, it's man that belongs to the earth […] Everything is connected like the blood that unites a single family. Everything is connected. Everything that happens to the earth happens to the threads of the earth. Man did not weave the web of life, he is only a thread of fabric. Everything that he does to the web, he does this to himself' (234; my trans.). The short story "Pawana" does not only give a voice to the Cosmic Other which contemporary society incessantly attempts to appropriate for monetary gain, but it also presents the ecocentric worldview of many Amerindian voices that the forces of globalization have silenced. The rending plea that Seattle delivered to his European counterparts reflects ecological realities that modern science is just now beginning to comprehend. For this reason, perhaps articulating a new worldview that more accurately represents recent scientific discoveries should begin with a re-valorization of indigenous thought that derives from a close relationship with the natural world.

The barren wasteland that epitomizes Le Clézio's Punta Bunda also demonstrates that human manipulation of the biosphere cannot simply be undone by future generations. As the biologist David Ehrenfeld elucidates, "Irreversibility is the third ecological constraint […] the tendency is to deny that anything so final, so thoroughly beyond our control, can occur. But we are causing irreversible changes all the time. Species are extinguished wholesale, and no genetic prowess will ever bring them back" (115). Both narrators of "Pawana" clearly express their understanding that this secret lagoon which was teeming with life will never be the same again. As the narrator Captain Scammon explains, "j'ai découvert ce passage, et plus rien ne sera jamais comme avant [...] j'ai lancé mes chasseurs assoiffés de sang, et la vie a cessé de naître. Maintenant, tout est renversé et détruit [...] Le ventre de la terre s'est desséché et flétri, il est devenu stérile" / 'I discovered this passage, and now nothing will be as it was before [...] I put forth my bloodthirsty hunters, and then life ceased to be born. Now all was reversed and destroyed [...] the womb of the Earth dried up and perished, became sterile' (92–93; 13). Clearly cognizant of the irreversible repercussions of their actions, Charles Melville Scammon and John de Nantucket express their remorse for their complicity in this crime against existence itself years after the carnage from which neither one of them ever seems to recover.

The final lines of the narrative concretize the failure of neoliberal fantasies to provide the whalers with any personal satisfaction or greater appreciation of their ephemeral existence. Although the crew does indeed appear to become "immensely rich" beyond their wildest imagination, their original dream quickly faded into a nightmare. For this reason, the desire that now fuels their quotidian reveries is to turn back the hands of time and to preserve this secret. Affirming his belated realization concerning the significance of the young John de Nantucket's visceral reaction after the pillage of the earth had begun, the narrator Charles Melville Scammon reveals,

> Je pense à lui, comme si je pouvais arrêter le cours du temps, l'étrave de la chaloupe, refermer l'entrée du passage. Je rêve à cela, comme autrefois j'avais rêvé d'ouvrir ce passage. Alors le ventre de la terre pourrait recommencer à vivre et les corps des baleines glisseraient doucement dans les eaux les plus calmes du monde, dans cette lagune qui enfin n'aurait plus de nom.
>
> I think back to him, as though I could stop the course of time, the stem of the launch, as though I could close up the entrance of the passage once again. I dream of all that, just as I once dreamed of opening this passage up. Then the womb of the earth could begin to live again, and the whales would softly glide through the calmest waters of the world, in this lagoon which at last would no longer have a name (93; 13).

Similar to other Leclézian characters, such as Alexis in *Le Chercheur d'or*, the two narrators from "Pawana" now realize that money cannot buy happiness nor can it fulfill basic human needs. Consumerist virtues are both chimerical and deceiving, despite messages to the contrary that bombard the modern subject. Much like Alexis as noted by Lotte Garsdal, Charles Melville Scammon and John de Nantucket are struck by the epiphany that "l'or n'est pas tout" / 'money is not everything' (23; my trans.). For the inhabitants of the global village, indoctrinated by birth with the new religion of consumption, this simple lesson represents an important piece of the puzzle in terms of feeling compassion for both marginalized individuals that are not reaping the fruits of unprecedented prosperity and for other sentient and nonsentient beings which suffer from the nefarious effects of human-induced cosmic anguish.

In the short stories "Villa Aurore" and "Orlamonde," which are part of the collection *La ronde et autres faits divers* (*The Round and Other Cold Hard Facts*), Le Clézio broaches many of the same ecological themes as in "Pawana." However, as the overarching title of this work unequivocally underscores, the narratives which comprise this volume are to be interpreted as bittersweet, unembellished slices of reality. Similar to "David" and "Ô voleur, voleur, quelle vie est la tienne?" which are examined in chapter two and which realistically portray the ugly underbelly of the urban ghetto, "Villa Aurore" and "Orlamonde" were inspired by actual events. Whereas "Pawana" is a fictitious account of a legendary passage where female whales give birth, Le Clézio offers more concrete examples of the war that globalization has waged upon the earth in *La ronde et autres faits divers*. "Villa Aurore" and "Orlamonde" are profoundly destabilizing texts because the reader immediately thinks about similar true stories that have taken place in his or her own backyard.

Returning to his former childhood playground of which he has fond memories years later after beginning law school, the narrator of "Villa Aurore," Gérard Estève, reminisces about an enigmatic lady Marie Doucet who owned spectacular gardens and a fake Greek temple bearing the mysterious name Ouranos[21] in which he spent a considerable amount of time. However, the majority of the breathtaking trees that he remembers have now been replaced by edifices of concrete and steel. Mortified by the disappearance of this once privileged space, the narrator explains, "Il n'y avait plus d'oiseaux dans le ciel, et les vieux chats errants n'avaient plus de place pour vivre. Moi aussi, je suis devenu un etranger " / 'There were no more birds in the sky, and the old stray cats had no place to live now. I too had become a stranger' (125; 95). Given his state of shock related to the vanishing of these natural wonders, Gérard is unable to knock on the now elderly Marie's door until a convenient pretext presents itself approximately one year later. Responding to an advertisement in the paper for student housing that also entails taking care of what remains of this residence, the narrator essentially speaks to Marie under false pretenses. The old lady confides that although entrepreneurs have taken nearly all of the land that she used to own with the exception of the house itself, they will not be satisfied until they have commercially developed every last parcel of her property. Marie is seeking assistance in fighting these voracious businessmen given the aggressive nature of the coercion techniques that they regularly employ in an attempt to evict her forcefully from her domicile. Realizing that one day these powerful men will not take no for an answer especially given laws such as eminent domain that justify government seizures of private land in the name of progress, Marie is lonely and desperate for an ally.

In this now rather sinister space that more closely resembles Punta Bunda than the lost paradise of his childhood where the grandeur of the elements, especially light, filled him with a sort of pantheistic euphoria, a profound sense of loss reverberates from the earth itself. Juxtaposing the elemental inebriation that this privileged space used to trigger during his youth to the deep, inner void that he now feels after the destruction, the narrator affirms, "Je restais assis des heures, à l'entrée de ce monde […] sentant le pouvoir de la lumière et l'odeur […] Elle (l'odeur) a plus de force que le réel, et la lumière […] dans le jardin, brille encore à l'intérieur de mon corps, plus belle et plus intense que celle du jour. Les choses ne devraient pas changer" / 'I would sit for hours at a time on the threshold of that world […] feeling the power of the light and smells […] It's more powerful than reality, and the light […] in the garden still shines within me more clearly and more intensely than the light of day. Things shouldn't change' (115–116; 87–88). Although those who laud globalization euphorically claim that the modern urbanized world represents the pinnacle of human civilization, it is evident that for Gérard these irreversible changes to the natural cosmic landscape should be lamented rather than celebrated.

Underscoring the "vide qui était maintenant dans les choses" / 'emptiness that pervaded everything' (118; 89), the narrator elucidates,

> Tout était tellement différent! […] Ce qui existait aujourd'hui avait effacé d'un seul coup tous mes souvenirs d'enfance, laissant la sensation douloureuse d'un vide, d'une mutilation […] Dépossédé, exilé, trahi […] alors il y avait pour moi ce goût de mort, ce goût de néant. Le béton et le goudron […] tout cela avait une forme, était plein d'une lueur d'angoisse, chargé d'un sens mauvais.
>
> Things were so different! […] The present reality had suddenly erased all of childhood memories, leaving only a painful sense of barrenness, of mutilation […] Dispossessed, banished, betrayed […] I sensed an aura of death, an aura of emptiness surrounding the world. The concrete and the asphalt […] all of it had form, was filled with a glimmer of apprehension, was laden with ill will (118–119; 89–90).

Similar to the sterility that characterizes Punta Bunda after its discovery and subsequent annihilation, Villa Aurore now wreaks from the pungent odor of death. Gérard not only expresses the painful memories related to his childhood as a lost paradise, but he also importantly highlights a more universal, existential trauma from which the modern subject often suffers. Given that the global village continues to urbanize rapidly leaving few places that have not been radically transformed by a very large human footprint, how can one re-establish a meaningful connection with elemental cosmic forces that created and which sustain life when nothing exists but human artifice and planetary alterations? As Thibault notes in the context of Amerindian culture and the ecocentric worldview which many of these societies espouse in his analysis of "Pawana," "The European also destroys a part of himself, a part of himself he may never find again" ("Awaité Pawana" 726). Since human beings are interwoven into the same web as all life forms, large-scale ecological exploitation, predicated upon notions such as the genesis myth, removes us further from the only reality that nothing can transcend and from a deep existential awareness of our small place in the cosmic whole.

The rending final pages of the narrative cast little doubt upon Le Clézio's point of view concerning the destructive, ecocidal notion of progress that is inseparable from the global village concept and from the ideology of consumerism. In his essay related to *Onitsha* and "Pawana," Robert Alvin Miller affirms that an important aspect of Le Clézio's literary project is to deconstruct "toute rhétorique reposant sur la notion du progrès des civilisations humaines" / 'any rhetoric that is based on the notion of progress of human civilizations' (36; my trans.). Indeed, both "Pawana" and "Villa Aurore" compel the reader to question deeply ingrained ideological constructions that many people take for granted. However, it should be noted that the actual incidents which Le Clézio depicts in "Villa Aurore" are not purely imaginative as in "Pawana." Underscoring that much of Marie's property was taken by force, which was justified by controversial eminent domain legislation that exists all around the world, the narrator elucidates, "Ils ont pris le terrain pour la route, pour l'école, et puis ils ont loti ce qui était en trop, ils ont construit les immeubles. Mais il y a encore cette maison, c'est cela qu'ils veulent maintenant, ils ne me laisseront pas en repos tant qu'ils n'auront pas eu la maison, pour quoi faire ? Pour construire encore, encore" / 'They took the lot for the road, for the school, and then they parceled out what was left; they built apartment buildings. But there's still this house; that's what they're after now, and they won't leave me a moment's rest until they've got it, and what for? To build more, still more' (130; 98). After political figures from a given community deem that a certain site is essential to maximize the prosperity and happiness of the citizenry, the soon-to-be displaced individual which owns the land in question has little legal recourse but to accept whatever monetary compensation that he or she receives. These aggressive laws, which claim to serve the best interests of the majority, silence all opposition and take away any semblance of personal freedom. Thus, the neoliberal vision of contentment continues to be imposed upon everyone eliminating all dissent or viable alternatives to the current system.

The eminent domain seizure in "Villa Aurore" is also indicative of humanity's insatiable zeal to control, possess, conquer, and domesticate the entire universe. The interconnected forces of globalization and urbanization pose the question of whether this materialistic desire has any limitations whatsoever. Will anything eventually survive this unhealthy compulsion, or is the actualization of the global village the final frontier which leads to complete and utter oblivion? The reader ponders whether the apocalyptic no man's land of Punta Bunda and Villa Aurore is the future of humanity unless we deviate from our current path of destruction. Given that what has transpired at Villa Aurore is emblematic of ongoing global processes, the scars to which the narrator refers represent a metaphor or even an ethical summons which urge the reader to protect the environment. Offering a rather frank assessment of the modern world and its hollow values, the narrator explains, "la ville moderne avait rongé la villa Aurore, car rien ne pouvait cacher la plaie, la douleur, l'angoisse qui régnaient maintenant ici [...] Les forces destructrices de la ville, les autos, les autocars, les camions, les bétonneuses, les grues, les marteaux pneumatiques, les pulvérisateurs, tout cela viendrait ici, tôt ou tard" / 'the modern city had eaten into Villa Aurora, for nothing could hide the wound, the pain, the anxiety that reigned here now [...] the destructive forces of the town— the cars, the buses, the trucks, the concrete mixers, the cranes, the pneumatic drills, the pulverizers—would all come here sooner or later' (131; 99). Villa Aurore is a thinly-veiled microcosm which the author employs to express his anxiety related to humanity's stewardship of planetary resources. Moreover, just as in "Pawana," Le Clézio asserts that the effects of human-induced ecological change are irreversible. This is the only planet that we have and if we succeed in "civilizing" every parcel of it, no magical remedy exists to cure these sores.

The somber tone of the final pages of the narrative underscores the existential emptiness created by anthropocentric dominion highlighted earlier by Thibault. Although Villa Aurore used to be a privileged site that was teeming with life, it will now forever be an apocalyptic wasteland like Punta Bunda. Elucidating the cosmic, ontological trauma that reverberates this sense of irreversible loss, the narrator affirms, "Il y avait un tel silence en elle (Marie), et ici, dans cette villa qui mourait [...] Alors c'était le silence à présent qui enserrait la vieille maison, qui la faisait mourir" / 'There was so much silence in her and here, in this dying villa [...] So now it was the silence that was crushing the old house, killing it' (132; 100). Questioning deeply entrenched neoliberal notions which assert that the increasingly interconnected, intertwined, globalized world has irrefutably increased the quality of life for all of the earth's citizens thereby creating a more profound appreciation of existence, Gérard does not see progress, hope, and unprecedented prosperity but rather destruction, alienation, and death.

Summarizing the short story Villa Aurore in his appropriately named essay "Vie urbaine-mort urbaine: *La Ronde et autres faits divers* de Jean-Marie Gustave Le Clézio" / 'Urbain life-urban death: *The Round and other cold hard facts* by Jean-Marie Gustave Le Clézio,' Fredrik Westerlund explains that the narrative "côtoie le lyrisme et la nostalgie d'enfance, tout en évoquant la violence de la ville grandissante" / 'mixes lyricism and the nostalgia of childhood while at the same time evoking the violence of the expanding city' (77; my trans.). As Westerlund astutely notes, urban life is indicative of aggression and disconnection rather than inner peace and fulfillment in Le Clézio's fiction. Similar to numerous other Leclézian protagonists such as Alexis, Gérard's profound cosmic anguish deconstructs the neoliberal view of happiness. Moreover, by refusing to share the land with other material beings, as advocated by Aldo Leopold in *A Sand County Almanac*, and accepting the naïve, misguided rhetoric of the genesis myth, Le Clézio illustrates that the alienated inhabitants of the global village are not even cognizant of the crimes against existence which render their narcissistic lifestyle possible. Given that the neoliberal economic model is predicated upon constant economic expansion and appropriation of natural resources, the reader is left to ponder if the end game of this vicious cycle will result in utter oblivion for every creature that is an important part of the biotic community of life including the human population.

The concluding lines of the text concretize the author's understanding of the ongoing processes of globalization and his anxiety concerning the ideology of the genesis myth that justifies the exploitation of everything around us in the name of progress. Imagining that perhaps Marie's Villa Aurore is on the brink of vanishing entirely giving way to even more urban development, the narrator laments,

> Peut-être que c'était ce soir, le dernier soir, quand tous ils allaient monter à l'assaut de la maison Aurore [...] avec leurs couteaux et leurs chaînes [...] ils lanceraient sur le toit plat leurs bouteilles de Coca-Cola vides, et peut-être que l'une d'elles contiendrait de l'essence enflammée. Tandis que j'entrais dans la foule des voitures et des camions [...] il me semblait que j'entendais très loin les cris sauvages des hommes de main de la ville, qui étaient en train de faire tomber l'une après l'autre les portes de la villa Aurore.
>
> Maybe this evening was the very last evening, when the young boys and girls from the juvenile home would go into the sleep-filled garden with their knives and chains [...] they would throw their empty Coca-Cola bottles on the flat roof, and maybe one of the bottles would be filled with burning gasoline...As I went into the crowd of cars and trucks [...] I thought I could hear, off in the distance, the wild cries of the city's thugs bringing down the doors of Villa Aurora one after the other (132–133; 100).

It should first be noted that the overt reference to the transnational giant Coca-Cola is not made by chance. The international company Coca-Cola, which has created a market for its products in nearly all corners of the planet, is emblematic of the widespread influence of globalization that undermines traditional cultures and ways of life. Drinking "Pils"[22] or rather Coca-Cola is synonymous with living the neoliberal dream that has intoxicated the masses leading to unparalleled destruction of the earth's limited natural resources.

Furthermore, the end of the narrative concretizes the insatiable thirst for material possessions that allegedly maximize human contentment which reinforces the neoliberal global village paradigm. Describing the self-centered actions of the entrepreneurs that wish to expand the city and their control of it, the narrator refers to them as "savages." The author's word choice is quite revealing because it deconstructs the traditional nature versus civilization dichotomy. Blinded by avarice, these unscrupulous businessmen have incessantly denigrated everything around them to have access to the good(s) life. Additionally, they have sometimes forcefully attempted to marginalize all resistance to their consumerist ideology by whatever means necessary. Instead of representing intellectually and ethically superior sentient beings that were meant to govern the biosphere due to their unheralded moral compass and great erudition, Le Clézio underscores that humanity's current stewardship of the planet is ill-founded, barbaric, selfish, and auto-destructive. Given that "la 'nature' est totalement bonne" / '"nature" is entirely good' in the writer's fiction and hence "le mal vient de l'homme" / 'evil comes from man,' perhaps human beings should adopt a more humble, ecocentric worldview which posits that we can learn from other life forms (Onimus 516; my trans.). Instead of denying what and who we are in an ill-fated attempt to transcend the physical realities of the universe, would it not be more positive and realistic to accept the bittersweet human condition and the smallness that this entails? Moreover, will we one day pay the ultimate price for the comforting illusions of anthropocentrism and our uncivilized, short-sighted behavior motivated by zealous greed?

The short story "Orlamonde" / 'Yondaland' from the same collection as "Villa Aurore" poses similar disconcerting questions related to the modern world and its hollow, superficial values. For a well-read "Leclé-ziste," the autotextual relationship between the female protagonists Annah and Lullaby from *Mondo et autres histoires* is quite evident. Both Annah and Lullaby are latchkey children that decide to skip school in order to commune with the elements in an abandoned building that is in a state of ruin. Moreover, the mothers of both young female adolescents suffer from serious illnesses and are consequently unable to play an active role in the lives of their daughters. As the narrator explains, "Annah pensait parfois à sa mère qui était malade, dans le grand hôpital en haut de la ville […] Personne ne lui disait qu'Annah manquait l'école presque tous les jours depuis trois mois, pour aller regarder la mer et le ciel" / 'Annah sometimes thought of her mother, who was sick, in the big hospital above the town […] No one told her that Annah had been skipping school almost every day for the past three months so that she could go and watch the sea and the sky' (241; 182). Similar to "Villa Aurore," the plot of "Orlamonde" is a realistic portrayal, mingled with the aforementioned lyricism highlighted by Westerlund, of a commonplace event that perhaps transpires somewhere every second in the global village.[23] In an effort to expand the ever-growing city, entrepreneurs have decided that the old abandoned theater in which Annah spends much of her time must be destroyed in order to pave the way for progress and to stimulate the local economy. As she is hiding inside of the condemned structure, the wrecking crew arrives to reduce the theater to rubble. Although Annah is upset with her friend Pierre at the end of the narrative who reveals her presence to the authorities, Pierre perhaps saves her life given that the demolition of this site had already begun.

Westerlund also notes that Annah follows a long line of Leclézian characters that deliberately flee modern civilization in an effort to recenter themselves and to live more authentically. As Westerlund affirms, "voilà la recette qu'emploient les personnages de Le Clézio [...] pour ne pas avoir à vivre dans la société occidentale" / 'Here is the recipe that Le Clézio's protagonists employ to not have to live in Western society' ("La vie urbaine-mort urbaine" 77; my trans.). Referring to the young female protagonist's threatened privileged space that is soon to be obliterated in which she can momentarily escape modernity, the narrator elucidates, "C'est l'endroit qu'elle aime le mieux au monde. Elle l'aime parce que c'est l'endroit du monde où l'on voit le mieux la mer et le ciel, rien d'autre que la mer et le ciel, comme si la terre et les hommes avaient cessé d'exister" / 'This is the place she loves most in the whole world. She loves it because from here you have the best view in the world of the sea and the sky, nothing but the sea and the sky, as though the earth and people had ceased to exist' (239; 181). "Orlamonde" is a sacred site for Annah because she is able to liberate herself for a few fleeting instants from the ideological walls in addition to those of concrete and steel that modern society has erected in an attempt to maximize human prosperity and happiness and to provide a sense of meaning. The tragic end of the narrative underscores the grim reality of globalization's far-reaching sphere of influence. In a global environment characterized by rapid urbanization, very few spaces exist that have not been radically transformed by humanity for materialistic reasons.

Before the old theater is completely demolished, this serene place served as an existential remedy that momentarily effaced the cosmic alienation of an ephemeral being disconnected from the nexus of life itself. Removed from the sterility and artifice of modern society and its many barriers, Annah re-establishes a primordial relationship with the cosmic whole because of the grandeur of the elements that pervade the ruins of Orlamonde. Explaining this form of cosmic spirituality and the protagonist's affective state when she attempts to fuse with other forms of matter, the narrator reveals, "Alors elle ne pensait plus à rien, tout pouvait s'effacer. Elle n'oubliait pas, non, mais les gens et les choses de l'autre monde n'avaient plus la même importance" / 'Then she didn't think of anything anymore; everything could just fade away. No, she didn't forget, but people and things in the other world weren't so very important here' (240; 182). Cognizant of the reality that human beings do not exist in a cosmic vacuum despite erroneous ideology that claims otherwise, Annah rejects a consumerist global village that is incapable of fulfilling its grandiose promises or offering any type of lasting meaning.

As she communes with elemental matter from which all life originally emanates, artificial human constructions that have led the modern subject further from fundamental truths related to the human condition appear to vanish temporarily. In his doctoral thesis entitled "Les Fleuves dans l'œuvre romanesque de Jean-Marie Gustave Le Clézio," Fredrik Westerlund explores literary interpretations of these intense instants of euphoria, actuated by sensorial contacts with the pantheistic divine, proposed by numerous researchers such as Keith Moser[24] and Isabelle Roussel-Gillet. Summarizing popular theories concerning these ecstatic experiences of divergent Leclézian protagonists in which the contingencies of time and space seem to disappear, Westerlund elucidates, "L'inscription de ces états physiques dans l'identification des différents espaces ajoute une force explicative à leur valorisation. L'autre versant de l'effet de syncope, le figement du temps, est d'une pertinence primordiale. Les moments d'effets de syncope dans l'analyse de Roussel-Gillet correspondent à ce que Keith A. Moser appelle 'privileged moments'" / 'The inscription of these physical states in the identification of different spaces adds an explanatory force to their valorization. The other side of the syncope effect, the freezing of time is of primordial importance. The syncope effect moments in Roussel-Gillet's analysis correspond to what Keith A. Moser calls "privileged moments"' (40; my trans.). Given that Orlamonde is on the brink of destruction and the ongoing effects of urbanization in this unnamed town offer little consolation that similar sites could trigger the same ecstasy and a sense of cosmic belonging, the reader ponders if the disconnection from which Annah suffers in the city will now be complete.

Confirming the protagonist's growing fears that Orlamonde will soon cease to exist, the narrator explains, "Le temps passe lentement, quand il apporte la destruction. En clignant des yeux, Annah voit le ciel qu'elle aime se couvrir d'oiseaux, de mouches, de toiles d'araignée [...] Le vent souffle avec force, un vent froid qui glace le corps de la petite fille, qui brouille ses yeux de larmes" / 'Time goes slowly by when it brings destruction in its wake. By blinking her eyes, Annah can see the sky that she loves fill with birds, with flies, with spider webs [...] A strong wind is blowing, a cold wind chilling the little girl to the bone, clouding her eyes with tears' (244; 185). In this passage, the foreshadowing which had been progressively taking shape since the beginning of the narrative crystallizes as it becomes evident that the theater and the surrounding landscape will soon be forever transformed. Annah closes her eyes and attempts to fix all of the natural wonders in her memory including the many organisms that call this place home. In stark contrast to the shortsighted entrepreneurs that are immune to virtues that do not directly equate to dollar signs, the protagonist realizes that this act of aggression will leave gaping wounds that will never heal. Similar to Charles Melville Scammon and John de Nantucket in "Pawana," it is improbable that the ephemeral riches that the businessmen seek to attain will actually be anything more than what Alexis in *Le Chercheur d'or* calls "l'or du sot" / 'fools' gold' that has consumed the masses but failed to deliver on its lofty ideals (359; 324).

Clearly reminiscent of John de Nantucket's aforementioned question "Comment peut-on tuer ce qu'on aime?" / 'How can we kill what we love?,' the narrator of "Orlamonde" asks, "Pourquoi veulent-ils tout détruire?" / 'Why do they want to destroy it all?' (246; 186). Given that her close connection with this privileged space has awoken dormant sensibilities stifled by contemporary urban life, Annah can no longer understand how modern society is so indifferent to the terrestrial sublime that surrounds them and to which everything is connected. When the inevitable destruction of Orlamonde begins, Annah feels an immeasurable existential void like the sentiments of John de Nantucket and Gérard examined earlier in this chapter. Painting a vivid portrait of this trauma, the narrator elucidates,

> Soudain, elle entend les détonations. Ce sont des coups terribles qui résonnent dans la muraille de pierre, qui font tomber de la poussière sur ses cheveux [...] les coups viennent [...] si violents que le corps de la petite fille tressaute et souffre. Le bruit des premiers murs qui s'écroulent est terrible [...] Annah voudrait crier, pour que tout s'arrête, mais la peur l'en empêche, et les vibrations la poussent vers le vide.
>
> Suddenly, she hears explosions. They are tremendous blasts that shake the foundations of the stone escarpment, bringing dust down into her hair [...] But the blows come [...] so intense that the little girl is bumped about and bruised. The sound of the first walls crumbling is terrifying [...] Annah would like to cry out so that it will all stop, but she is paralyzed with fear, and the vibrations are jarring her out toward the precipice (247; 187).

Although Annah is undoubtedly paralyzed in fear because she is afraid for her life, her cosmic awareness related to the potential ramifications of the actions of the demolition crew induces far greater anguish. The young female protagonist realizes that excessive urbanization does not automatically improve the quality of life for everyone caught in its snares, but rather this destruction leaves behind a trail of spiritual and material death. Incessant economic development might ensure that certain material comforts are maintained, but global human society is at the crucial point of deciding if the cost is too great.

Similar to Marie in "Villa Aurore," Annah wonders if anything will be spared from the taint of financial greed. Affirming her comprehension that Orlamonde will not be the last place decimated by the powerful forces of globalization, the protagonist speculates, "Ils vont tout détruire, peut-être, toute la terre, les rochers, les montagnes, et puis enfouir la mer et le ciel sous les décombres et la poussière" / 'They're going to destroy everything, maybe the whole world—the rocks, the mountains—and then bury the sea and the sky under the rubble and the dust' (247; 187). Expressing similar sentiments to those of other Leclézian protagonists previously examined, Annah elucidates her profound anxiety concerning whether the human zeal to conquer and possess everything can only be quenched when nothing else exists to be appropriated. The rather somber end of the narrative does provide, however, some semblance of hope. As she is being placed into a police car to remove her from danger, the protagonist turns around one last time. Mingling the destabilizing realism that disturbs the reader throughout the text with a faint glimmer of optimism, the narrator asserts, "Orlamonde n'existe plus, ce ne sont que des ruines couleur de vieille poussière [. . .] Mais le reflet du soleil sur la mer brille sur le visage et dans les yeux sombres de la petite fille, avec la lumière qu'on n'éteint pas de la colère" / 'Yondaland is no more, it is a mere pile of ruins, the color of old dust [. . .] But the reflection of the sun on the sea shines upon the little girl's face and fills her dark eyes with a light that anger cannot dim' (249; 189). The annihilation of this privileged site is now complete and irreversible, but Annah will never forget the spiritual force of the elements that have forever permeated her to the core. Even if she is forced to witness additional ecological crimes from a race that cannot accept the existential implications of the physical realities of the universe, the protagonist will always be sustained by whatever material remnants remain.

## CONCLUSION

For nearly half a century, Le Clézio's extremely diverse narratives have urged the reader to renounce anthropocentrism and to embrace cosmic humility. Although the debate in the literary community concerning whether his works should be divided into distinct stages or simply considered to be indicative of a natural evolution will continue to rage, Le Clézio's fascination with deep ecology and its existential implications has always been evident. Indeed, the writer's earlier texts, such as *L'Extase Matérielle*, *Terra Amata*, "Arrière," "L'homme qui marche," and "Le monde est vivant" offer an invaluable theoretical framework for understanding the enigmatic euphoria that his later protagonists experience after re-establishing an intimate, sensorial contact with the universe. Moreover, Le Clézio's entire literary repertoire appears to be more important than ever given the severity of the environmental crisis that threatens the web of life itself.

In his fiction, speeches, and recent interventions in support of ecological causes, Le Clézio urges global society to deconstruct centuries of narcissistic, misguided, and false homocentric logic that contradicts fundamental physical realities. In a global village permeated with the ideology of consumption and neoliberal virtues, the modern subject has alienated himself from the greatest truth of all and from which no escape exists: matter. In addition to the religion of consumerism, certain notions such as Descartes's *bêtemachine* theory are appealing ideas, but modern science has effectively debunked many antiquated and destructive intellectual paradigms. On a final note, this study has clearly elucidated that Le Clézio's narratives should be further analyzed with other ecocritical texts that attempt to answer questions, such as "Where must the limit to human rights lie?" and "Is it possible to pursue absolute biotic egalitarianism?" (Yen Yu 94). Le Clézio does not pretend to have definitive answers to these complex issues. Yet, his works remind us all that perhaps our future in addition to that of the entire planet depends on a deep appreciation of and a dialogue concerning the environmental problems that plague the global village.

## NOTES

1. I first addressed the "genesis myth" in the context of French literary engagement in an essay published by *Sprachkunst* (Volume 42, issue 1). However, this chapter delves into this notion in a different context and at much greater length.

2. This citation can be found on page 110 of the 2003 edition of the text originally published by Gallimard in 1992. This edition includes supplementary materials written by Bruno Doucey. All subsequent references to this work will refer to the 2003 edition.

3. It should also be noted that Sueza Espejo's preliminary ecocritical analysis of Le Clézio's fiction is limited to the narrative *Désert*. This dearth of research clearly highlights a gap that this present study attempts to begin to fill. Yet, more comprehensive investigations are needed by the part of the international literary community given both the urgency of the ecological crisis and the complexity of the author's work that transcend the limitations of this specific exploration.

4. A term used by ecocritics, such as Lance Newman. See Newman, Lance. "Marxism and Ecocriticism." *Interdisciplinary Studies in Literature and Environment* 9 (2): 1–23.

5. For a more comprehensive discussion of the paradoxes and ambiguities of Christian theology concerning the relationship between humanity and the rest of the material universe, see Buell, Lawrence, *The Environmental Imagination* and Ehrenfeld, David, *The Arrogance of Humanism.* It should also be noted that Ehrenfeld explains the ethical principle related to environmental accountability in the book of Genesis as the "Noah principle" (207–209).

6. As part of our personal interview conducted at his home in Albuquerque, New Mexico, Le Clézio underscores the importance of stewardship. The complete transcript of this discussion serves as the postscript to this study.

7. Ecocritics often employ the terms non-anthropocentric humanism and soft anthropocentrism as well which have similar implications.

8. It should be noted that it is because of narratives such as *Terra Amata* that critics often probe the influence of the *nouveau roman* upon the young Le Clézio and his writings.

9. The title of this short story is indicative of the author's fascination with cosmogony and the impossible yet alluring "reverse voyage" which appeals to many of his divergent protagonists for existential reasons that are rather apparent. See Mezade, Jean-Paul. "Le voyage à rebours." *Sud* 85–86: 149–154.

10. In his doctoral thesis entitled "Les Fleuves dans l'œuvre romanesque de Jean-Marie Gustave Le Clézio," Fredrik Westerlund underscores the importance of the organic musical sonorities of the universe.

11. The journalist Maya Jaggi notes that the author's entire literary project entails the promotion of a "healthier approach to ecology" (n.p.).

12. (e.g.) Dutton, Jacqueline. "Entretien privé avec J.M.G. Le Clézio." *Le Chercheur d'Or et Ailleurs*: *L'Utopie de J.M.G. Le Clézio.*

13. Several critics have also noted that Le Clézio seems to have adopted the Amerindian cosmic worldview which venerates the forces of nature that sustain all life, but which also underscores the indifference of the universe. Frequent and deadly environmental catastrophes which undermine any notions of human superiority offer a concrete example of this philosophical paradigm. See also the author's interview published in *A Chacun sa France* by Nadine Dormoy and Liliane Lazar in which he discusses this nuance directly in addition to the reflections of the narrator of *Terra Amata* related to the sun Kax or the "monstre sans pitié qui cherche à détruire le monde" / 'pitiless monster that seeks to destroy the world' (13; my trans.).

14. (c.f.). Azam Zanganeh, Lila. "Une œuvre mal comprise aux Etats-Unis." *Le Monde*, 11 Oct. 2008: 23.

15. The word "diasporic" in this sense refers to what is perhaps the most profound inner trauma of all from which a sentient being can suffer. It is indicative of the cerebral pain of a conscious living creature that has been entirely disconnected and uprooted from its veritable cosmic roots. Both Elisabeth Ravoux-Rallo and Elena Real in addition to many other Le Clézio scholars have analyzed this anguish. Specifically, Ravoux-Rallo affirms, "L'œuvre de Le Clézio est depuis quelques années une sorte de quête d'une patrie de l'âme où guérir des maux causés par le monde moderne" / 'Le Clézio's work has been for several years a sort of quest for a homeland of the soul to heal from the evils caused by the modern world' (81; my trans.).

16. Agnès Clavareau asserts that Leclézian protagonists seek privileged spaces far from the globalized world in which "Les âmes sont à nu, et il n'y a pas d'obstacles entre le cosmos et sa créature" / 'Souls are naked, and there are no obstacles between the cosmos and its creature' (402; my trans.).

17. Numerous Le Clézio scholars divide his works into two distinct phases. The first stage begins in 1963 with the publication of his first novel *Le Procès-verbal* and ends with texts such as *Voyages de l'autre côté* (1975) and *Mondo et autres histoires* (1978). The influence of both the *nouveau roman* and existentialism are quite apparent in the first phase, whereas narratives from the latter period are often described as being more poetic, lyrical, and even mystical.

18. For a more comprehensive investigation of Leclézian spirituality, see Moser's essay "Rending Moments of Material Ecstasy in the Meditative Essays of Two Nobel Laureates: Le Clézio and Camus." *Romance Notes* 49 (1): 13–21.

19. "Pawana" originally appeared for the first time in 1988 in the form of a play directed by Georges Lavaudant.

20. Although the action takes place in Punta Bunda in California, the references to Nantucket including one of the narrator's names, John de Nantucket (the punctuation

is also revealing) are quite deliberate given that Nantucket was the global center of the whaling industry during a certain time frame.

21. In addition to the evident autotextual connections to the text *Ourania,* this Greek temple reminds the reader of a similar abandoned house in the short story "Lullaby" which fueled this protagonist's reverie and in which she also established an intimate relationship with the natural world.

22. This soft drink is mentioned in *Les Géants*. See chapter three.

23. The author's enigmatic epigraph which states "Toute ressemblance avec des événements ayant existé est impossible" / 'Any resemblance to events having actually taken place is impossible' appears to be an intentionally ironic statement intended to destabilize the reader. (239; 181).

24. See Moser, Keith. *"Privileged Moments" in the Novels and Short Stories of J.M.G. Le Clézio: His Contemporary Development of a Traditional French Literary Device*. New York: The Edwin Mellen Press, 2008.

# FIVE

# Resisting Global Hegemonic Domination in Le Clézio's Narratives and the Importance of Interculturality

Given that J.M.G. Le Clézio's narratives concretize why the original euphoria related to globalization has faded all across the planet as illustrated in the preceding chapters, numerous critics have correctly underscored his bleak assessment concerning the current state of the modern world. However, the Nobel Laureate's recent texts, such as *Raga, Ourania,* and *Histoire du pied et autres fantaisies,* reveal a more nuanced point of view that encourages the reader to envision what a more just and egalitarian global village might encompass. Although these latest works dismiss neoliberal fantasies and simplistic consumerist ideology that have justified the systematic exploitation of everyone and everything in the name of progress, they also urge the modern subject to be resilient in the face of tremendous adversity. Instead of accepting the imposition of a monolithic socioeconomic model that is riddled with inequality and injustice and which serves the interests of the "happy few," Le Clézio appears to suggest that the first step is to resist integration into the global village by stoically confronting reality and having the necessary courage to propose another dream which counterpoints McLuhan's evaporated one.

In a contention that is emblematic of the anguish from which his human and nonhuman protagonists suffer in a globalized world that is ever expanding its hegemonic planetary stranglehold, Le Clézio asserts in the context of recent failed attempts to create various utopian societies, "Ce sont les souffrances des hommes qui rendaient ces rêves légitimes et urgents" / 'It is human suffering that renders these dreams legitimate and urgent' (Garcin 2006 n.p.; my trans.). For Le Clézio, even if certain efforts which endeavored to construct ideal societies undoubtedly culminated in unmitigated failure, their eventual collapse should be best understood in the greater context of the dire realities that inspired these experiments. If neoliberalism would have been able to keep its lofty promises of a world in which everyone would enjoy the fruits of unprecedented prosperity and happiness, then no one would desperately strive to remove themselves from the system. Expressing his profound concerns related to the modern world, Le Clézio explains,

> On parle de "libération," de "démocratisation," et au même instant se développent les nouveaux racismes, le machismo, le tourisme sexuel, la prédation en tout genre des puissants sur les plus faibles. Je ne sais s'il y a lieu d'être pessimiste ou optimiste [...] c'est aussi la mondialisation, la diffusion des images et des idées reçues, l'intolérance intellectuelle, l'intégrisme, l'insolence d'un certain libéralisme qui ne tient pas compte des minorités, les usines offshore, l'affirmation de la supériorité de l'investissement sur les nécessités humaines.
>
> We talk about "liberation," "democratization," while at the same time new types of racism are developing, machismo, sexual tourism, the predation of all different types by the powerful against the weak. I don't know whether we should be optimistic or pessimistic [...] It is also globalization, the diffusion of images and accepted ideas, intellectual intolerance, integrationism, the insolence of a certain type of liberalism that disregards minorities, offshore factories, and the affirmation of the superiority of investment over human necessities (Garcin 2006 n.p.; my trans.).

Affirming his awareness that billions of people in the universe are not living a dream but rather a recurring unsustainable nightmare which the powerful forces of globalization have only served to exacerbate, the author questions the deeply entrenched notion that the current socioeconomic paradigm represents the pinnacle of human civilization. Given that the worldwide distribution of wealth is more inequitable than at any other point in history because of exploitative ideology and practices that claim to improve everyone's quality of life, exploring any and all alternatives to the neoliberal global village becomes more essential than ever with each passing day.

## INDIGENOUS EFFORTS AT MAINTAINING AUTONOMY AND TRADITIONAL CULTURAL IDENTITIES IN THE FACE OF GLOBALIZATION

In addition to the endemic problems that Le Clézio outlines in his interview with Jérôme Garcin, the author's fiction also portrays the pressure that many indigenous communities feel to abandon their ancestral practices and to embrace the universal values of a consumerist, monolithic culture. In the face of a global village whose very economic structure necessitates continual growth leading to the threat of cultural imperialism, how can indigenous societies maintain their identity and resist mounting pressure to assimilate? Although Oceania has often been called the "invisible content," the past, present, and future impact of the modern world is undeniable in Le Clézio's text *Raga*. As the author clearly outlines in this essay, another world is perhaps possible given that certain communities are returning to their traditions in a clear rejection of the Western values of progress and civilization. Yet, it should be noted that *Raga*[1] is a complex work full of apparent paradoxes and *aporia* that caution the reader to avoid oversimplifying complicated issues for which no easy solution exists. In the absence of infallible truths related to the ongoing processes of globalization and their impact upon the rest of the world, *Raga* poses disconcerting questions concerning the re-appropriation of cultural identities in modern society.

Published by *Editions du Seuil* in November 2006 in a special edition directed by the renowned Caribbean writer and *creolité /antillanité*[2] theorist Edouard Glissant, *Raga* is an homage to the resilience of Polynesian and Melanesian peoples and to the contributions of their divergent cultures. Similar to *Haï* ,[3] Le Clézio's appreciations of this "continent invisible" / 'invisible continent' and this "lieu sans reconnaissance internationale" / 'place without international recognition' (9; my trans.) are based on his personal experiences in the region. As Mark Andrews elucidates, "Lorsque Le Clézio accepte en 2005 l'invitation d'Édouard Glissant [...] à rejoindre la cinquième expédition maritime du trois-mâts La Boudeuse 'au pays des Saa,' son rôle sera celui d'écrivain du bord. Au cours de cette croisière dans le Pacifique sud, Le Clézio fera escale à l'île de la Pentecôte, et en profitera pour rédiger un court journal de voyage intitulé *Raga : Approche du continent invisible*" / 'When Le Clézio accepted Edouard Glissant's invitation to join this fifth maritime expedition of the three-master *La Boudeuse* in "Saa country," his role would be that of anboard writer. During this cruise in the South Pacific, Le Clézio would stop over at Pentecost Island and would take advantage of this to compose a short travel journal entitled *Raga: Approche du continent invisible*' (246; my trans.). A travel diary that intertwines Polynesian and Melanesian history, myth, legends, and religion, *Raga* is actually a much more complex and nuanced text than it initially appears to be at first glance. Mingled with Le Clézio's astute observations related to a culture that he greatly admires but which receives little international attention is a destabilizing realism concerning the ongoing, nefarious effects of the sinister practice of blackbirding[4] in addition to his awareness of the serious contemporary problems that continue to persist in the region, such as the HIV/AIDS epidemic and patriarchal domination. As Isabelle Roussel-Gillet underscores, "La 'réalité agressive' est bien présente, à la fois actuelle et historique, avec l'exploitation par les *blackbirds* [...] Le Clézio raconte aussi la vie contemporaine et en particulier celle des femmes, dont l'une a le sida" / 'The 'agressive reality' is ominpresent, at the same time historical and current, including exploitation by the *blackbirds* [...] Le Clézio also depicts contemporary life and in particular that of women, one of whom has AIDS' ("Ecrivain de l'incertitude" 118 ; my trans.).

These serious issues that plague contemporary Polynesian and Melanesian society noted by Roussel-Gillet, specifically the present impact of blackbirding whose repercussions are still quite visible, concretize how globalization has united divergent peoples against the romantic idealism associated with McLuhan's global village concept. Given that the forces of globalization are driven in essence by the same monolithic culture that is responsible for colonial exploitation all around the world in addition to blackbirding in Oceania after the abolition of slavery in the United States, it is evident why the indigenous societies that call this region home would place little faith in the harbingers of "progress" since the scars of the past have yet to heal. In other words, why would these communities accept neoliberalism's lofty promises at face value given that the so-called developed and civilized world has a dubious track record of exploiting vulnerable, disenfranchised prey with its enticing yet illusory ideological snares?

Adopting a point of view that is reminiscent of that proposed by Gayatri Spivak examined in chapter one related to the global village concept as "colonialism's newest trick" in reference to contemporary Polynesian and Melanesian resistance to globalization, Le Clézio elucidates, "Parfois le retour aux valeurs ancestrales, qui a inspiré les révoltes successives, jusqu'à l'indépendance. Non par la conviction des Mélanésiens que leur ancienne culture était supérieure, mais par la certitude du mensonge et de la fourberie qui accompagnaient tout commerce avec les étrangers" / 'Sometimes (it was) the return to ancestral values which inspired subsequent revolts that led to independence. (This was not motivated by) a conviction by Melanesians that their traditional culture was superior but by the certainty of lies and deception that accompanies all commerce with foreigners' (54; my trans.). In this passage, the author explains that although globalization was allegedly supposed to improve the quality of life for everyone and to unite cultures like never before, the profound skepticism of divergent Melanesian cultures, which is grounded in unpleasant historical realities, has forced these diverse communities to band together in an effort to resist integration into the global village. Moreover, these concerted efforts by Melanesian peoples to determine their own destiny and to choose for themselves how they would like to live is an expression of their dissatisfaction with the current situation of inequality and injustice. The cultures that Le Clézio discovers during his travels to Oceania provide concrete examples of the "discontents" to which Stiglitz and researchers from many different fields refer.

Yet, it should be noted that although Le Clézio freely admits that indigenous thought and other worldviews fascinate him and perhaps even offer better models for global society,[5] this valorization of other types of knowledge is not a naïve expression of "political correctness"[6] as some misinformed scholars would contend. Despite his deep appreciation of the numerous cultures with which he has been in intimate contact, Le Clézio realizes that a true utopia[7] in the traditional sense of this word is impossible. For this reason, the author reveals in a recent interview in which he describes his experiences with the Embreras and Waunanas in the Darien region of Panama, "I am not idealizing them, but the society is so much better balanced than the one I came from" (Jaggi n.p.). Furthermore, Le Clézio elucidates in a separate interview, "le Darién panaméen est devenu, selon Lonely Planet, 'l'endroit le plus dangereux du monde'" / 'The Darien region of Panama has become, according to Lonely Planet, "the most dangerous place in the world"' (Garcin n.p.; my trans.). Although Le Clézio often expresses his firm conviction that each culture has something important to offer the modern world, he is also cognizant that every society has fundamental problems that need to be addressed.

In addition to the aforementioned HIV/AIDS epidemic[8] which has devastated Oceania, Le Clézio poignantly underscores the quotidian struggles that women face in this region and in many other places in the world to liberate themselves from centuries of patriarchal governance and abuse. It is evident that the author believes that Western civilization has much to learn from rich Polynesian and Melanesian cultures, yet he is also aware that these social structures often have glaring imperfections. Describing his encounter with Charlotte Wèi Matansuè, an ardent promoter of female emancipation, and recounting her tragic story, the narrator of *Raga* explains,

> Mariée très jeune selon la coutume, son mari s'est révélé jaloux et brutal. Il la roue régulièrement de coups [...] Un jour, quand ses enfants ont grandi, elle décide qu'elle en a assez, elle quitte l'homme, et emmène ses enfants avec elle dans le village de sa grand-mère [...] A Pentecôte, cela ne se fait pas. L'homme a payé le prix pour le mariage, la famille de sa femme est liée par un contrat [...] Toutes ces années de douleur, de larmes, de honte, elle les évoque en souriant, sans appuyer [...] Il n'y a pas eu de divorce [...] Mais la rupture est maintenant définitive.
>
> Married very young according to customs, her husband proved to be jealous and brutal. He regularly beat her [...] One day after her children were grown, she decided that she had had enough, she left this man and took her children with her to her grandmother's village [...] On Pentecost Island, this does not happen. This man had paid the price for this marriage, his wife's family was bound by a contract [...] All of these years of pain, tears, and shame, she evokes them as she smiles

> without putting her head down [...] There was no divorce [...] But the breakup is now definitive (34; my trans.).

Le Clézio's rending portrait of this intelligent, resilient, and determined woman that is able to smile when reflecting upon her traumatic past illustrates that the author's reflections concerning Vanuatu transcend superficial cultural comparisons. Given the patriarchal nature of this society in which women are treated like possessions and second-class citizens, Charlotte's sinister and abusive husband thinks that he can do whatever he wants to his wife since he "legitimately" owns her according to traditional Vanuatu values. It should also be noted that in much of the world these conjugal mores which force young girls to marry sometimes even before the onset of puberty would be considered to be nothing less than statutory rape. Moreover, Le Clézio notes that Charlotte's struggle to free herself from the patriarchal chains that bind her to a life of servitude is emblematic of the universal efforts of women all around the planet to control their own destiny. The writer further elucidates "La grande difficulté que les femmes ont à faire valoir leurs droits, quelle que soit la société dans laquelle elles se trouvent. Je pense aussi à ces femmes africaines qui sont aujourd'hui sur le devant de la scène pour la lutte, pour affirmer leur droit au bonheur, leur droit à la parole" / 'The great difficulty that women have in asserting their rights regardless of the society in which they find themselves. I also think about the African women that are taking center stage for this fight in order to affirm their right to happiness, their right to speak' (35; my trans.).

As evidenced by his keen awareness of the grave issues that exist in contemporary Polynesian and Melanesian society including the HIV/AIDS pandemic and patriarchal power structures, the notion that Le Clézio idealizes traditional civilizations is clearly misleading and simplistic. However, he does firmly believe that each culture has something to offer the modern world despite its inherent faults. For this reason, Le Clézio lauds the diversity and accomplishments of various peoples from Oceania. Specifically, the writer first notes that the influence of island societies from the South Pacific is apparent all around the world. Although the "invisible continent" to which the title of *Raga* alludes appears to be quite isolated at first glance, Le Clézio reveals that the myriad of cultures that call this part of the world home have been deliberately spreading their culture and sharing their way of life for centuries. Explaining the inventions that have made these cultural exchanges possible even centuries before the dawn of the industrial age, Le Clézio affirms, "Pour réussir cette aventure, les Mélanésiens et les Polynésiens durent mettre au point une série d'inventions géniales, qui ont encore cours aujourd'hui : la pirogue à balancier, le *ruerue,* la double pirogue transportant bétail et provisions [...] la navigation en 'tirant les bords' alternant la voile et la rame [...]" / 'To realize these exploits, Melanesians and Polynesians had to develop a series of great inventions, which are still around today : the outrigger canoe, the *ruerue*, the double pirogue that transports both livestock and provisions [...] navigation by maneuvering and alternating between sailing and rowing [...]' (13; my trans.). Far from being passive receptacles that were waiting to be enlightened by European imperialists, Melanesian and Polynesian peoples had already made considerable maritime advances that required a tremendous amount of ingenuity. Moreover, these island cultures from the Central and South Pacific had been systematically disseminating this knowledge all throughout the region for centuries.

In addition to their numerous pragmatic maritime feats, Le Clézio valorizes the considerable amount of erudition that these divergent island societies already possessed well before the arrival of colonial conquerors. The popular myth of a legendary voyage which recounts the efforts of the protagonists Matantaré and Tabitan to leave their island in search of a better life eventually arriving in Raga (Pentecost Island) offers a concrete example of this knowledge. Recognizing the fact that human beings do not exist in a cosmic void and are therefore linked to the rest of the material universe, the indigenous peoples of Oceania observed and studied the cosmos. For this reason, their understanding of astrology, ecology, and of the physical realities of existence itself far surpassed that of their European counterparts. Referring to this deep cosmic awareness, which is also inseparable from their ecocentric worldview and spiritual belief system, Le Clézio explains, "Tabitan connaît bien les étoiles [...] L'étoile qui palpite au plus près de l'horizon, c'est le Premier Précurseur, comme on l'appelle, qui est suivi après minuit par le Précurseur Médian" / 'Tabitan knows the stars very well [...] the star that flickers closest to the horizon that is what we call the First Precursor, which is followed after midnight by the Median Precursor' (22; my trans.). Although the European invaders often scoffed at indigenous religious thought describing it as naïve and magical, recent scientific discoveries outlined in the preceding chapters have validated many fundamental pantheistic concepts. Given their primordial relationship with the cosmic forces that created all life, traditional cultures from the Central and South Pacific were in some ways philosophically, intellectually, and spiritually more advanced than the European societies that tried to "civilize" and educate them according to a certain homocentric paradigm.

The Western anthropocentric and scientifically flawed *weltanschauung*, which Le Clézio calls the genesis myth, perhaps represents the origin of the ecological crisis that threatens the entire biosphere. For this reason, James Fenelon and Thomas Hall elucidate in their sociocultural analysis of several distinct indigenous societies that are resisting integration into the global village, "We discuss four sets of issues that not only exemplify resistance and revitalization for indigenous peoples, toward globalization and cultural dominance, but that actually offer potentially better worldviews for the future of humanity" (1). In this same vein, the sacred myth of Matantaré and Tabitan's saga was undoubtedly dismissed by the colonizers as naïve and unrealistic. However, if the invaders would have heeded the ecocentric messages that are inherent in the narrative itself, then it is possible that the ecological calamity would not be so dire. In a clear affirmation of his respect for other material life forms that is indicative of his understanding that the universe cannot truly be appropriated, the narrator explains that the family attempted to establish a connection with their natural surroundings upon their arrival in Raga after many precarious days at sea. As the author reveals, "Demain, ou plus tard, ils seront à Raga, ils retrouveront ceux qui les ont précédés, ils prendront possession des champs en défrichant la forêt, ils prieront les esprits du lieu de les accepter sur leurs terres" / 'Tomorrow, or later, they will be in Raga, they will meet those that have preceded them, they will take possession of the fields and cultivate the forest, they will pray to the spirits of this place to accept them on their land' (26; my trans.). First, it should be noted that this story is emblematic of an ecocentric worldview which affirms that the earth does not belong to humankind alone, but rather to larger forces that transcend the needs and desires of one given species.

Additionally, although the notion of becoming acquainted with deceased others who used to inhabit this space might have seemed mystical and even absurd to European conquerors, the law of conservation of energy does unequivocally stipulate that "energy is never created nor destroyed." Understanding that nothing truly ever disappears because of their intimate relationship with nature, as articulated by Le Clézio in *L'Extase Matérielle,* the "first" legendary or even mythical inhabitants of Raga realize that the earth incessantly recycles the energy of dead organisms to create new life. At least on a very basic level, the cosmic sensibilities of Matantaré and Tabitan are actually quite logical given that they correspond to a deep ecological knowledge of the universe. As researchers such as Fenelon and Hall hypothesize, perhaps this type of erudition represents the only remedy that could save the planet from the voracious appetite of the neoliberal global village. Furthermore, since Western ideological notions related to human superiority have been thoroughly debunked by modern science as outlined in the preceding chapter, should Le Clézio be accused of "scientific correctness" instead of "political correctness"? Regardless, it is evident that if modern society wishes to pick up the pieces of McLuhan's shattered dream, then it has much to learn from rich indigenous cultures all across the planet in terms of shifting from an anthropocentric to an ecocentric worldview. Moreover, their basic understanding of deep ecology is one of the contributing factors that urges many indigenous peoples to resist globalization. If a necessary condition of integration into the global village entails embracing a cosmic disconnect thereby losing a part of oneself and one's connection to a universe to which everything is inextricably linked as Bruno Thibault and other Le Clézio scholars have underscored, then both cultural autonomy and existential identity are at stake. Given that the hollow virtues of neoliberalism and its boulevard of broken dreams cannot replace fundamental affective ontological needs, such as a sense of cosmic belonging and purpose, it should come as no surprise that many traditional societies are not convinced that the current situation represents the greatest crowning achievement of human civilization.

Given their profound skepticism related to modernity, Le Clézio highlights the concerted efforts of leaders from Oceania which represent divergent communities to fight back against the powerful forces of globalization. Offering a historical backdrop that illustrates the nefarious effects of colonialism upon the region, such as wide-scale depopulation, the author explains, "Et lorsqu'on lit les récits de voyages des ethnographes de la première moitié du XX$^{e}$ siècle, c'est cela qui frappe: l'enfermement des survivants, leur continuelle défiance à l'égard de la société occidentale, l'hostilité vis-à-vis des tentatives de colonisation et de l'introduction des techniques nouvelles" / 'And when one reads the travel diaries of ethnographers from the first half of the 20th century, this is what is striking: the imprisonment of survivors, the continual mistrust of Western society, their hostility concerning attempts at colonizing and the introduction of new techniques' (54; my trans.). Providing statistics to support his contentions related to the catastrophic population depletion which transpired as a direct result of brutal colonial exploitation, Le Clézio recounts how those that survived united in a common effort to expel the foreign invaders and to rediscover their own identity. Although the European conquerors devastated their region as many Melanesians and Polynesians lost their life during the occupation according to official historical records, the obstinate individuals that were still alive continued to resist in the face of seemingly insurmountable odds. Moreover, the European superpowers that governed Oceania made no attempts whatsoever to create any type of postcolonial transition after they left the area.

Noting the dire consequences of both colonial exploitation and subsequent abdication, Mark Andrews asserts, "Parmi les pages les plus émouvantes de *Raga* se trouvent celles qui évoquent la résistance des îliens face aux cycles d'exploitation et d'abandon par les Européens du vaste continent invisible que forment les îles du Pacifique" / 'Among the most moving pages of *Raga* are those that evoke the resistance of these island peoples in the face of exploitation and abandonment by the Europeans of the vast invisible continent that is formed by the islands of the Pacific' (248; my trans.). Andrews reiterates, "L'un des textes récents de l'auteur, *Raga : Approche du continent invisible,* pose une question analogue, celle de la relation à tisser entre les avancées de la mondialisation et les survivances culturelles et économiques ancestrales (par exemple celle de la pratique du *kastom* à l'île de la Pentecôte en Mélanésie)" / 'One of the author's recent texts, *Raga: Approche du continent invisible,* asks an analogous question, that of the interwoven relationship between the advances of globalization and the survival of cultural and economic ancestral traditions (for example the practice of *kastom* on Pentecost Island in Malaysia)' (243; my trans.). Indeed, Andrews correctly identifies the central focus of this complex travel journal which is inseparable from the ongoing processes of globalization all around the planet.

Similar to other postcolonial societies thrown into a globalized world, the peoples of Oceania have been left with the following three fundamental choices concerning how to reconstruct their torn social and cultural fabric: 1) Embrace the values of the neoliberal global village entirely thereby losing centuries of cultural identity and erudition, 2) Reject the romantic universalism associated with McLuhan's vision and return to their cultural roots, and 3) Create a "hybrid" culture that simultaneously endeavors to protect certain rudimentary ideals that have defined their society for countless generations, but which also attempts to improve the quality of life for its citizens by borrowing elements from the dominant monolithic paradigm. The islanders' decision related to their postcolonial situation in addition to the pervasive influence of globalization initially appears to be rather clear in *Raga*. Describing the eroding of modernity and a return to traditional cultural values that is emblematic of many Melanesian and Polynesian societies, Le Clézio asserts, "La différence entre Raga et Maurice, c'est qu'ici le temps semble s'être arrêté au premier chapitre de l'occupation humaine [...] Il n'y a pas [...] ces gros villages dans les vallées, et pratiquement-hormis le couvent des sœurs de Melsissi et le Toyota tout-terrain de Noël qui m'a amené de l'aéroport—aucune trace du monde moderne" / 'The difference between Raga and Mauritius is that here time seems to have stopped during the first chapter of human occupation [...] There are no [...] large villages in the valleys and practically outside of the sisters' convent in Melsissi and Noël's all-terrain Toyota that picked me up at the airport—there is no trace of the modern world' (32; my trans.). The author later clarifies that when the edifices of concrete and steel which were erected by the colonizers collapse because of frequent natural disasters that plague tropical islands or from progressive deterioration caused by the elements, nothing is rebuilt to replace these structures.

Instead, many islanders have chosen to reject the excesses and artifice of the modern world and to live in traditional huts like their ancestors. Furthermore, the author notes that these so-called primitive shelters are often able to withstand nature's fury, whereas the European buildings have crumbled. These omnipresent ruins are indicative not only of a colonial system that eventually fell apart, but they also refute simplistic notions of cultural supremacy. Explaining how the divergent cultures of Oceania have rejected the ethnocentric neoliberal "one size fits all" mentality, Le Clézio affirms,

> les habitants de ces lieux se sont détournés du progrès et de la vie moderne, ils se sont retournés vers ce qui les avait toujours soutenus, la connaissance des plantes, les traditions, les contes, les rêves, l'imaginaire—ce que les anthropologues ont schématisé sous le nom de *kastom*, la tradition [...] pourquoi ces gens habiteraient-ils si loin de la côte, obstinément dans ces hauts inaccessibles [...] comme jadis au temps de leur première arrivée sur l'île.
>
> the inhabitants of these places have turned away from progress and modern life, they have returned to what has always sustained them, their knowledge of plants, traditions, stories, dreams, imagination—that which anthropologists have simplified under the name *kastom*, tradition [...] why would these people live so far from the coast, stubbornly in these inaccessible heights [...] like in the days of yore when they first arrived on the island (32; my trans.).

Embracing a different definition of social progress and revealing their skepticism concerning the neoliberal vision of happiness and prosperity, numerous Melanesian and Polynesian societies actively seek to revitalize and restore their traditional cultural heritage to its original vigor.

It is in this context in which Le Clézio frames his thoughts concerning an important social movement known as the "Naked Cult" in Vanuatu. As the name of this project unequivocally implies, one of the basic tenets of its philosophy was returning to a nudist lifestyle. Le Clézio explains, "Sous l'autorité du chef religieux Tsek, les habitants de la rivière Ora devaient vivre nus, sans objets modernes ni argent, sans relations sexuelles, sans sacrements. Dans son extrémisme identitaire, le Naked Cult visait à retrouver l'état d'avant le péché—avant l'arrivée des Européens—et avant la propriété privée du sol" / 'Under the authority of the religious leader Tsek, the inhabitants of the Ora River had to live naked, without modern objects or money, with no sexual relations, without sacraments. In its extremism related to identity, the Naked Cult aimed to rediscover a time before sin—before the arrival of the Europeans—and before private ownership of land' (109; my trans.). Although this movement led by John Frum eventually disappeared in the 1980s according to Le Clézio, the author expresses a considerable amount of respect concerning the efforts of Frum and his followers to affirm their inalienable right to self-determination. As the writer further elucidates, "le Naked Cult parlait surtout de cette extraordinaire capacité de résistance des Mélanésiens" / 'The Naked Cult especially spoke about the extraordinary capacity of the Melanesians to resist' (109; my trans.). Adopting a hostile attitude vis-à-vis Western culture similar to that of several *négritude* writers, Frum contended that the only solution was to "purify" his culture of all occidental contamination.

However, despite Le Clézio's admiration for Frum and his supporters given their courage to stand up against the forces of hegemonic domination that have conquered much of the world, it is also evident that the author considers the ideology that spurred this movement to be a bit extreme. Although Le Clézio understands the frustration articulated by Frum related to the threat of sociocultural imperialism, he appears to espouse a point of view that is closer to that of Edouard Glissant. As an ardent defender of *créolité* which deconstructs simplistic notions of cultural "purity," Glissant would undoubtedly reveal the ideological naïveté that drives such logic. Moreover, in an aptly named essay entitled "On ne peut pas faire barrage au métissage" / 'We cannot put up a roadblock against miscegenation,' Le Clézio reveals, "En fait, les cultures sont toutes métisses, mélangées, y compris l'occidentale, faite de nombreux éléments venant d'Afrique, d'Asie. On ne peut faire faire barrage au métissage. Et la modernité est aussi bien japonaise, coréenne, chinoise qu'européenne ou américaine" / 'In fact, all cultures are hybrid, mixed including Western society, made up of several elements from Africa and Asia. We cannot put up a roadblock against miscegenation. And modernity is also Japanese, Korean, Chinese as well as European and American' (Dufay n.p.; my trans.). For Le Clézio, "creoleness" is not only a positive phenomenon given that every culture has something to offer the modern world, but it also appears to be unavoidable. Similar to Jan Nederveen Pieterse,[9] he affirms that the notion itself of an untainted culture that has not been influenced by other civilizations is an illusory product of the human imagination. Moreover, Le Clézio is also cognizant that the complex phenomenon of globalization transcends superficial dichotomies that oversimplify indigenous resistance to a homogenized Western socioeconomic model.

Although Frum somewhat naively attempted to restore his culture to what he perceived to be its original roots, Le Clézio also notes that intercultural exchanges in Oceania have created a rich mosaic of spiritual, social, linguistic, and intellectual paradigms. Rejecting simplistic ideology that places divergent cultures into isolated categories or boxes and which cautions individuals to protect the integrity of a given belief system from outside influence, the author lauds the presence of what could be described as a hybrid form of animistic Catholicism that thrives in the region. Painting a portrait of the major Catholic convent of Melsissi, the author asserts, "Le couvent de Melsissi est un lieu impressionnant [...] Il parle de la puissance de l'Eglise catholique, du rôle joué par les missionnaires dans cet archipel lointain. Il symbolise aussi la transformation que traverse la communauté catholique dans le monde. Non d'un déclin, mais d'un changement fondamental qui doit aboutir à une institution nouvelle" / 'The Melsissi convent is an impressive place [...] It speaks to the power of the Catholic church, of the role played by missionaries in this far away archipelago. It also symbolizes the transformation that the Catholic community is going through in the world. Not a decline, but a fundamental change that should lead to a new institution' (29; my trans.). Although Christian missionaries are often blamed for the eradication of traditional indigenous beliefs all around the world, Le Clézio affirms that different forms of spirituality can coexist and even complement each other. Expressing a hopeful tone concerning these natural hybrid creations that result from intimate contact amongst distinct cultures, the author rejects the rigid cultural divisions outlined by Samuel Huntington in his seminal work *The Clash of Civilizations*.[10]

Le Clézio portrays the Catholic sanctuary at Melsissi as one of the salient features of their contemporary culture. It is evident that the imposition of Catholicism by Westerners was initially motivated by ethnocentric ideological attempts to "civilize savages." However, the ancestral pantheistic beliefs of Melanesian and Polynesian peoples have continued to thrive as they constitute a vital part of the ethical underpinning of these diverse societies. As the author elucidates, "Les habitants de Pentecôte, après le départ des colons, sont retournés à leur système traditionnel, dans lequel la terre n'est plus une propriété mais plutôt un accord mystique passé entre les hommes du lieu et les esprits des ancêtres" / 'The inhabitants of Pentecost, after the departure of the colonizers, have returned to the traditional system in which the earth is no longer a possession but rather a mystical pact between the peoples of this place and the spirits of their ancestors' (68–69; my trans.). Although the inhabitants of Pentecost Island were probably forced to be rather discrete when practicing traditional religious customs during the colonial occupation of their land, now they are free to worship how they please. Moreover, as dedicated parishioners still continue to fill the pews of the Catholic church in Melsissi, many of these same devotees cling to traditional spiritual beliefs that have guided their society for generations. Reacting to the postcolonial situation in a much different fashion than Frum and his followers, they have borrowed several aspects of Western society that they find useful and combined them with a spiritual system that has sustained them throughout their entire history. This new hybrid religion which appears to function quite well in this given situation dismisses Huntington's assertion that violent cultural clashes are often inevitable and irreconcilable in a globalized world. On their own terms, the citizens of Melsissi have successfully re-constructed their identity and decolonized their psyche while simultaneously refusing to accept certain ideological concepts of the neoliberal global village that are detrimental to both the human and nonhuman population.

Nuancing his earlier contention that practically no trace of the modern world is visible in Oceania, Le Clézio recounts his experiences with a native man named Willie whose balanced worldview reveals that both resistance and reconciliation are indeed possible for indigenous peoples that seek alternatives to the current situation. Although cultural theorists that espouse radical views on both sides of the debate express convictions that are emblematic of an "all or nothing" attitude concerning globalization and its values, Willie exemplifies the positive virtues of cultural hybridity. Underscoring that intercultural exchanges in Melanesian and Polynesian societies are not limited to the spiritual realm, Le Clézio explains,

> Willie, malgré sa volonté de participer au monde moderne (téléphone, Internet), me conte une anecdote qui me montre le lien qu'il continue d'entretenir avec les esprits de la terre. Etant malade, et souffrant beaucoup, il avait rêvé d'une plante, une liane sans nom, qui l'attendait dans la forêt. Il était parti à sa recherche et l'avait trouvée à l'endroit qu'il avait vu en rêve, l'avait broyée et avait fabriqué un onguent qui l'avait guéri de son mal. Il parle de cette liane non comme d'une feuille ou d'une médecine, mais comme un don que l'esprit de ses ancêtres lui avait laissé dans la forêt.
>
> Willie, despite his desire to participate in the modern world (telephone, Internet), told me an anecdote which showed me the connection that he continues to maintain with the spirits of the earth. Being sick and in tremendous suffering, he had dreamed about a plant, a creeper without a name, that was waiting for him in the forest. He left to look for it and he found it at the spot which he had seen in his dream, he grinded it and made an ointment out of it which cured him of his illness. He spoke about this creeper not as a plant or as a medicine, but as a gift that the spirit of his ancestors had left for him in the forest (70; my trans.).

Willie gives credence to the theory that embracing certain aspects of modernity which can indeed improve one's lifestyle does not necessarily entail losing everything that encompasses a cultural identity of a given society. Perhaps the problem with the global village, which is dominated by the interests of transnational corporations, is that the exchange is considered to be a one-way street. If all peoples were to be given a voice, then potentially a more humane and sustainable interconnected and interdependent world would be possible. Willie does not indignantly reject everything that the Western paradigm has to offer given that he valorizes certain technological advances which render communication and the rapid dissemination of information possible, but he still remains connected to a universe that created and which sustains all life.

In addition to this spiritual *métissage*, which is characteristic of several Melanesian and Polynesian societies, Le Clézio defends Bislama creole which is the official language of Vanuatu. According to Le Clézio, creole languages should not be considered to be bastardizations or imperfect dialects of a certain language. Not only are creoles complex linguistic systems in which any thought can be expressed, but they are also emblematic of a form of resistance to colonial tyranny. At a recent conference in Montreal dedicated to the subject of globalization, Le Clézio affirms, "Lorsqu'on parle du créole en France, on a un peu l'impression que les gens étendent *patois*, ils entendent une sorte de jargon, qui aurait été le langage des serviteurs, quelque chose de dépréciatif, c'est tres récent que l'on considère le créole pour ce qu'il est, la dernière langue indo-européenne apparue sur cette planète"[11] / 'When one talks about creole in France, one has the impression that people think of *patois*, they understand this to mean a type of jargon, which would have been the language of servants, something derogatory, it's only very recently that we consider creole for what it actually is, the last Indo-European language to have surfaced on this planet' ("Les littératures de langue française à l'heure de la mondialisation" n.p.; my trans.). Reminding the reader of the context in which *Raga* was written, Mark Andrews asserts, "En citant abondamment les écrits de son hôte à bord de la Boudeuse, Édouard Glissant, Le Clézio fait l'éloge des langues créoles créées dans la violence de l'oppression" / 'By abundantly citing the writings of his host, Edouard Glissant, while on board la Boudeuse, Le Clézio praises creole languages that were created by violence and oppression' (248; my trans.). For societies that have been decimated by decades or generations of colonial exploitation, creole languages are a reflection of the resilience of indigenous peoples that have begun the arduous process of reconstructing their shattered identity from the ashes.[12]

Underscoring the cultural hybridity that is indicative of several contemporary civilizations in Oceania, the writer elucidates, "Au Vanuatu, en Océanie, de même. Longuement, patiemment, les peoples autochtones ont recouvré leur indépendance. Ils se sont libérés des tutelles coloniales, ils ont inventé une nouvelle langue créole, le bislama. Ils ont édifié une nouvelle culture, une nouvelle religion, issues de la rencontre" / 'In Vanuatu, in Oceania, as well. After much reflection, patiently, autochthon peoples disguised their independence. They freed themselves from colonial trusteeship, they invented a new creole language, bislama. They edified a new culture, a new religion, resulting from an encounter' (123; my trans.). Although Le Clézio acknowledges that creole languages originally were born out of necessity given that two divergent cultures needed to communicate with each other on a basic level in his aforementioned speech at Montreal, they are not emblematic of indigenous complicity related to colonial governance. Instead, creating a new hybrid linguistic system in which every sentiment could be expressed should be considered to be a subversive act calculatingly designed to undermine the power structure of the oppressor. This linguistic resistance or refusal to assimilate was perhaps the first step that paved the way for eventual self-determination. Moreover, this stubborn and resilient attitude in the face of adversity is a microcosmic reflection which illustrates how fragmented identities maligned by ethnocentric hegemonic forces are being re-appropriated and re-constructed in a globalized world.

Echoing the sentiments of Edouard Glissant, Le Clézio also lauds "mental" creoleness as a manifestation of intercultural citizenship that is indicative of a genuine openness toward the Other and a willingness to engage in dialogue. Articulating how this intellectual and affective malleability has resulted in the creation of successful hybrid societies which have protected the traditional virtues which are most essential to them while embracing certain aspects of the neoliberal global village paradigm, Le Clézio explains, "Quelques gadgets […] peuvent rendre la vie plus facile […] Et surtout, la connaissance, par les livres, les journaux, les cassettes vidéo […] Le métissage mental, à propos de quoi le poète Edouard Glissant dit que les gens des îles ont cens ans d'avance sur tous les autres peuples de la terre" / 'Some gadgets […] can make life easier […] And especially, knowledge from books, newspapers, video cassettes […] Mental miscegenation, about which the poet Edouard Glissant says that island people are one hundred years in advance of all of the other people of the earth' (129–130; my trans.). First, it should be noted that there appears to be a visible shift to a more moderate point of view concerning technology in Le Clézio's recent fiction.[13] Moreover, the author clearly advocates in favor of hybridity as perhaps the best solution to cultural imperialism and hegemonic domination. For this reason, perhaps rebuilding a more just and egalitarian global village entails dismissing extremist neoliberal logic which asserts that no alternatives to the current system are possible or even warranted and examining how indigenous societies have created a slightly different model that incorporates major tenets of Western thought while simultaneously safeguarding centuries of erudition inherited from their ancestors. Given that many earlier Leclézian protagonists appear to reject Western civilization entirely, recent texts such as *Raga* also seem to suggest the possibility of reconciliation. However, in order for this process to achieve significant results on a more global scale, the voices of traditional peoples must first be valorized and heard even if they threaten the deeply entrenched narcissistic interests of the "happy few."

In addition to the spiritual, linguistic, and intellectual flexibility that epitomizes several contemporary Melanesian and Polynesian societies, Le Clézio highlights the efforts of Charlotte Wèi Matansuè to take advantage of the free market economic system to liberate Vanuatu women from centuries of patriarchal dominance while simultaneously preserving elements of their cultural heritage. As the narrator asserts, "Charlotte a contribué à la reconnaissance marchande de la valeur de la natte—donc du travail des femmes. Elle est surtout parvenue à une reconnaissance de leur statut dans la société traditionnellement machiste du Vanuatu […] La natte est devenue pour elles un moyen d'accès au pouvoir" / 'Charlotte contributed to the market recognition of the value of the braid—therefore the work of women. She has especially managed to make their rights recognized in the traditionally chauvinistic society of Vanuatu […] The braid has become for them a means to access power' (41; my trans.). Le Clézio reiterates, "Ce n'est pas un petit progrès, et il ne doit rien à la mission catholique, ni aux discours des hommes politiques. C'est l'œuvre des femmes de Raga, et d'elles seules" / 'This is not a small step towards progress, and it owes nothing to the catholic mission or to the speeches of politicians. It is the work of women from Raga and (it comes) from them alone' (41; my trans.). Expressing his admiration from the emancipation movements that have come from within and which exemplify the strength and courage of women like Charlotte, Le Clézio underscores how blending different cultural elements from divergent models can create better global societies. Although cultural purists might contend that the citizens of Vanuatu should attempt to purge their community of any and all forms of outside contamination, this extreme position is rather problematic given that their traditional culture is profoundly misogynistic. Would it not be more productive to espouse a more humble intercultural view which posits that different peoples can and should learn from each other? By realistically portraying both the negative and positive facets of Vanuatu society, this mentality is precisely what Le Clézio seems to promote.

However, perhaps the most important way in which the modern subject must resist integration into the monolithic global village as it is currently being managed is to replace the neoliberal dream of the good(s) life outlined in the preceding chapters with a different vision for humanity. In other words, the first step to creating a more humane and democratic global community that reflects the humanistic aspirations associated with McLuhan's euphoric view is to envision what a better world might encompass. As the narrator states referring to movements such as Frum's aforementioned Naked Cult, "La résistance, c'était l'action désespérée, ultime, de ceux qui se voyaient condamnés à l'asservissement ou à l'extinction. Les mouvements [...] prenaient naissance dans des rêves plutôt que dans des projets révolutionnaires" / 'Resistance was in the form of the desperate and last-ditch action of those who saw themselves condemned to servitude or to extinction. The movements [...] were born in dreams rather than in revolutionary projects' (107; my trans.). Although Le Clézio deconstructs the ideological naïveté that fueled Frum's organized resistance, the author admires this leader for having the courage to admit that the global village is hardly a dream for the vast majority of the earth's inhabitants. Furthermore, Frum at least endeavored to propose a solution to the litany of problems that plague modern society using his imagination. Without a new vision to replace McLuhan's evaporated aspirations, the situation will only continue to degenerate further with each passing day.

The end of this complex narrative, which concretizes the complicated debates surrounding globalization perhaps more than any of the author's works, expresses a similar point of view to that of Joseph Stiglitz albeit in a different context. Le Clézio contends that the world in which billions of human beings live is likely going to keep metaphorically shrinking. The tone of the final pages of the essay *Raga* is reminiscent of Stiglitz's affirmation that "We cannot go back on globalization; it is here to stay. The issue is how can we make it work" (*Globalization and Its Discontents* 222). As Mark Andrews states, "Vers la fin de son récit, Le Clézio paraît accepter la modernité comme une réalité non seulement inévitable, mais souhaitable" / 'Toward the end of the narrative, Le Clézio appears to accept modernity as a reality that is not only avoidable but desirable' (249; my trans.). Andrews notes that Le Clézio is not naïve enough to think that the processes that have connected most of the planet could somehow magically be reversed. Moreover, Le Clézio reiterates near the end of the narrative that different cultures and value systems can successfully coexist when common people, instead of transnational corporations, from a given region are in control of their own destiny.

Clearly nuancing his earlier affirmation that the peoples of Oceania have apparently turned their back on modernity entirely, Le Clézio clarifies,

> C'est le monde moderne. On peut regretter le temps où les villages vivaient leurs traditions, sans témoins, sans caméscopes ni calendrier official. Mais c'est la réalité [...] La société mélanésienne a certainement beaucoup changé, mais elle maintient le respect des aînés, et cela me plaît [...] On dit de ses habitants qu'ils ont gardé les traits de la culture mélanésienne originelle. C'est bien possible. En même temps, ils sont très impliqués dans l'économie touristique.
>
> This is the modern world. We can lament the time when villages lived their traditions, without any witnesses, without camcorders nor an official calendar. But this is reality [...] Melanesian society has certainly changed a lot, but it has maintained its respect for elders and I like this [...] One says about its inhabitants that they have kept aspects of their original Melanesian culture. This is quite possible. At the same time, they are very implicated in the tourist economy (113; my trans.).

Contending that "back to nature" movements such as Frum's organized resistance are unrealistic, the author expresses that Melanesian culture will never exist as it once did before the arrival of the Europeans. However, Le Clézio also implies that the hybrid cultures that divergent civilizations from Oceania have created have found a way to preserve the most important elements of their cultural identity and to benefit from what globalization has to offer. In the final pages of *Raga,* Le Clézio reveals his aspirations that a veritable intercultural exchange, grounded in mutual respect and humility, will begin to take place between Melanesian and Polynesian cultures and the Western world. The author contends that if we can overcome our willful blindness concerning indigenous thought, then perhaps a reconciliation that could potentially benefit the inhabitants of the entire global village, human and otherwise, could begin to take place.

## WHAT CAN BE LEARNED FROM MODERN FAILED UTOPIAS: INTERCULTURAL DIALOGUE, CREOLIZATION, AND HYBRIDITY

In addition to his deep admiration for traditional civilizations from all corners of the globe, which have much to contribute to the modern world if we are willing to listen, Le Clézio is also fascinated with historical and present-day attempts at creating utopian societies. *Ourania* recounts the collapse of two distinct contemporary efforts to build such communities, as examined in chapter two. Although neither of these ideal societies is able to actualize its lofty goals, this failure does not mean that these endeavors have no merit. Every society has its inherent flaws, as Le Clézio articulates in *Raga,* but this unpleasant reality should not be misinterpreted to signify that alternatives to the current situation are nonexistent. Despite their undeniable faults, it is indeed plausible that other socioeconomic models represent valid points of departure for re-conceptualizing the global village paradigm.

In addition to his astute observations that dismiss the naïve euphoria of supporters of neoliberal globalization in its current form, *Ourania* contains a plethora of autobiographical and autotextual elements that strike the reader. As Thierry Léger explains, "Publié en 2006, *Ourania* est un roman divisé en trois parties très inégales qui décrivent trois étapes de la vie du narrateur-protagoniste Daniel Sillitoe, personnage qui ressemble en de très nombreux points à son créateur. La première partie, longue d'une dizaine de pages, raconte l'enfance de Daniel dans un village de l'arrière-pays niçois pendant la Seconde Guerre mondiale, période pendant laquelle il invente le pays d'Ourania" / 'Published in 2006, *Ourania* is a novel divided into three very unequal parts that describe three stages in the life of the narrator/protagonist Daniel Sillitoe, a character that resembles its creator in numerous ways. The first part, approximately twelve pages long, recounts Daniel's childhood in the backcountry around Nice during World War II, a period during which he invented the country of Ourania' (263; my trans.). It is virtually impossible to read *Ourania* without thinking of *Etoile Errante* and *Ritournelle de la faim*. Indeed, the parallels between the first three autobiographical pages of *Ritournelle de la faim* which precede the actual narrative itself and the beginning of *Ourania* are difficult to ignore. Furthermore, the imaginary utopia that the narrator creates in *Ourania* to escape the dire realities of Nazi occupation, Vichy France, and the Shoah itself are reminiscent of Georges Perec's *W ou le souvenir d'enfance*. However, it should be noted that *Ourania* is not an ironic caricature of a despotic genocidal regime that progressively reveals itself to be anything but a perfect society.[14]

In stark contrast to the antithesis of utopia that is emblematic of Perec's complex and experimental novel, Le Clézio sincerely respects the efforts of the dreamers that endeavored to create *campos* and *emporio* with the best of intentions. Moreover, as Le Clézio confides in an interview with Jérôme Garcin, his first-hand knowledge of numerous indigenous communities in addition to his admiration for historical utopists such as Sir Thomas More are at the very core of his ideas concerning what a better world could encompass. As the writer elucidates,

> J'ai écrit *Ourania* en référence et dévotion au livre qui a le plus compté dans la pensée européenne du XVI siècle, l'*Utopie* de Thomas More. Ce livre a été admiré, critiqué, et aujourd'hui délaissé, alors qu'il porte en lui toutes les questions et les angoisses de notre modernité [...] J'ai rêvé moi-même de ce pays d'Ourania quand j'étais enfant [...] J'ai quitté Nice pour aller [...] rejoindre au Nigeria mon père [...] il n'y avait pas d'école, nous vivions, nous les enfants, en bande et en totale liberté [...] Autrement dit, d'une certaine façon, pour moi Campos a réellement existé.

> I wrote *Ourania* in reference and in devotion to the most important book representing European thought of the 16th century, *Utopia* by Thomas More. This book was admired, criticized, and today has been abandoned even though it contains all of the questions and anguish concerning modernity [...] I dreamed myself of this country called *Ourania* when I was a child [...] I left Nice to go [...] rejoin my father in Nigeria [...] there was no school, us the children we lived as a group and in total freedom [...] In other words, in a certain fashion, for me Campos truly existed (Garcin n.p.; my trans.).

Reiterating his contention that clearly resonates in this interview and in his fiction that globalization has disenfranchised billions of people across the planet in spite of its positive aspects, Le Clézio also expresses the necessity of a new vision that could come closer to creating the promised win-win scenarios.

Given that the very notion itself of a utopia is at the heart of *Ourania,* numerous researchers have attempted to explain the author's nuanced viewpoints concerning the realization of so-called terrestrial paradises. Thierry Léger underscores, "*Ourania* est indéniablement un roman qui problématise l'utopie, mais c'est une utopie qui se déroule à l'époque postmoderne, c'est-à-dire à une époque où l'idée même de pensée absolue, de société idéale est difficilement concevable, sauf dans l'imaginaire, loin de la réalité quotidienne" / '*Ourania* is undeniably a novel that renders utopia problematic, but it's also a utopia that unfolds during the postmodern era, that is to say during a period in which the notion itself of absolute truth of an ideal society is difficult to conceive, except for in one's imagination, far from daily reality' (266; my trans.). Echoing similar sentiments, Bruno Thibault asserts, "De nombreux critiques ont donc vu dans la disparition de Campos le symbole de la fin des utopies dans le monde contemporain et l'expression du pessimisme de l'auteur. Est-il encore possible, aujourd'hui, dans un monde gagné aux valeurs de la modernité et de la globalisation économique, de rêver à une société idéale

et indépendante, même à l'échelle réduite" / 'Numerous critics have therefore interpreted the disappearance of Campos as a symbol of the end of utopias in the contemporary world and an expression of the author's pessimism. Is it still possible today in a world won over by modern values and economic globalization to dream about an ideal and independent society even on a reduced scale' (*La Métaphore Exotique* 214; my trans.). Given that Le Clézio is cognizant that the powerful forces of globalization have perhaps already impacted the entire planet, as evidenced in *Raga*, many literary theorists wonder if the author believes that successful resistance to hegemonic domination is even possible.

Confirming Thibault's assertion concerning standard interpretations of the novel *Ourania* by the literary community, Fredrik Westerlund states, "Le livre transmet une vision pessimiste sur les possibilités de vivre ses rêves, de trouver de la paix dans le monde moderne" / 'The book transmits a pessimistic vision concerning the possibility of living one's dreams and of finding peace in the modern world' (*"Les Fleuves dans l'œuvre Romanesque"* 72; my trans.). The deconstruction of the neoliberal dream outlined in the preceding chapters in the context of Le Clézio's varied fiction concretizes the fact that the actualization of McLuhan's euphoric vision has destroyed much of humanity's aspirations. As narratives such as *Le Chercheur d'or, Désert,* and *Poisson d'or* illustrate, neoliberal fallacies have been woefully unable to provide the modern subject with any semblance of existential meaning or satisfaction. However, Le Clézio's recent narratives including *Raga* and *Ourania* also possess hopeful tones that serve to temper his disconcerting questions related to the modern world. Specifically, both of these texts seem to imply that even if the stoic, fraternal struggle against the injustice and inequality that is emblematic of the global village is difficult at best, this unfortunate reality does not mean that the uphill fight is in vain.

It is perhaps in the interview with Jacqueline Dutton in which Le Clézio most clearly articulates his fascination with the notion of a utopia. In reference to Peter Matthiessen, the American novelist and environmental crusader, the author reveals, "Je suis un peu de son avis, je crois qu'il faut tendre à réaliser le paradis sur terre, c'est-à-dire enfin réaliser l'utopie" / 'I agree with his opinion for the most part, I think that we should attempt to realize paradise on earth or in other words try to finally realize utopia' (282; my trans.). However, this statement should not be removed from its global context. Earlier in this same conversation in response to Dutton's question "Vous voyez une distinction entre le paradis et l'utopie?" / 'Do you see a distinction between paradise and utopia?' Le Clézio answers, "Oui, parce que le paradis n'est pas réalisable sur la terre, c'est le contraire même pratiquement de l'utopie" / 'Yes, because paradise is not able to be realized on earth, it's practically even the opposite of utopia' (281; my trans.). Although Le Clézio readily admits that a true utopia in the traditional sense of the word is unattainable, human beings should nonetheless endeavor to create the best society possible. As Le Clézio's fiction illustrates, the dominant socioeconomic paradigm which has been exported all across the planet can and should be improved to serve the interests of everyone including ethnic and moral minorities. Moreover, even the slightest chance that a meaningful victory is in reach justifies the act of resistance itself.

The two divergent utopian societies that the narrator Daniel Sillitoe discovers in Mexico possess major fundamental flaws. As Léger correctly notes, the author himself admires such efforts but he does not idealize them. In addition to the realistic portrayal of academic backstabbing and intellectual pretentiousness that characterizes Emporio explored in chapter two, it is evident from the beginning of the text that the other defiant community in question, Campos, is already on the brink of disappearing. When Daniel is asking for directions, an unidentified individual reveals, "Si vous voulez savoir, ils ne vont pas habiter encore longtemps par ici" / 'If you really want to know, they are not going to be living around here much longer' (88; my trans.). The narrator reiterates, "Il était clair que, pour cet homme, les habitants de Campos n'étaient pas légitimes" / 'It was clear that that for this man, the inhabitants of Campos were not legitimate' (88; my trans.). These revelations destabilize the reader and create what Westerlund and other researchers have identified as a pessimistic tone given that we are witnessing an ill-fated dream that has already begun to de-crystallize from the onset. The reader inevitably ponders the ultimate significance of a project that will soon culminate in what could only be described as an unmitigated failure to the outside world.

However, both of the seemingly doomed modern utopias in *Ourania* which clearly do not epitomize "heaven on earth" reflect ideals that are important to the author. For this reason, these communities, although not perfect by any stretch of the imagination, could potentially represent a type of initial blueprint for creating a global village that corresponds more closely to McLuhan's original humanistic vision. From this standpoint, the socioeconomic and moral foundation of Campos is quite revealing. Underscoring the ethical principles that deem what is considered to be positive for society, Thierry Léger asserts, "Il nous propose une utopie communautaire dans le village de Campos où règnent la liberté, le respect d'autrui et de la nature" / 'He proposes to us a communitarian utopia in the village of Campos where freedom, respect for the Other, and nature reign supreme' (266; my trans.). Given Le Clézio's dedication to interculturality as evidenced by the preface that he contributed to Issa Asgarally's *L'Interculturel ou la guerre* and the philanthropic organization that they founded together[15] in addition to the author's deep ecological sensibilities explored in the preceding chapter, it is hardly surprising that a community which valorizes these same virtues would appeal to him. Furthermore, this isolated enclave, comprised of discontents which represent majority and indigenous cultures from all parts of the globe, welcomes everyone. Affirming this openness, the spiritual and political leader of Campos Jadi explains in reference to the rather unsavory character Efrain, "Si nous ne pouvons pas accepter cet homme, en faire notre frère, c'est que notre communauté ne vaut rien" / 'If we cannot accept this man, make him our brother, then our community is worthless' (170; my trans.). Efrain arouses much suspicion amongst the citizens of Campos and he undoubtedly craves power, but no one can be excluded in an ideal society.

In addition the unconditional acceptance and valorization of the Other that undergirds the moral fabric of Campos, this community which functions nearly outside of the system entirely similar to social groups such as the Amish[16] espouses a different conception of education. Whereas the quest for knowledge itself in Western society is purely utilitarian as the modern subject is conditioned to value education only when it directly correlates to helping one procure the good(s) life, the inhabitants of Campos emphasize the importance of knowledge for vastly different reasons. Like many traditional societies with which Le Clézio is familiar, this intercultural community maintains that the greatest form of erudition is a type of awareness that helps one better understand the universe and his or her place in it. As the narrator clarifies, "La vie, on y enseigne la vie. A Campos on n'enseigne rien d'autre que la vie" / 'Life, we teach life there. At Campos, we teach nothing else besides life' (96; my trans.). Instinctively aware of the scientific reality that human beings do not exist inside of an ecological vacuum given their close relationship with the natural world, the citizens of Campos live a fulfilling life without illusory, homocentric ideology that leads one further from the truth. Perhaps this pedagogical paradigm which dismisses the notion that education is only useful in terms of affirming the intellectual superiority of the individual over the group, actualizing narcissistic materialistic desires, or exercising even greater dominion over the universe represents a healthier model for humanity to begin to heal the cosmic disconnect and counterpoint the genesis myth.

Perhaps the Western world could learn from an ecocentric pedagogical system in which no gap exists between theory and practice. Although recent scientific discoveries have disproven outdated philosophical and ideological notions inherited from Renaissance humanism, our thought systems must also evolve given that the very future of the planet is at stake. The geologist Daniel Sillitoe clearly articulates the first law of ecology and a keen understanding of the physical laws of the universe in a speech that he gives at the Emporio. Explaining the dire significance of protecting a fragile planet, the narrator professes, "Le sol et le 'nœud' de l'écosphère [...] Si vous ne le traitez pas bien, vous le perdrez, car un sol dégradé ne se récupère pas. Quand il est détruit, il faut des milliers d'années pour que la terre en invente un nouveau" / 'The soil is the 'knot' of the ecosphere […] If you do not treat it well, you will lose it, because a degraded soil will not be able to recover. When it is destroyed, it will take billions of years for the earth to invent a new one' (81; my trans.). The apocalyptic tone of Daniel's public discourse resembles the stern warning issued by the narrator of "Pawana." The ecocentric value system, influenced by indigenous Amerindian thought,[17] of Campos possesses the necessary spiritual and philosophical worldview that is urgently required to articulate the material realities of the biosphere to the masses.

Not only does the ecological humility espoused by numerous traditional societies offer an invaluable ideological alternative to the destructive and perhaps even lethal genesis myth, but the intellectual modesty that is emblematic of their fragmented understanding of the universe and their small role in it also fosters both cosmic and social cohesion. In stark contrast to the Western model which emphasizes ascertaining absolute truths, the inhabitants of Campos are cognizant of their epistemological limitations and are thus able to embrace ambivalence in addition to other divergent points of view. As Jadi explained to Raphaël the first night that he arrived in Campos, "Laisse-toi entraîner dans un autre monde, devine-le à la manière de la cigale, par les pores de ta peau, pas seulement avec les chambres noires de tes yeux, mais avec tout ton corps. Respire-le, bois-le. Si tu crois savoir quelque chose, oublie-le" / 'Let yourself enter into another world, make guesses about it like a cicada, by the pores of your skin, not only with the dark chambers of your eyes, but with your entire body. Breath it, drink it. If you think that you know something, forget it' (187; my trans.). In a contention that is reminiscent of the narrator of *L'Extase Matérielle* which urges the reader to "Chercher au-delà des mots, chercher au-delà de l'intelligence. Chercher avec tous les sens grands ouverts, et avec les autres moyens inconnus, la voie de la communication avec la matière" / 'look beyond words, look beyond intelligence. Look with all of your senses fully opened and by other unknown means, the path of communication with matter,' Jadi underscores the importance of establishing an intimate, sensorial connection with the material world which transcends the limitations of rational thought (185; my trans.). Moreover, it is difficult to hone intercultural sensitivity when a given subject thinks that he or she possesses definitive answers for all of life's greatest questions. Since Campos was founded upon the very notion that each individual and every culture has invaluable insights to contribute, it is no surprise that this imperfect society appears to be much more balanced than the global village paradigm. Perhaps the alleged universality of the Western intellectual model also explains the obstinate resistance of many people to admit that centuries of homocentric logic are not only misleading but entirely false. Ironically, it is Western civilization that has been guilty of wishful thinking, such as Descartes's *bêtemachine* concept, which has alienated humanity from the universe and from the greatest truth of all: matter.

In addition to the educational structure of Campos, Isabelle Roussel-Gillet notes another important intercultural dimension of this community which is actually much more outside of the system than the inhabitants of Raga. Describing this unconventional language or the "rêve d'Elmen chez Le Clézio" / 'Le Clézio's Elmen dream,' Roussel-Gillet specifies that this linguistic code is "un langage puisant dans plusieurs langues balbutié" / 'a language of babble that draws from several different languages' ("Ecrivain de l'incertitude" 170; my trans.). Moreover, numerous critics, such as Bruno Thibault, Fredrik Westerlund, and Claude Cavallero have examined the autotextual references between *Ourania* and the author's short story "Martin" given that the child prodigy of this earlier narrative also creates a language called Elmen. In the beginning of *Ourania*, the reader is initially befuddled concerning the significance of the "Elmen dream" to which Roussel-Gillet refers given that the official language of Campos does indeed appear to be nothing but gibberish. Elucidating the linguistic structure of Elmen, the narrator states, "Dans elmen, chacun parle comme il veut, comme cela lui convient, en changeant les mots, ou bien en se servant des mots des autres [...] cette langue ne sert pas seulement à parler, mais à chanter, à crier, ou à jouer avec les sons. Parfois tu as simplement envie de faire des sons, pour rire, pour imiter" / 'In Elmen, everyone speaks however they wish, as it suits him or her, by changing words, or rather by using other people's words [...] This language is not only used for speaking, but to sing, to yell, or to play with sounds. Sometimes you just want to make sounds, to laugh, to imitate' (165; my trans.). Although this lighthearted linguistic exercise that is emblematic of speaking Elmen perhaps does not appear to serve the traditional purpose that explains why human civilizations created these codes in the first place, this unorthodox method of communication reflects Le Clézio's philosophical problems with language itself.

Given the profound concerns that Le Clézio expresses related to the hegemonic forces that deliberately manipulate linguistic systems for their own benefit in *Les Géants*,[18] it is evident why the writer would attempt to imagine what other forms of communication could encompass. In a certain sense, the author appears to be proposing a sort of purification that would allow languages to fulfill their original design of establishing a deeper connection with the Other and the universe. Poetically revealing what such a linguistic project could entail, the narrator of *L'inconnu sur la terre*, a text which could also be described as the universal story of humanity, similar to *Terra Amata*, asserts "Je voudrais vous parler loin, longtemps, avec des mots qui ne seraient pas seulement des mots, mais qui conduiraient jusqu'au ciel, jusqu'à la mer" / 'I would like to speak to you from afar, a long time, with words that would not only be words, but which would lead to the sky and the sea' (9; my trans.). Le Clézio deliberately employs the conditional tense in these opening lines of *L'inconnu sur la terre* to express a type of idealistic, linguistic vision which corresponds to the "dream" noted by Roussel-Gillet in *Ourania*. Furthermore, the goal of every utopia is to eliminate injustice, inequality, and oppression. If language itself is being used and carefully disseminated by the "happy few" and the corporate entities that they control such as the neoliberal media to solidify their governance of the entire planet, then a different form of communication must be invented. The first step in reappropriating language itself would be to ensure that all civilizations have an equal voice in this process. This is precisely the function that Elmen, which is comprised of elements from dominant and indigenous languages, attempts to achieve. In a global atmosphere dominated by a few select economic powers and institutions such as the IMF and the World Bank which protect their interests, the voices of minority societies have been systematically stifled.

In his monograph entitled *Le Clézio: Témoin du monde,* Claude Cavallero reveals in a footnote, "Selon une confidence de l'auteur, le mot 'elmen' est celui qu'il a trouvé dans son enfance pour imaginer une supra-langue, une langue internationale auxiliaire à l'image de l'Esperanto" / 'The author personally confided to me that the world 'elmen' is the one that he created in his childhood to imagine a super-language, an international auxiliary language in the image of Esperanto' (52; my trans.). The humanistic intentions that inspired Jadi and his followers to invent Elmen are similar to those of the founders of Esperanto who hoped to create a more cohesive and peaceful world. Many people have contended that such efforts are naïve, however, these aspirations clearly negate the consumerist smokescreen that is the new opiate of the masses by expressing a vision that counterpoints the neoliberal pipe dream that has failed to deliver on its lofty promises. Moreover, given that the proponents of globalization in its current form are willing to use all hegemonic tools at their disposal, including the hostile media takeover concerning how knowledge is conveyed to the general populace, to expand their supremacy, linguistic resistance is a vital part of the struggle against tyranny.

Similar to his elegy of creoles as hybrid innovations of oppressed peoples attempting to redefine themselves in a complex, globalized landscape on their own terms in *Raga,* Le Clézio also implies that the cultural and intellectual miscegenation that is at the core of Elmen and the society that it reflects is a positive phenomenon. The connection between creole and Elmen becomes explicit near the end of the narrative after the group has been expelled from Campos and is attempting to resettle in Belize. When Raphaël overhears *bogo bogo,* he initially naively assumes that these individuals are speaking Elmen. As the narrator explains, "Et les langages, l'anglais, l'espagnol, le maya, et cette langue créole qui résonne comme une musique, le *bogo bogo* venu d'Afrique, et quand il l'entend Raphaël a cette réflexion naïve: 'ils parlent elmen comme nous!' Pas exactement, mais il lui semble qu'ils sont enfin arrivés dans un pays où tout se mélange, où tout est inventé" / 'And the languages, English, Spanish,

Mayan, and this creole language that resonates like a music, *bogo bogo* from Africa, and when he heard it Raphaël had this naive thought: 'They speak Elmen like us!' Not exactly, but it seemed to him that they had finally arrived in a country where everything is mixed together, where everything is invented' (246; my trans.). Despite the obvious humor in this passage and others designed to make the reader laugh, cautioning us to not make light of what Elmen itself represents, Roussel-Gillet declares, "Prenons au sérieux ce babil" / 'Let's take this babble seriously' ("Ecrivain de l'incertitude" 88; my trans.). Underneath the veil of comedy, Le Clézio once again describes creoleness or cultural hybridity in a positive context. For both Le Clézio and Glissant, *Métissage* and the intercultural openness that it represents should be lauded not shunned. Moreover, this cultural exchange has helped numerous civilizations, whose social fabric has been torn by slavery, colonialism, blackbirding, and the neoliberal global village, to recreate their fractured identities. Inventing another form of expressing oneself is not indicative of complicity, but instead it is a form of resistance that finds its roots in historical persecution and exploitation.

Although the naïve dreamers of Campos appear to have created an isolated intercultural community in which the vast majority of its inhabitants enjoy a better quality of life than those who live in modern society, powerful outside influences will prematurely eradicate Jadi's vision. Summarizing the inevitable downfall of this failed utopia, Fredrik Westerlund affirms, "Les habitants de cette société sont chassés par les capitalistes qui veulent exploiter leurs terres riches pour l'expansion de leurs cultures de fraises, et les habitants sont éparpillés" / 'The inhabitants of this society are chased away by capitalists that want to exploit their valuable land in order to expand their strawberry plantations, and the inhabitants are scattered' (72; my trans.). Given that the citizens of Campos are a peaceful people that have irrefutably harmed no one, they are undeniably the victims of materialistic avarice and a narrow conception of progress. The same corporations examined in chapter two which have ruthlessly exploited everyone and everything in this region seek to tighten their financial stranglehold. Since their economic resources wield them considerable political and social power, nothing stands in the way.

In his review of *Ourania*, Alexander Hertich notes that the ultimate collapse of Campos is a realistic microcosm that reflects the author's deep concerns related to what transpires on a daily basis in the global village. Specifically, Hertich asserts that this disquieting text poses the following questions: "Have we lost our way in this mercantilist society, where profits outweigh other concerns? Are we stripping the Earth of its longterm natural resources in order to ensure immediate shareholder approval? [...] Does globalization result in homogenization where all forms of rebellion and individuality are erased?" (628). As Hertich underscores, the failure of Campos illustrates the grim reality that it is becoming more difficult with each passing day for common people to defend themselves against an integrated political and social elite that nearly owns everything. Unable to stand the thought that one little parcel of land exists that they have yet to develop to extend their economic dominion even further, the respected businessmen successfully remove the final barrier that had stood between them and total usurpation of power.

The corporate tycoon that is most emblematic of the unfettered greed to which Hertich refers is Aldaberto Aranzas or Don Aldaberto. Before officially introducing the narrator Daniel to this baron, the founder of Emporio Don Thomas reveals, "Tout ce que vous voyez là appartient ou appartiendra un jour à Aranzas […] Surtout Campos. Il a l'intention de tout reprendre, de planter en avocatiers, ou de créer des lotissements. C'est un homme très riche" / 'Everything that you see there belongs or will belong one day to Aranzas […] Especially Campos. He intends to take everything, to plant avocado trees and to create lots. He is a very rich man' (191; my trans.). This passage underscores the pessimism highlighted by Thibault and Westerlund. Even the beginning of the narrative indicates that it is not a question of will Campos disappear but rather when will this community be displaced. For this reason, throughout the entire narrative, the reader is simply waiting for the proverbial *coup de grâce* that will evict Jadi and his followers from this land. Moreover, given that the funding for Don Thomas's humanitarian utopian project depends on the "generosity" of Aranzas, a clear conflict of interest emerges. How is it possible to question authority when the system controls everything and stifles any type of meaningful subversion? When research is funded by corporations whose only real objective is to maximize profits, academicians must carefully filter or minimize any findings that could potentially undermine the interests of the integrated political and social elite. Explaining this predicament, Hertich poses the following question: "Are universities turning away from a tradition of academic freedom to keep board members and alumni content?" (628). In *Ourania*, Aranzas's money and his zeal to control everything will undermine the humanistic and intellectual integrity of Emporio despite the sincerity of its founder. Instead of fostering an intercultural exchange between all facets of society as originally intended, many of Emporio's researchers appear to disseminate propaganda that only benefits *les maîtres*.

In fact, the region's most influential newspaper, *La Jornada*, is far from "fair and balanced." Aranzas's intellectual henchmen appear to contribute regularly to this publication. Total hegemonic domination is within Aranzas's grasp because this propaganda outlet carefully frames public perception and manufactures consent.[19] Articulating how information related to Campos is systemically filtered and distorted to manipulate public opinion thereby reinforcing the dominant socioeconomic power structures, the narrator affirms, "Quelques jours plus tard, *La Jornada* a lancé l'attaque finale contre Campos […] La république idéale du Conseiller y était décrite comme un refuge de vagabonds venus de l'étranger, où avaient cours la drogue, la promiscuité, et les pratiques les plus condamnables de l'ex-mouvement hippie nord-américain. Le conseiller lui-même était peint sous les traits d'un gourou fantastique et dangereux" / 'A few days later, *La Jornada* launched its final assault against Campos [...] The ideal republic of the Counselor was described as a refuge of foreign vagabonds, where drugs, promiscuity, and the most wretched practices of the North American ex-hippie movement ran rampant. The counselor himself was painted with the characteristics of a ridiculous and dangerous guru' (197–198; my trans.). The interlocking and interdependent structures that serve to maintain Aranzas's corporatocracy drive the final nail in the coffin of Jadi's humanistic vision of a better society. Although Anthony Martin had much purer intentions than the ruthless capitalists who only care about generating colossal profits for their shareholders, his people are vilified and expelled.

Yet, despite the predictable collapse of both utopias in *Ourania* which profoundly destabilize the reader, the narrative closes with a slight glimmer of hope. After the inhabitants of Campos have been banished, Daniel's lover Dahlia realizes, "ils n'étaient que des rêveurs immatures et naïfs, des proscrits venus de partout, qui avaient essayé de vivre différemment. Ils étaient une tribu perdue" / 'They were just immature and naive dreamers, outcasts that came from everywhere, that tried to live differently. They were a lost tribe' (208; my trans.). Dahlia's belated epiphany causes her much emotional distress. The narrator Daniel wants to console her but he is unable to share his thoughts concerning "ces gens de Campos (qui) avaient fait le rêve d'un monde meilleur, un peu fou, mais [...] leur rêve n'enlevait rien aux autres" / 'those people from Campos that had the dream of a better world, a little crazy, but their [...] dream didn't take anything away from other people' (214; my trans.). In stark contrast to the narcissistic neoliberal vision for humanity, exemplified by Aldaberto Aranzas, which intentionally exploits human prey at market value, the actualization of Jadi's dream did not harm anyone. The fact that Aranzas is lauded as a reputable member of society and Jadi is objurgated reflects the hollow virtues of consumerist ideology. The bankrupt moral system which is indicative of modern society, as evidenced by the unfathomable recent Supreme Court decision that corporations are people, explains this apparent paradox. If artificial social creations whose sole purpose is to generate revenue are individuals, then it should come as no surprise that the intrinsic value of human beings has been debased to such an extent. The ideology that we are in essence machines whose importance is solely determined by how much money we make for ourselves or for unscrupulous others renders it even more difficult to resist global hegemonic domination.

The end of the narrative clearly articulates Le Clézio's keen awareness that the global village nightmare is getting worse. Daniel Sillitoe returns to Belize twenty-five years after the collapse of Campos to follow the traces of this community. After he realizes that Jadi's dream has completely vanished and no remnants remain, the narrator decides that he will not travel to Mexico given the disturbing indirect information that he receives about the region. As the narrator elucidates, "J'ai bien compris que le people arc-en-ciel n'avait laissé aucun souvenir, que le vent les avait emportés. J'ai décidé de ne pas retourner à la Vallée [...] Les nouvelles que j'en ai reçues de seconde main ne sont pas bonnes. La crise économique, l'émigration, le pouvoir grandissant des banques ont fait leur œuvre. L'Emporio a changé de domicile" / 'I understand all too well that the rainbow people had left no memory, that the wind had carried them away. I decided to not return to the Valley [...] The second-hand news that I had received was not good. The economic crisis, emigration, the increasing power of the banks had left their mark. Emporio had changed locations' (277; my trans.). Recent events that have transpired a few short years after the publication of *Ourania* in 2006 have validated Le Clézio's concerns related to the expanding influence of financial institutions and the consolidation of power. The same anxiety that Le Clézio expresses in his fiction mirrors the frustration of billions of people around the globe concerning government bailouts that to this point have only benefited the top one percent of the social ladder.

Despite the poignant realism identified by numerous critics which is clearly evident throughout the text related to the current state of the modern world, the novel culminates with an affirmation of hope. As Thierry Léger explains, "Cependant, la dernière phrase du roman conclut sur une note positive, une invitation à réaliser notre propre idéal, notre Ourania" / 'However, the last sentence of the novel concludes on a positive note, an invitation to realize our own ideal (society), our Ourania' (271; my trans.). Reaching a similar conclusion as Léger, Alexander Hertich states, "Like the narrator, we learn a great deal over the course of the novel, about globalization, agro-business, Latin American politics and culture [...] Le Clézio's latest novel is highly rewarding. It pushes us to reevaluate our surroundings and question the status quo, forever searching for our own Ourania"[20] (629).

Elucidating the author's nuanced ideas concerning the significance of the notion of utopia for perhaps recreating the global village paradigm, the narrator affirms, "Il n'y a pas de quoi être optimiste. Pourtant ce qui nous unit encore, Dahlia et moi, ce qui nous permet d'espérer, c'est la certitude que le pays d'Ourania a vraiment existé, d'en avoir été les témoins" / 'There is no reason to be optimistic. Nonetheless what still unites Dahlia and I, what allows us to hope is the certainty that the country of Ourania really existed and to have been the witnesses' (283; my trans.). The uphill battle against hegemonic forces that continue to consolidate their power with each passing moment might be doomed to failure, but this regrettable reality does not mean that the ill-fated dreams of admirable humanists like Jadi and Don Thomas are futile. Although both of these utopias were fundamentally flawed from the onset, they still appear to be better models for human civilizations than the neoliberal vision of happiness. Despite affirmations to the contrary, reforming globalization is both possible and essential for the future happiness and prosperity of billions of people across the planet. Perhaps unsuccessful utopian communities, such as Campos, can provide invaluable insights to begin this long awaited process.

## RE-APPROPRIATING TECHNOLOGY TO DEFEND THE OPPRESSED AND DISENFRANCHISED

In addition to the cultural, spiritual, linguistic, and intellectual miscegenation that is emblematic of intercultural exchanges grounded in mutual respect for the contributions of the Other which Le Clézio appears to propose in *Raga* and *Ourania* as a way of resisting hegemonic domination and creating a better global society, subversion presents itself in a rather unlikely form in the short story "Barsa, ou Barsaq." In this recent narrative from the *Histoire du Pied et autres fantaisies* collection, the hopeful *dénouement* perhaps suggests a significant paradigm shift concerning the author's views related to technology. Whereas earlier texts, such as *La Guerre* and *Les Géants* (examined in chapter three), deconstruct the notion of the media as a type of benevolent fourth estate and express serious misgivings that echo Richard Pickard's notion of the global village as a "techno-evil" economic malevolent entity, modern technology plays a crucial role in the happy ending of "Barsa, ou Barsaq." Moreover, given that Willie from *Raga* embraces devices such as computers and telephones while still adhering to a rather pantheistic worldview, perhaps the value and impact of technological advances should be best understood in the same context of cultural *métissage* in Le Clézio's diverse, complex, and ever-evolving *œuvre*.

Published in 2011 by Gallimard, *Histoire du Pied et autres fantaisies* is the writer's latest work to date. The newspaper *L'Express* describes the varied stories that comprise this collection as follows: "Le nouveau recueil de nouvelles de J.M.G Le Clézio, *Histoire du pied et autres fantaisies,* rassemble des portraits de femmes qui refusent le cynisme et la brutalité du monde" / 'The new collection of novellas by J.M.G. Le Clézio, *Histoire du pied et autres fantaisies,* unites portraits of women that refuse the cynicism and the brutality of the world' (n.p.; my trans.). Indeed, an overarching theme that links together several of these independent short stories is a valorization of the efforts of determined women from all around the world to overcome tremendous obstacles in order to liberate themselves and to affirm their right to happiness in the modern world. The aforementioned positive resolution of a crisis is entirely due to the resilience and courage of a Senegalese woman named Fatou who refuses to give up on her lover Mahama and her vision of a life that they will share together. Summarizing the plot of this text, Le Clézio explains in a recent interview with France 5, "Elle va à la recherche de son amant qui est parti et qui a quitté le Sénégal pour se rendre en Espagne pour trouver du travail. Elle veut aller au bout de cette recherche" / 'She leaves in search of her lover who has gone and has left Senegal to go to Spain to look for work. She is determined to persevere in this search to the very end' (n.p.; my trans.). Similar to Ouma and Alexis in *Le Chercheur d'or,* Fatou will attempt to save Mahama from materialistic narcissistic obsessions which threaten to undermine the quality of both of their lives.

Given that she has heard nothing from her lover that left his homeland in search of the good(s) life like numerous immigrant Leclézian protagonists outlined in chapter two, this situation explains why she stares at the ocean every single day hoping to see Mahama somewhere on the horizon. Mahama's affirmation "je vais aller à l'étranger, et quand je reviendrai, je serai riche et je pourrai t'épouser" / 'I am going to go abroad, and when I come back I will be rich and I can marry you' is quite revealing (82; my trans.). Similar to other immigrants from developing societies that leave in search of a better life in the Western world, Mahama is enticed by seductive images of fame and fortune that are often antithetical to the harsh realities that foreigners discover in their host country. Clearly expressing Mahama's naïveté, the narrator elucidates, "Quand il reviendra, il sera riche, il lui dira, je t'aime, tu n'auras plus jamais besoin de travailler" / 'When he comes back, he will be rich, he will tell her, I love you, you no longer will need to work ever again' (94; my trans.). Seduced by what Baudrillard terms the cult of the film star, Mahama is unaware that in the vast majority of modern families, both parents must work full time, given the exorbitant cost of living that continues to exacerbate all across the planet. Indeed, very few individuals will ever have the opportunity to live the life of luxury lauded by the consumerist mainstream media. Yet, this illusory ideology in addition to the neoliberal view of happiness which posits that there is an automatic correlation between happiness and material wealth has consumed the masses. For this reason, Mahama decides to leave Senegal in the hope of procuring a lucrative position in Barcelona, Spain.[21]

Similar to the portraits of anguish examined in chapter two which confirm Bruno Thibault's assertion that the immigrant is the emblematic figure of contemporary exploitation in Le Clézio's fiction, Mahama will not discover a welcoming land that is freely flowing with milk and honey for all. Moreover, the self-proclaimed philosopher Omar, whose role is to convince young Senegalese men that a vast array of highly rewarding opportunities await them in the "promised land," is an important cog in a systematic network that ruthlessly exploits the local population and the acute poverty from which it suffers. As the narrator explains, "Fatou voit parfois le philosophe [...] Fatou le hait, c'est lui qui a convaincu Watson[22] de s'en aller, c'est lui qui a organisé le passage. Fatou est sûre qu'il est un rabatteur [...] qu'il dirige un réseau de passeurs qui envoient les jeunes à la mort" / 'Fatou sometimes goes to see the philosopher [...] Fatou hates him, it's him that convinced Watson to leave, he's the one that prepared his passage. Fatou is sure that he is a supplier [...] that he directs a network of smugglers that send young people to their death' (97; my trans.). In his review of *Histoire du Pied et autres fantaisies* in *Le Magazine Littéraire*, Joseph Macé-Scaron affirms in reference to this unsavory character, "Démasqué dans 'Barsa, ou barsaq,' Omar, le philosophe qui s'est rebaptisé Simon Frantz Fanon, hommage à l'auteur des *Damnés de la terre*, qui rêve et fume sur son rocher et encourage les jeunes à quitter Gorée. C'est un minable rabatteur qui envoie les candidats au départ vers l'enfer" / 'Demasked in "Barsa, ou barsaq," Omar, the philosopher who renamed himself Simon Frantz Fanon, homage to the author of *The Wretched of the Earth*, who dreams and smokes on his rock and encourages young people to leave Gorée. He is a pathetic supplier who sends people wanting to leave straight to hell' (n.p.; my trans.).

Given that she understands the philosopher's true intentions for sending unknowing victims to unscrupulous profiteers who are eager to exploit them for financial gain and since "La vie est longue, monotone sans son ami" / 'Life is long and monotonous without her friend,' Fatou will go to Europe in search of Mahama (96; my trans.). Although the female protagonist has no idea where her lover might be because she never received any correspondence, she is resolute in her conviction that she will somehow eventually find him. Courtesy of her friend le Zambo that she encounters during her search, Fatou uncovers that the vessel which was supposed to transport Mahama and other immigrants to Europe capsized in the ocean. Even though Fatou originally fears that Mahama might have perished during this catastrophic shipwreck that le Zambo discovers using the Internet, she now at least knows where to look for her companion. It should also be noted that the protagonist intuitively interprets le Zambo's virtual discovery as a mystical sign that her quest must continue. As the narrator asserts, "C'était de la magie, un don de Dieu, un miracle. Le Zambo avait reçu une intuition de l'au-delà, une vision, et l'écran de son ordinateur s'était allumé sur la page du naufrage" / 'It was magic, a gift from God, a miracle. Le Zambo had received an intuition from the great beyond, a vision, and the screen of his computer had lit up to the page of the shipwreck' (116; my trans.). Whereas the experience that Fatou describes would be interpreted by most people in modern society as a rather banal event rendered possible by mega–search engines such as Google, Fatou appears to believe that certain mystical forces thrust her into contact with le Zambo thereby making this occurrence possible.

Regardless of how Fatou incorporates the role of technology into her existing worldview, it is evident that the Internet quite literally saves the day for both the female protagonist and Mahama. Whereas the *maîtres du langage* and their powerful media outlet Varioum to which the author refers in *Les Géants* are cast in a very negative light given that they represent the hegemonic forces that control the dissemination of (mis)information in a concerted effort to consolidate their socioeconomic dominance, Le Clézio appears to have adopted a more moderate point of view concerning technology in his recent fiction. This more nuanced and balanced conception of industrial advances is quite striking given the deep concerns that the author articulates related to technology being in the service of the "happy few" in works such as *La Guerre* and *Les Géants*. Highlighting the systematic exploitation of the indoctrinated masses by the corporate elite rendered possible by the myriad of powerful devices at their disposal, Stephen Smith affirms, "*La Guerre* pictures humanity as subdued and exploited by technology and the language of technology, the result of which is an inevitable muteness" (54).[23] Although Le Clézio is hardly what Tatic terms a "technological optimist" that naively affirms that "technology can resolve all problems," the writer clearly expresses his aspirations that specifically the Internet might one day play a crucial role in reshaping the global village (6).

This noticeable paradigm shift in Le Clézio's complex *œuvre* which seems to valorize the utility of certain devices in terms of improving the quality of one's life and allowing the modern subject to maximize his or her happiness is rather perplexing initially. However, recent events such as the Orange Revolution in the Ukraine and the undeniable impact of social media networks such as Facebook that successfully organized resistance to totalitarian regimes have perhaps compelled the author to refine his views concerning technology. Le Clézio's latest fiction appears to espouse what the ecocritic Robert Spencer calls a Marxist perspective of technology. As Spencer elucidates in the context of environmental ethics, "Marxists have maintained [. . .] the environment is not imperiled by technology but by capitalism and by capitalism's deployment of technology in the service of exploitation" (34). Although Spencer's essay specifically explores how powerful, hegemonic forces have used certain inventions to expand their worldwide domination of natural resources, his principles are applicable to the role of technology in society as a whole. In fact, the reader can logically surmise that Le Clézio implies in "Barsa, ou Barsaq" that the Internet has tremendous potential to be a prevailing force for good if everyone is given an equal voice in this cyber environment. In other words, if common people are in control of this innovative virtual tool and not corporations whose only motivations are monetary, then perhaps the Internet can have a vital part in the process of reconstructing a global village that no longer disenfranchises billions of people across the planet.

In addition to the author's recent works which unequivocally suggest a slight evolution concerning the purpose and utility of technology for the modern subject, Le Clézio's Nobel acceptance speech "Dans la forêt des paradoxes" / 'In the Forest of Paradoxes' provides further evidence that a visible shift has begun to take place. In an affirmation noted by numerous critics, the laureate affirmed from the highest literary stage, "La mondialisation n'est pas une mauvaise chose en soi. La communication rend le progrès plus rapide [...] Peut-être que la généralisation de l'information rendra les conflits plus difficiles. S'il y avait eu internet, il est possible que Hitler n'eût pas réussi son complot mafieux—le ridicule l'eût peut-être empêché de naître" / 'Globalization is not a bad thing in and of itself. Communication has accelerated progress [...] Perhaps the generalization of information will help to forestall conflicts. Who knows, if the Internet had existed at the time, perhaps Hitler's criminal plot would not have succeeded—ridicule might have prevented it from ever seeing the light of day'[24] (80). Indeed, this personal and philosophical conviction sheds light on the hopeful amorous reunion at the end of "Barsa, ou Barsaq."

Moreover, as Mark Andrews notes in the essay *Raga* as well, for Le Clézio's latest protagonists, reconciliation with globalization now seems to be possible. In his speech "In the Forest of Paradoxes," Le Clézio clearly and passionately articulates a humanistic point of view that is similar to that of Joseph Stiglitz. As outlined in the preceding chapters, Le Clézio is cognizant that the current situation is anything but a dream for the vast majority of the earth's human and nonhuman population, but he also steadfastly expresses a sincere hope that globalization with a more humane face can be achieved. Echoing similar sentiments, Stiglitz declares, "While globalization poses challenges, it also offers powerful opportunities for the higher education community to play a key role in shaping and reshaping the future" (649). Additionally, Stiglitz also highlights in both *Globalization and Its Discontents* and *Making Globalization Work* that all civilizations need to have an equal voice in important political decisions that affect everyone in an interconnected and interdependent world. Given that numerous critics have noted that this effort to defend the marginalized has been a salient aspect of Le Clézio's fiction from 1963 to the present, it comes as no surprise that Le Clézio contends that the neoliberal global village must be drastically reformed in order for it to actualize its lofty goals of a better world for all.

Despite his cautious optimism that one day technology could help lead the way to resist global, hegemonic domination and to demand social justice and equality, the 2008 Nobel Laureate in Literature realizes that certain issues must be resolved in order for this vision to come to fruition. Although the Internet played a major role in the aforementioned geopolitical conflicts, will the ever-widening gap between the haves and have-nots limit its philanthropic potential? As the author ponders in his acceptance speech, "Alors ne sommes-nous pas en train de créer une nouvelle élite, de tracer une nouvelle ligne qui divise le monde entre ceux qui ont accès à la communication et au savoir et ceux qui restent exclus du partage?" / 'Are we not, therefore, in the process of creating a new elite, of drawing a new line to divide the world between those who have access to communication and knowledge, and those who are left out?' (80). These disconcerting questions are emblematic of the dire realities underscored in chapter one related to the global distribution of wealth. Given that millions of people in the most affluent country in the world, the United States, do not even have regular access to the Internet, this is a serious concern that needs to be addressed to create the promised "win-win" scenarios lauded by euphoric supporters of neoliberalism. Modern innovations have a lot to offer humanity, but not if they are only available to those that possess the necessary economic means to take advantage of their benefits.[25]

## CONCLUSION

Le Clézio's latest fiction in addition to his recent epitexts underscore that it is imperative to explore alternatives to the current situation. In *Raga*, the author portrays the efforts of indigenous communities to reconstruct their splintered identities in the wake of centuries of exploitation including slavery, blackbirding, colonialism, and neoliberalism. On their own terms, Melanesian and Polynesian peoples have found a way to create rich and diverse hybrid cultures that maintain crucial aspects of their traditional way of life while simultaneously benefiting from modernity. Furthermore, this linguistic, cultural, and intellectual miscegenation has become a powerful form of resistance for many primordial civilizations. In *Ourania*, the reader witnesses the inevitable collapse of two failed utopias that appear to have no place in modern society because of the shallow virtues of consumerism that have intoxicated the modern subject with empty promises. However, these flawed utopian communities seem to offer better models for humanity despite their numerous faults. For this reason, perhaps an invaluable first step in reshaping the global village should involve re-examining unsuccessful attempts at creating terrestrial paradises. In addition to embracing intercultural and mental *creoleness* and re-envisioning what a utopia might encompass, Le Clézio proposes in "Barsa, ou Barsaq" that technology can and should be reappropriated to liberate oppressed peoples caught in the snares of the neoliberal nightmare. In the face of seemingly insurmountable exploitation by the "happy few" that continues to intensify, Le Clézio encourages each of us to confront reality stoically while daring to dream of a better world for all.

## NOTES

1. On page 9 of the text, Le Clézio indicates that the word "Raga" to which the title alludes refers to Pentecost Island in the *apma* language.

2. This importance nuance will be developed in a later section of this chapter in reference to how debates related to *la négritude* and *la créolité* reflect attempts at reconstructing traditional cultural identities after the forceful imposition of another allegedly superior socioeconomic paradigm and way of life.

3. It should be noted that Le Clézio's extended stay with the indigenous cultures that inspired this Amerindian text was of a much longer duration than his travels in Oceania.

4. In *Raga,* Le Clézio offers the following historical explanation of blackbirding: "le *blackbirding* s'est développé au moment où la fin de la guerre de Sécession a marqué l'arrêt de la traite avec l'Afrique [...] Paradoxalement, ce furent la campagne abolitionniste aux Etats-Unis et la guerre civile qui déclenchèrent le trafic humain dans le Pacifique" / 'Blackbirding developed at the moment when the War of Succession marked the end of trading with Africa [...] Paradoxically, it was the abolitionist campaign in the United States and the Civil War that triggered human trafficking in the Pacific' (49; my trans.). Mark Andrews further elucidates, "Abolir l'esclavage en Amérique du Nord a eu pour conséquence de déplacer la culture esclavagiste des plantations aux antipodes. Le prix du coton et le prix du sucre étant montés en flèche par suite de l'effondrement de la production aux États-Unis, il fallait développer d'autres sources" / 'Abolishing slavery in North America consequently displaced the slavery culture of the plantations to the antipodes. The price of cotton and the price of sugar rose drastically because of the breakdown of production in the United States, other sources had to be developed' (247; my trans.).

5. In this vein, the following exchange between Jacqueline Dutton and Le Clézio is quite revealing: "Serait-il possible qu'au début, vous n'étiez pas conscient des possibilités d'imaginer une meilleure société, donc vous avez cherché à créer une meilleure société ailleurs, ou serait-il plutôt qu'au fur et à mesure que vous vous êtes éloigné de l'Europe, vous êtes devenu capable d'imaginer une meilleure société? (LC) Je crois que c'est plutôt cette deuxième hypothèse" / 'Would it be possible that in the beginning, you were not conscious of the possibilities of creating a better society, so you looked for a better society elsewhere, or would it be better to say that the further that you got away from Europe, you became capable of imagining a better society? (LC) I think that the second hypothesis is more appropriate' (284; my trans.).

6. See note from the previous chapter concerning these unfounded criticisms/oversimplifications of Le Clézio's works.

7. The author's fascination with various failed attempts at creating utopian societies will be analyzed in relation to *Ourania* in a later section of this chapter.

8. Pages 92–95 of the text offer a detailed explanation of the devastation that this epidemic has caused.

9. For a comprehensive investigation of Pieterse and his theory of cultural hybridity that far exceeds the scope of this specific study, see Pieterse, Jan, *Global Mélange: Globalization and Culture,* Rowman & Littlefield, 2003. It should also be noted that Katharine Harrington applies the concept of a rhizome to Le Clézio's fiction in her discussion of nomadism. See Harrington, Katharine, "Writing between Borders: Nomadism and Its Implications for Contemporary French and Francophone Literature," *Contemporary French and Francophone Studies* 10 (2): 117–125.

10. The co-founder of the "fondation pour l'interculturel et la paix" with whom Le Clézio created this humanitarian organization, Issa Asgarally, vehemently attacks the Manichaean logic that is indicative of Huntington's distinct cultural categories in his essay *L'Interculturel ou la guerre.* See pages 53–60. As evidenced by his decision to contribute a preface to Asgarally's work, Le Clézio seems to have adopted a similar point of view.

11. In this same speech, Le Clézio asserts that French people should not shun creole or poke fun at its alleged imperfections, but rather thank creole for its contributions and for ensuring that French/Francophone culture continues to thrive all across the planet.

12. Le Clézio's ardent defense of divergent creoles is part of his larger concerns related to threatened languages all around the world that are on the brink of disappearing because of the nefarious effects of globalization. In this context, Claude Cavallero states, "Cette sensibilité à la problématique des langues se mêle dans les premiers ouvrages aux défis formels que se pose l'écrivain face aux excès d'une modernité qui l'exacerbe" / 'This sensibility concerning the language problem is mingled with formal challenges that the writer poses related to the excesses of modernity that has exacerbated it' (*Le Clézio, Témoin du monde* 142; my trans.).

13. This noticeable shift will be systematically explored in a later section of this chapter.

14. From the standpoint of literary devices, the relationship between these two texts should be developed further by the literary community. However, this investigation surpasses the scope of the present study.

15. For more information concerning the "Fondation pour l'interculturel et la paix," visit the official website: www.fipinterculturel.com. Additionally, Keith Moser's recent article in *Les Cahiers Le Clézio* (Vol. 3–4: 41–46) chronicles the launching of this organization.

16. Perhaps a parallel even exists between the Amish rite of passage *rumspringa* and the voyage during which Daniel meets Raphaël.

17. It is not by chance that the leader of this group "Jadi" or Anthony Martin is a Choctaw Indian.

18. For a more comprehensive discussion related to the paradoxes and nuances of Le Clézio's linguistic convictions, see Moser, Keith, "Le paradoxe du langage ou le 'terrible privilège' de l'humanité selon J.M.G. Le Clézio," *J.M.G. Le Clézio dans la forêt des paradoxes*, eds. Bruno Thibault and Keith Moser, Paris: L'Harmattan, Collection Études transnationales, francophones et comparés, 2012.

19. See the discussion in chapter three related to Herman and Chomsky's Propaganda Model (PM).

20. Although Hertich clearly appreciates *Ourania* as a whole, he does refer to the work using the pejorative terms "pedantic" and "polemical." Given the inherent word limitations of a book review, he unfortunately is not able to develop this minor criticism much further.

21. It becomes evident later in the narrative that the "Barsa" or "Barsaq" to which the title alludes is Barcelona.

22. On the first page of the narrative, the author indicates that Fatou and Watson have anglicized their names to appeal to tourists. As the narrator explains, "Fatou se fait appeler Vanessa, comme Mahama se fait appeler Watson. Ils se sont choisis ces prénoms pour les touristes" / 'Fatou calls herself Vanessa, like Mahama calls himself Watson. They chose these first names for themselves for tourists' (77; my trans.).

23. In a similar vein, Nadine Dormoy and Liliane Lazar assert, "Refusant la société technologique des grands ensembles, des aéroports, des autoroutes et des supermarchés, Le Clézio cherche refuge dans les civilisations anciennes et disparues" / 'Rejecting the technological society of shopping centers, airports, interstates and supermarkets, Le Clézio seeks refuge in ancient civilizations and in those that have already vanished' (*A Chacun sa France* 121; my trans.)

24. This English translation in addition to all of the subsequent ones is taken directly from the www.Nobelprize.org website.

25. In addition to his Nobel speech, the author also briefly outlines the benefits of modern technology including the Internet in an interview entitled "The World Has No Center," *NPQ* (Summer 2009): 78–81.

# Conclusion

The disquieting anxiety expressed by J.M.G. Le Clézio in his fiction concerning the actualization of the global village nightmare is a reflection of the author's astute observations related to the current state of the modern world. Le Clézio reminds the reader that it is only after directly confronting the cold hard facts which dismiss neoliberal fallacies and simplistic consumerist ideology that global society can begin the arduous process of picking up the shattered pieces of McLuhan's failed vision for humanity. The selected title for the English translation of *La Ronde et Autres Faits Divers* (*The Round and Other Cold Hard Facts*) is quite revealing. Indeed, the realistic portraits of sheer anguish depicted in narratives, such as "David" and "Ô voleur, voleur, quelle vie est la tienne?" clearly negate the misguided and unfounded euphoria associated with the neoliberal global village concept. Moreover, these somber slices of quotidian reality also counterpoint simplistic interpretations of Le Clézio's complex and ever-evolving prose.

In *J.M.G. Le Clézio et la Métaphore Exotique*, Bruno Thibault notes in his concluding remarks, "Le Clézio souligne l'esprit de dissidence qui caractérise l'écrivain contemporain" / 'Le Clézio underscores the spirit of dissidence that epitomizes the contemporary writer' (228; my trans.). Given his rather humble vision of the artist in society,[1] the author does not claim to possess definitive answers for the myriad of grave issues that plague the modern subject on a daily basis in a world that is more interconnected and interdependent than at any other point in the history of human civilization. However, Le Clézio's extremely diverse *oeuvre* does pose a plethora of disconcerting questions concerning the ongoing processes of globalization which echo the concerns of many other contemporary artists and thinkers. Additionally, organized resistance to globalization as it is currently being managed by organizations like the World Bank and the IMF is becoming more widespread on a worldwide scale given the dire inequalities that are emblematic of the modern world, as evidenced by what transpired in Seattle in November 1999 in addition to various "Occupy" movements. The rending pain of numerous LeClézian protagonists, which are deliberately exploited at market value, should be understood in this context. Le Clézio's fiction reveals the unfortunate truth that manipulative, albeit alluring ideology, which announced the dawning of a new era for both human prosperity and cultural relations has only served to solidify the hegemonic domination of the "happy few."

This interdisciplinary investigation of an evaporated dream in the context of Le Clézio's narratives has also clearly elucidated that much of the author's work could be described as an attempt to explain all facets of the human experience including what existentialists call the human condition. In fact, the aforementioned philosophical universality of texts, such as *Terra Amata* and *L'Inconnu sur la terre*, is rather transparent. In this vein, perhaps more than any other contemporary writer, Le Clézio's narratives urge the reader to reflect upon what it means to be a sensuous, ephemeral being thrown into the chaos of existence in a planetary landscape that is constantly being transformed in the name of progress.

Furthermore, this interdisciplinary study intentionally endeavors to transcend cancerous, academic insularity in an effort to reconnect the disciplines and to foster a meaningful dialogue related to the dominant hegemon of our time. Specifically, the writer's deep ecological sensibilities, which are indicative of an acute awareness of the existential ramifications of recent scientific discoveries outlined in both chapter one and four, beckon the entire higher education community to unite in order to combat the scientifically erroneous genesis myth which has placed every living creature on this earth in serious peril. Moreover, Le Clézio's ecophilosophical essay *L'Extase Matérielle* exposes false and misleading dualities, in addition to homocentric notions such as Descartes's *bêtemachine* theory, as illusory products of the human imagination. In an age defined by an exacerbating ecological calamity, the humanities are more essential than ever for articulating a more ecocentric worldview which is required to inhabit this earth more sustainably and to respect both the human and cosmic Other. Although many people question the importance of literature in a technocratic, globalized world, the voices of inquisitive and well-informed writers must be heard now more than ever. As Njemanze Ugochi affirms, "the study of literature has inestimable values attached to it while globalization is the symbol of our age" (49).

Given that many contemporary scientists, despite their great erudition and monumental achievements, have failed miserably to articulate the urgent paradigm shift that is essential for the future vitality of all the earth's inhabitants, disciplines which emphasize critical thinking skills must fill this void. The "petitesse" to which Le Clézio's narratives often refer is perhaps the only viable remedy that can save humanity from the voracious, egotistical appetite of the neoliberal global village that threatens to eliminate everyone and everything in its path. Highlighting the importance of cosmic humility, the narrator of *L'Inconnu sur la terre* asserts, "Il faut devenir soi-même petit, si petit qu'on est à l'ombre d'une herbe et d'une fleur, et vivre au soleil, dans la poussière, sous le vent, dans une seule journée longue comme une saison" / 'One has to become small himself, so small that he is in the shadow of an herb and a flower and he must live in the sun, in the dust, underneath the wind, in a single long day that is like a season' (15; my trans.). This apparent biotic egalitarianism, explored in various texts in chapter four, clearly expresses a much healthier and more sustainable worldview than the thoroughly debunked genesis myth whose disproven ideology continues to justify relentless exploitation of finite natural resources. Moreover, the very future of the planet and every sentient and nonsentient being in it could very well depend on how far our thought systems evolve in order to reflect what modern science has discovered.

Yet, Le Clézio's recent texts such as *Raga* and *Ourania* also provide a faint glimmer of hope which affirms that despite the recurring nightmare that has imposed itself all across the planet, resistance is indeed possible. Although the probability that those who fight back will ultimately fail becomes stronger with each passing day given that the hegemonic forces outlined in chapter three continue to solidify their global governance, alternatives exist and they should be explored. The time has come to replace McLuhan's naïve vision and the romantic universalism that it entails with another dream that could perhaps create a more egalitarian and just world for all. Nuancing his earlier views concerning technology and globalization itself, the author's latest works attempt to re-conceptualize what such a society could encompass and the values that it would reflect. A noticeable shift has occurred in Le Clézio's fiction given that modernity appeared to have nothing to offer the author's earlier protagonists. Espousing a more moderate position concerning globalization itself, the writer's latest narratives seem to propose that intercultural dialogue in addition to cultural, linguistic, spiritual, and intellectual *métissage* represent invaluable points of departure for envisioning a better world. For Le Clézio, every culture despite its glaring imperfections has something to contribute that could potentially create a better socioeconomic model for the majority of the earth's inhabitants.

Similar to other modern artists that have decried injustice in all of its different forms, Le Clézio stoically urges the reader to dream in the face of seemingly insurmountable adversity. Even if victory might be out of reach, this unpleasant reality does not mean that the uphill struggle is in vain. Despite the efforts of transnational corporations to expand their global dominance and to eradicate all obstacles in their way, as underscored by the successful attempts of the integrated political and social elite to curtail the humanistic ambitions of Campos and Emporio in *Ourania,* too much is at stake to abandon the collective fight against systematic exploitation, oppression, and tyranny. As odd as it might sound on the surface, perhaps the first step is to dare to *imagine* what globalization with a more humane face would entail to echo the words of the legendary British songwriter John Lennon.[2] Although this study has clearly established that Le Clézio's balanced worldview reflects the disconcerting gravity of the sinister realities that are antithetical to the ideology espoused by the supporters of the neoliberal global village, the author's aspirations for the future parallel those of artistic humanists such as Lennon.

It should be noted that the writer expresses his admiration for the "ex-hippies" who attempted to create a terrestrial paradise in *Ourania*. This isolated enclave living on the periphery of society hardly realized an actual utopia, but these naïve dreamers did appear to build a much better society than the neoliberal model that has been exported all across the planet. Similar to other artists which refuse to deny harsh realities that negate the elation still associated with McLuhan's vision, Le Clézio's fiction endeavors to eradicate all of the artificial geopolitical, sociocultural, linguistic, spiritual, and cosmic borders that continue to polarize contemporary society at the beginning of a new millennium. For both Le Clézio and Lennon, uniting humanity means deconstructing the neoliberal definition of happiness and the incessant images of fame and fortune that incessantly bombard the modern subject. For this reason, Le Clézio's diverse protagonists, such as Alexis, Lalla, and Laïla discover that the hollow virtues of consumerism are a poor substitute that cannot replace fundamental human needs, such as a sense of belonging and existential meaning. Moreover, the author's characters often realize that these enticing materialistic snares have been created and are carefully managed by those at the top of the social ladder that are unwilling to share the fruits of their prosperity with others.

Despite what the Supreme Court and other influential organizations affirm, we must constantly be reminded that human beings are not empty machines whose only value is purely instrumental or monetary. Given this vile debasement of humanity which equates the worth of a sentient being to that of an artificial entity whose only purpose is to generate revenue for the *maîtres* explored in chapter three, the study of literature and the humanities in a globalized world is more vital than ever. The undeniable severity of the current situation compels us to put basic necessities above the narcissistic desires of the "happy few." Examining Le Clézio's inexhaustible *oeuvre* summons the reader to reject exploitative and potentially even lethal anthropocentric and consumeristic ideology. By leaving McLuhan's outdated and simplistic vision in the ashes of the past, perhaps a new subversive dream might one day be born that could save every living organism on this planet and restore human dignity.

## NOTES

1. Keith Moser systematically explores this subject in an article entitled "The Decentered Humanism and Cosmic Engagement of J.M.G. Le Clézio: Posing Questions in an Age of Suspicion," *Sprachkunst* 42 (1).

2. Numerous critics, such as Marina Salles (*Le Clézio: notre contemporain*), have explored musicality in all of its divergent forms in Le Clézio's fiction. In addition to the music of traditional societies and the rhythmic cycles of the cosmos itself that are often present in the author's narratives, Le Clézio's works contain a myriad of references to popular culture as well. The song "Nowhere Man," written by John Lennon and recorded by the Beatles, appears in *Voyages de l'autre côté*. Moreover, the Beatles, given their message of peace, harmony, and social cohesion, are listed as an example of what the aforementioned *Fondation pour l'interculturel et la paix* promotes as "musique sans frontières" / 'music without borders.' (www.fipinterculturel.com/pdf/catalogue_fip.pdf).

# Postscript: "Doubting Must Be the Beginning of Wisdom"

## *A Conversation with J.M.G. Le Clézio, Albuquerque, New Mexico, July 2011*

**KM:** First of all, I would like to thank you for taking time out of your busy schedule to meet with me today to discuss the importance of intercultural values in the era of globalization in addition to other issues associated with the modern world. I would also like to express my sincere gratitude for allowing me to live interculturality firsthand from Mauritius last summer during the launching of the *Fondation pour l'interculturel et la paix*. Before we begin to delve into this complex and nuanced subject is there anything that you would like to convey to the reader concerning the foundation that you created with the renowned intercultural theorist Issa Asgarally?

**JMGLC:** Well, it has been a concern for me for many years because being from Mauritius. . . I mean my family being from Mauritius, I know the value and necessity of intercultural relations. Mauritius being a very small place if people don't get together and they are not able to live together then there would be a bloody war there, people would keep trying to subdue others. It has been like that for some time, I myself am from the colonial, the so-called French-Mauritians who descend from slave owners and landowners who were growing sugar cane in the plantation system. Of course, those people were not multicultural; they were not cultural at all, their only culture was cultivating sugar cane. So, I think that I was born with the germ of criticizing that society. It's probably something like what Faulkner expresses in his work that I was born in such a society and I must acknowledge it. I cannot deny it. But then I was sensitive to all of the faults of this society. This led me naturally to doubt the superiority of a culture over another. I am (currently) reading Rousseau's essay concerning the origin of inequality. It is a strong text that is still just as alive today. Rousseau says that there are two types of inequality: the one which is natural, some people are stronger, more intelligent, or more agile than others but you can say that the leaders have naturally inherited a superiority (complex). It's society that gives them that (feeling of) superiority. They have to criticize it and they have to acknowledge the fact that it's not natural it is something that has been constructed by the social system. So, from a very early age I was sensitive to those questions. When Dr. Asgarally and Mrs. Sarojini were thinking of taking action, I think that we all agreed together that we should do something that would be more official. This is the reason why this foundation was created from this encounter.

**KM:** What can we do to support this initiative?

**JMGLC:** The interesting thing is that before it existed no one would have said that it was necessary but now that it exists some people say "Well, it's not a bad thing that it exists." For instance, in Mauritius, there is a law that businesses must give a certain percentage of their revenue to cultural activities. This initiative was perfect for that. The law was just created two years ago and it was about the same time that the foundation was created. This was a good opportunity and the foundation has also received some benefits from these businesses.

**KM:** Some intercultural theorists have suggested that perhaps humility is the most important intercultural virtue of all in terms of creating a more just and empathetic global village and you mentioned the superiority complex. What is your take on the importance of both literature and interculturality in helping one appreciate the Other and what he/she has to offer?

**JMGLC:** Well, this question of the global village that you mentioned is a question which has yet to be solved. We have no idea what it means. What is the meaning of that (expression)? In fact, we see more and more that this village is not able to be found. When I mention interculturality to French intellectuals, there is a slight sarcasm. They say "Don't you think that now interculturality is over and we have to talk about something called transculturality?" I try to understand what they mean by transculturality. They mean that culture has no definitive boundaries. Culture is always on the move . . . In fact, if all cultures are always on the move and I strongly believe this we have not solved the question that some cultures can't express themselves. They don't have any echo in globalization or in the global village. In fact, the global village looks more like a private sector where some people have all of the power to express themselves and some people are outside of that private space and they have no access to freedom of expression.

**KM:** You mentioned *Discourse on the Origin and Foundations of Inequality among Men* by Jean-Jacques Rousseau. Are there any other books that have had this transformative effect upon you?

**JMGLC:** Well, yes, a lot of books. The fact that you can read, you can have access to other languages and expressions through translations it gives you the idea that literature, thought, or philosophy has no nationality. It doesn't belong to a nation. It belongs to something much more general. This can provide the feeling that we are communicating one with the other. I had that feeling when I was reading Cervantes. Because I read this in French in a very old book that my parents had on their bookshelves. This very old book I read it as if it were written in French. One day I discovered that Cervantes was not French. [laughs] So I think that literature is a good terrain to realize we communicate (with each other) and that the essence of communication is between people and cultures. Of course, some books are easier to read than others. Translation offers very good access to interculturality. It's the reason why in Mauritius I thought that while giving books (to disadvantaged children) I brought translations of my books and other types of books in Russian, Chinese, and Japanese so that the children could see and put books from other languages in their hands. Even if they don't understand it, they might be interested in learning Arabic or Russian just because they saw those books. That is how I feel.

**KM:** In spite of the undeniable diversity of your literary repertoire from 1963 to the present, it seems as if certain elements have remained constant. For example, in both *L'Extase Matérielle* and *Terra Amata,* you underscore the importance of cosmic or ecological humility. Why is this form of humility so important?

**JMGLC:** Probably, it would be something like the concept of global responsibility and this might create the idea that literature belongs to this general feeling that we have not for nature but for life (itself). Personally, I have always been interested in this type of literature that not only deals with human beings, literature which gives a role to what we call nature or what Rousseau would have called nature. This is the real world, the world for dogs, the world for trees, how do they live? We are sharing the same world but sometimes literature does not express this. *L'Extase Matérielle* was an attempt to realize what is commonly called an out of body experience, getting out of your body. It's a basic experience that we have to go through. I was reading the ROTC manual; strangely enough the teaching of the ROTC is that the future soldier has to experience an out of body experience. For instance, he has to question himself about what rain means for other forms of life, for other cultures. This is very interesting to see that someone with a gun might suddenly doubt and reflect upon what is the meaning of rain. It was giving a basis for comparison that might seem naïve, but rainfall for human beings on the east coast could mean a lot of trouble but for animals or people living in the desert is a benefit. Suddenly, the man who has a rifle reflects about this. Water is so important where I am. I cannot have a weak reaction. I must first understand the people and their way of life in the terrain where I am. I found this very interesting. This was written during the hottest moment of the war in Iraq, and Iraq is a place where it does not rain a lot. I found it interesting that for the ROTC there was a need to reflect on the role of the soldier and trying to understand what something could mean for someone else or for another way of life. Or, maybe another species. Who knows? Suddenly, the soldier reflects about a camel, a horse, or that bird which seems so serious and has his own water. So, he reflects about this and he doubts, and doubting must be the beginning of wisdom.

**KM:** I would have never expected those elements in the ROTC manual.

**JMGLC:** Yeah, I was amazed to see that. In fact, interculturality is one of the elements that the American soldier has to deal with. But it is the American soldier. I am not sure that this would be good for the French Legionnaire. [laughs]

**KM:** During your speech at Mississippi State University, you used the term the "genesis myth" in the context of the relationship between humanity and the rest of the material universe. How would you define the genesis myth and how would you describe its past, present, and future ramifications for both humankind and other life forms?

**JMGLC:** Hmmm. . . . Why do you mention this?

**KM:** Because some of my current research relates to the genesis myth. It seems to be very similar to a term that I found by Simon Estok called ecophobia or that human beings have the biblical imperative to control everything that lives. I found it very similar to this notion. Is this what you were trying to convey?

**JMGLC:** I don't think that in my mind it has anything to do with biblical teachings. It more likely deals with the utilitarian philosophy of humanism which claims that human beings should only be interested with what deals with their own history. I have some doubts like the ROTC soldier. I have doubts in the face of such affirmations. Genesis has not always been expressed in the same way for some people. For instance, here the world preexisted the human being which emerged from the earth, they (human beings) were like the seas, they came from the earth. This for me has meaning because in the face of such secrets and the only way that we can deal with that is to have an approach which would be close to that which we feel for nature and the reality that we come from nature. Emerging from the earth is more convenient (of an explanation) for me than anything else. It's funny that you ask that question because I am writing a short story now which is exactly related to that theme. Apart from the human world how can life be defined if it is not by humans (themselves)? How can we define this (life)? If we do not create the words or if you use words with the intention to obtain another type of knowledge than what we have by language, how can we express that? One of the best writers in Mauritius is named Abhimanyu Anat. Did you meet him?

**KM:** No, I did not meet him unfortunately.

**JMGLC:** He is a good novelist that has written several novels. One of them is translated into English and French. He writes in the Hindi language. He does not write in English or in French. Once he was telling me that he was trying to write about a person or a human being that does not yet exist. This (notion) to me could be related to the genesis myth because the myth is about something which preexisted human beings. Genesis preexisted human beings. After all, we are here. We are like animals; we need fresh air. We need water when we are thirsty, but we do not question those things and all of these necessities. So, we are just products of the genesis but we are not able to know what it could be.

**KM:** You created an excellent segue way into my next question. Some intercultural narratives not only foster interspecies empathy and compassion, but they also promote biotic egalitarianism or the notion that every organism, human and otherwise, possesses the same intrinsic right to inhabit this planet. I would contend that many of your works support the basic principles of biotic egalitarianism, but how far do you think that the human family is willing or even capable of shifting our current homocentric worldview to a more ecocentric one?

**JMGLC:** I have no answer to that question. Maybe you have one. [laughs]

**KM:** [laughs] I definitely do not.

**JMGLC:** But definitely literature deals with that. It is one of the ways of dealing with that. Literature, it is not science, ecology, or a political system. It's just an approximation of the instinctive questions that you ask yourself. I mean after all a human being lives through all stages of life until his maturity. I am always amazed when I look at children that look especially like animals. They are very close to animals. The smaller, the younger they are the closer they are (to animals). They have immediate reactions. They shriek with a very strong powerful voice. They can immediately go from one emotion to another, from wrath to sorrow, and from sorrow to joy, it's so quick that you don't understand it. Literature has something to do with this apprenticeship.

**KM:** You mentioned humanism a few moments ago, so I would like to ask a question related to humanism. Renaissance humanism defined the notion of progress in a certain fashion. What does social progress mean to you? How would you define this concept?

**JMGLC:** The word is multifaceted. The word can mean progress in techniques and there are ways of producing fire which are easier than knocking two flints together. But there are also ways of getting rid of diseases of maintaining health and after all life has been defined as the "common forces that fight against death." So, evidently progress is in favor of those common forces, fighting against death. After that, if we want to define what progress could mean then it is much more complicated. Lévi-Strauss provided evidence that for some people in so-called primitive societies, they manage to keep a balance, old and necessary balances, balances between the human being and nature, balance inside of themselves, balance between war and peace, and even balance in not being too numerous or populated in one place. Those societies offer another face of progress because all of those balances they were not invented naturally. They had to reflect upon this. They constructed societies that were able to give a certain type of happiness to their people. But, of course, when you get inside of those societies, you realize that those societies are not perfect. They have injustice. The women are very often badly treated. You probably have the same amount of rapists, criminals, and crooks anywhere. But still, the balance exists and I have seen examples of this balance but these examples are true for a very small or limited society. In such a society as complex as the capitalistic world or the modern world it could not be done so easily, so we have to invent another meaning to progress.

**KM:** How would you describe the role of interculturality in a consumer society or republic?

**JMGLC:** I think that everything is linked in that field. Interculturality, which means the relationship between human beings as elements of a culture, but it also means the relationship to, in my opinion, the relationship with human beings to their world, to other life forms, to what we call nature. It is always very difficult to define nature, but cities are also part of nature. So, that relationship between the individual and the group and those elements of nature from which they are sustained and where they live. So, I definitely think that there is a connection. I am not myself a fanatic of the ecological movements. I do not belong to any political party or any association of militants in that area. But, I am always in favor of anything that favors a better understanding of the human world. I am interested only in ecology if it deals with human beings. After all, we know that human beings will not last very long but the earth will still live and probably some forms of life will survive. I am interested in that only because it is a recipe for survival for human beings. After all, it is an economy of life. This means that we have to care about everything that we do because we have to think about future generations or at least about our own survival. We are fragile and we might as well disappear. I am not sure that the earth will suffer so much from our disappearance. [laughs]

**KM:** Do you think that it is important to think of these ecological questions in terms of self-preservation for the human species?

**JMGLC:** Yes, exactly! Definitely! But human beings are concerned about other forms of life not so much because of something inherent in them but being on top of the food chain they have to be careful about everything. This is a form of responsibility. It's strange because when you read the bible you find those elements which say that the world has been given to human beings so that they can be nourished and take advantage of creation. In fact, the bible is an interesting book, but also other cultures favor that balance (as well). I always remember when I was in the Panama forest. I went with some Indians who were going to take a short trip. One man who was not an American Indian had a rifle and we ran into a wild turkey so the man with a rifle was aiming and one of the American Indians said, "No, we are traveling for three days what are we going to do with that turkey? We will kill the turkey when we come back." It was a good idea. [laughs] We didn't manage to find it again, but it was still a good reaction. I think that we need to learn about these simple behaviors.

**KM:** Actually, I find the bible to be a very nuanced text related to the debate between dominion and stewardship that you mentioned.

**JMGLC:** Yes, definitely. Because it is a book which is linked to a society of poverty which was the case at the time and this was revealed to the world. We can really find lessons in that, but sometimes I meet opposition to that from certain intellectuals who say that "No, nature is not at the service of human beings but to the contrary human beings are subservient to nature." But in fact, this is the wrong question. Both things are true. Human beings are at the service of nature because nature preserves them so it is a question of giving and getting back.

**KM:** How do you think that consumerism affects traditional values?

**JMGLC:** Well, as we were saying, the bible is a traditional book. In modern society, the modern world is totally anti-biblical. It is the reverse of what the bible says. It is also the opposite of what the Amerindians say, of what the people from Vanuatu say. There was this strange man, A Frenchman who came to Vanuatu in the 1940s and he tried to impose the monoculture of coffee because he found out that coffee trees could grow very well there. So, he tried to convince the people to do that. They managed to plant some coffee crops, but the money was nothing and it disappeared quickly. As soon as the European people left this part of the world, the people of the jungle took back everything. So, from time to time, you see a coffee tree choking in the middle of a huge forest. You know they don't see the use of having an industrial relationship to nature. On the contrary, they like to plant tara which is a root, the tara root, they do this in the middle of the forest in order to try to blend it in with the forest. They hide what they are doing with these huge leaves. So, they have to remove the leaves and you see the plantation and there are the leaves. It grows like a hidden, living secret in the forest. This is very interesting. I think that maybe we do not have enough secrets. This might be something that is wrong in our society. Everything is open; there are not enough secrets in life, in nature, in all of our relationships.

**KM:** I was wondering if we could discuss the media for a second. Your reflections on the media in works such as *La Guerre* and *Les Géants* seem to be more significant than ever. What do you think that the increasing corporate control of the mainstream media suggests for the future of the global village?

**JMGLC:** Well, when I was writing this, I was overwhelmed by society and it would make you laugh if I were to mention what motivated me to write books such as *Les Géants*. I wrote this because in a place not far from Nice in the mouth of a dry river, they were building walls to keep out the water and on this ground that they were getting from the river they were building what they called a hypermarket. Now, this would be a very small thing if you compare it with the U.S. I was so shocked by this that it immediately gave me the idea that I would have to fight against this and in order to fight against this, I had to read everything that was related to this type of wide scale industry. So, I read Gustave Le Bon and the publications from the Institute of Colors, not from Mississippi but from somewhere around there, and I was reading these publications and I was somewhat indignant about how they were treating their patrons. I learned that every car, before they sold a car, they would spray the new car smell. This kind of perfume smells good, so you buy the car. It smells new, but this is just fake. There were also a lot of debates at that time about subliminal communication in cinema, in advertisement, and even in books. In *Les Géants*, I tried to place something subliminal: "We must burn hyperpolis." [laughs] This was kind of naïve behavior, but I was young and full of illusions. I was surely not aware of what it meant, but this hypermarket was small in the grand scheme of things. I am still rather faithful to this time of my life, because I feel that there is something wrong in this type of egocentric behavior. If we go through (economic) crises, it's probably due to that and especially lately because of the fact that everything is related. This trade system is multinational. People are totally indifferent to the consequences for human societies. This is very strange. I recently met a distinguished economist and he was so indifferent to these consequences. There was an economic crisis and he is a good economist. He expressed in such a matter of fact way the way of thinking of economists in the U.S., indifferent to people of the world. I said to him, "Don't you think that people have been living with this crisis for ten years or twenty years in Pakistan. They live this daily. In Mauritius, they live this daily." They are just saying, "We went wrong with such and such and so it became the world crisis." But the world was in crisis and he was indifferent to these arguments. He did not react to this. I suppose that with his training he sees the main points and the rest of the world is of secondary importance to him. To me, this (mentality) is not so good.

**KM:** I would like to discuss your text *Raga* briefly and the efforts of certain communities to reject superficial consumer values and to return to traditional ways of life. Even if globalization is here to stay as some economists suggest, what can we learn from diverse and invaluable indigenous cultures that could enrich and improve our current society?

**JMGLC:** It is always difficult to discuss this because when you belong as I do to an industrial culture . . . I live in the industrialized world, in France, in the U.S., or even some places in Mauritius, the industrial age has arrived. It is so difficult to refer to people who live another type of life. This has something condescending in a way, and I would not like to express that. But, going to some places in Panama or some places in Mexico or even some places in Mauritius, you see that there is another world which lives according to other rules. These rules are rules which would probably make that (aforementioned) economist mad. Because, it seems so simple. But, it is a question of balance and preservation of the place where you live. It is also a question about thinking of future generations and trying not to be too aggressive because everything bounces back to you and your descendents will suffer from this aggression. Most of these places are interesting because they did not have wars, they have been apart from wars not only world wars but small wars, they never really knew war. I was reading Rousseau and I found out some very interesting things. This man was a kind of prophet. He was seeing the great difficulties of modern societies that are *jusqu'au-boutiste* when they wage war. It's war until the end. Until they wipe out the enemy, they are not satisfied. He was saying that and this comparison might be shocking that people who live according to nature and wild animals have the same knowledge. They don't fight until the end. They realize that there is a moment where it could be really bad. They stop and one of the parties accepts defeat and turns away. It is very true that those people have not really known war. They have been outside of this idea that we have to go to the end, this type of radicalism. They are not radicals. They are the opposite. They can accept a new religion. They can even accept the planting of coffee trees. They are willing to try anything new that nature or visitors offer. Then, they can make a choice. They don't have a preconceived idea of what the world should be. So, when we speak of tradition, we mean that something is blocked and at the same time, this is a frozen mental system. But, this is not the case, it's an openness, it's a way to be able to change. Tradition, at least for those people that we were talking about, is an open not a closed system. On the contrary, radicalism and especially when this radicalism is founded upon philosophical prejudices, then it is frozen, it doesn't evolve. This is why philosophy sometimes seems so dangerous.

**KM:** And it seems as if certain cultures are a bit more open to creolization or this cultural exchange and I think that your narratives such as *Raga* clearly highlight this fact.

**JMGLC:** They don't have this idea of ethnic purity. This doesn't exist. They have a natural mistrust of their neighbors because their neighbors might come and steal their children or steal things from them so they have this natural mistrust. But, they do not consider themselves to be the only human beings. They know that human beings are more or less all the same. They would rather build their myths and their traditions on this idea that human beings are all alike. This is completely different from what we inherited from the philosophical systems of Europe or in the U.S.

**KM:** Many critics have suggested that the immigrant is the emblematic figure of injustice and human exploitation in contemporary society. I would argue that many of your texts, such as *Désert*, *Poisson d'or*, *La Ronde et autres faits divers*, and *Coeur Brûle*, could be considered intercultural texts because they pose disconcerting questions related to how immigrant and migrant populations are treated and perceived in the modern world. How do you think that so-called noncitizens are treated in mainstream Western society?

**JMGLC**: Well, it depends on where you are. In Europe, it's very true that people are closed-minded in the awareness of their culture and they have historical prejudices that the outside world is dangerous even including North America. When you are in the U.S., it is rather different. I think that the benefits of immigration are something real in the U.S. They don't have the same kind of refusal of immigration. It is part of the system. We know that the U.S. was built on immigration. I think that it is still the country that receives the most immigrants in the world. I was looking at the numbers. I think that it is something like five million immigrants each year that enter the U.S. This is amazing. It proves that eventually a country can be built on those moving values. I am sure that this is something that the so-called old world has to admit. This will probably be the case. I think that literature has a role to play in that, because literature is made of encounters, it is made of different voices, not only different languages, but different origins. It is so evident in the U.S. but not so evident especially in France. But small countries like Mauritius are not open to immigration, they are so small and they are already so (densely) populated, but they are open to creolization of thought. They are very much open to this (mentality). They put their values at stake and each generation has to change. For instance, the people of my generation which were living at the time of the British Empire, they had to deal with British rule in Mauritius. The white portion of the population was very much closed-minded about their old values. But, this has changed now we are seeing that most of the members of that population emigrate. They go elsewhere because they do not find any jobs in Mauritius. They try the U.S. or Europe, or sometimes Africa or other places. They are adventurous. But not only that part of the population, but also the population of Indian descent, they were pretty sure that they would be the masters of Mauritius twenty years ago. But, now they are not so sure. Now they feel that they are very different from their motherland. They differ so much from India. Some people from Mauritius of Indian origin, they do not want to go to India. They don't accept being from India. They want to be something else. They want to mix their Indian values with the other values of Mauritius, with Muslim values, with Christian values.

**KM:** You mentioned the role of literature. Does intercultural literature have a role to play in terms of reframing public perception of these disadvantaged social groups?

**JMGLC:** Yes, I think so because literature is not totally useless. [laughs] Oscar Wilde was saying in the preface to *The Picture of Dorian Gray* that in his eyes literature was "perfectly useless." Perfect because it was perfect, but useless because it was useless. I think that he is a bit pessimistic. Of course, it is not perfect, but then it is not totally useless. It has some use. It allows people from other cultures or other family groups to see through other eyes when they read Abhimanyu Anat who describes plantation life from the point of view of the *coolies*. Then you enter this world, you better understand what it meant to live during this time. When you read a text by Mark Twain or other great writers, you enter another system of values. You have to accept them, otherwise you can't read this. Even Proust who is a difficult author because his milieu is so restricted, the renters who didn't work . . . This milieu doesn't exist today because everyone has to work. But, at this time, there was this society around Proust that never worked. Or, other authors at that time who never worked like Oscar Wilde. They never worked besides writing their stories or novels. This is hard to imagine today someone who lives by not producing anything. They were just producing words. This is hard to imagine. And still when you read Proust's books, you can forget about this dimension. You can get to the inner self of Proust, the discovery of the mechanism of memory, and the associations of words and ideas which is fascinating. When you enter a book, you leave a part of yourself and you gain a part of someone else. I think that (reading) literature is a necessary activity. It is a *métisse* or creole activity essentially.

**KM:** I agree and many people discuss the link between compassion and imagination given the limited scope of the human experience in terms of understanding the Other.

**JMGLC:** It would be simple if it was just compassion, but it could also be revenge or wickedness, it could be anything. But the interesting thing is that through books, I would not say that you can be better, that would be asking for too much from literature, but you can be someone else. You can be more understanding which does not mean that you are more generous but you probably have the potential to understand better, which is probably progress for human beings. I was reading the thoughts of Parmenides the other day. Parmenides lived in a time in which the nobility was not necessary. People did not really need to communicate. People had rather simple lives, at least people on top of the ladder. Of course, slaves were not a part of this (society). But for those people, they would just think about "What is the moon?" This is one of their questions. And they would sit outside of public places and people would be interested in this. Today you can't ask for this, it has to be slightly different.

**KM:** I would like to ask a question related to your recent text *Ourania* and with your permission I would first like to share the final lines of the work with the reader: *Ourania* ends with the following conclusion which I think is very important in the context of globalization: "En attendant, les régions les plus pauvres de la planète continuent à sombrer dans les guerres larvées et l'insolvabilité [...] il n'y a pas de quoi être optimiste. Pourtant, ce qui nous unit encore, Dahlia et moi, ce qui nous permet d'espérer, c'est la certitude que le pays d'Ourania a vraiment existé, d'en avoir été les témoins" (283). What I find significant about this passage is the combination of stark realism related to the current state of the global village with an affirmation of hope. Is this the sentiment that you were trying to convey?

**JMGLC:** Well, yes. Otherwise, I would not have written that book. It is not a sexist story; it is the opposite of a sexist story. I wrote that book because when I was in Mexico, I had the good fortune to encounter two different things, one was an abandoned field in the middle of nowhere where I was living. In that field, there were remains of an ancient society. So, I asked the people who lived there. It had nothing to do with pre-Hispanic society. There were the ruins of a church, the remnants of an old mill, the ruins of other dwellings. They told me about these civilians who tried to invent a new society there. This society lasted for several years. In fact, I think that it stood for around fifty years. Then, for political reasons, because it was the time of the Mexican Revolution, the organizers of this place had to leave. Everything was conquered by time, by politics, and also by the lack of money. They had to abandon this experience. Then the same year I was traveling by bus and I met this small group of post-hippies. We traveled together and they were led by an old man and they were trying to find a place to stay because they had been expelled I believe from the north of Mexico. They were expelled because they were under suspicion of smoking marijuana which at that time was a terrible thing. So, they had to go somewhere else. They learned that it might be possible to relocate to Belize. They were traveling south. I traveled with them for two or three days and I spoke with them. They were so naïve, but at the same time I was fascinated by their enthusiastic project of being somewhere where they could cultivate the land, grow their vegetables while at the same time trying not to offend Mother Nature. It was a mixture of different things. When I saw them, I was certain that it (their project) was doomed to fail. In my eyes, it was impossible that it would succeed. I don't know what happened to them. They probably failed. But speaking with them gave me the idea that sometimes dreams and reality can coincide and live together. During those very moments, it fills you with joy because after all there had been a lot of wars and a lot of other failures (during this time). Those people still had the illusion that they would succeed. At the same time, it also recounts another utopia which is a small college where I was working in Mexico. This college was undermined by rivalries and by ambitions. At the head of the college was a very good friend of mine Don Luis González, a historian, an admirable man, a real humanist in the twentieth century. He tried very hard to keep this institution alive. One of the main aspects of this institution was to be a utopia. It would open its doors once a week so that the people from the village could come and listen to both university professors and students and they would take part in these discussions. This was also totally utopian. It did not fail, but the open (to the public) part of the college does not exist anymore. So, some things are doomed to fail but it is good to know that they once existed.

**KM:** Speaking of dreams, at the beginning of a new millennium, what are your concerns and aspirations for the human family based on the present situation?

**JMGLC:** I don't believe that much in the global village because as we said earlier, there is evidence of its failure. The global village seems more and more like the global market instead of a global village. If you consider that most of the people who live on this planet lack basic necessities, they don't have enough drinkable water, the children don't get immunizations. Even in some places like Vanuatu that we were talking about, women don't have a good situation there. They have to gain their freedom. So, there is a general tendency to want the world to be better and at the same time there is the general tendency for this world to be more and more threatened by worldwide corporations and the personal motivations of businessmen. So, it is a fight. In fact, this fight that we are living has been going on for a long time, probably since the Renaissance. We are perhaps in the last chapters of that fight. Maybe we are going to find a way that is not idealistic or utopian which is not totalitarian to deal with those contradictions. I am not sure about the future of all of this or of the future of the human race. But, I am pretty sure that the little span of time in which human beings are going to be on this earth that literature is going to be very important to them. Don't ask me why. [laughs]

**KM:** The failure of the global village is that what you were trying to illustrate with the notion of the "happy few" in your Nobel acceptance speech in terms of the domination of the many by the few?

**JMGLC:** "Happy few" has another meaning in English. It means the people who know (have access to knowledge) who are in fact most of the time the people who benefit from the ignorance of the rest of the population. Definitely, providing education to children is a good solution for some of the problems. It (education) does not provide food but it will give many people the means to earn a living and to sustain themselves in a difficult world. Then, another possible solution is the belief that we need to have in art and culture and by culture I mean something which is multiple, not one culture. This global culture which would be made of so many different cultures would be a combination and an exchange of cultures. This is why I am rather militant in the intercultural arena.

**KM:** It has been a pleasure. Thank you for your time.

**JMGLC:** Thank you so much.

# References


Abensour, Gérard. "L'Épopée de la Fin de l'Insularité." *Critique* 41: 1106–1111.

Adams, Paul. "Television as Gathering Place." *Annals of the Association of American Geographers* 82 (1): 117–135.

Amar, Ruth. "Du regard *autre* et de la solitude dans l'œuvre le clézienne." *Lettres Romanes* 55 (3–4): 309–318.

———. "Le récit LeClézien ou l'écriture du vide." *Australian Journal of French Studies* 41 (1): 26–36.

Amin, Samir. "Exiting the Crisis of Capitalism or Capitalism in Crisis?" *Globalization* 7 (1–2): 261–273.

Archambault, Paul. "Jean-Marie Le Clézio and the 2008 Nobel Prize: Can France Really Claim Him?" *Symposium* 63 (4): 281–297.

Arnould, Eric. "Should Consumer Citizens Escape the Market?" *The Annals of the American Academy of Political and Social Science* 611: 96–111.

Asgarally, Issa. *L'Interculturel ou la Guerre.* Port Louis, Mauritius: MSM Limited, 2005.

Barber, Pauline. "Contradictions of Class and Consumption When the Commodity Is Labour." *Anthropologica* 46: 203–218.

Barnlund, Dean. *Intercultural Communication.* Eds. Larry Samovar and Richard Porter. New York: Wadsworth, 1997. 27–35.

Basu, Kaushik. "Globalization and the Politics of International Finance: The Stiglitz Verdict." *Journal of Economic Literature* 41: 885–899.

Batra, Nandita. "Dominion, Empathy, and Symbiosis; Gender and Anthropocentrism in Romanticism." *Interdisciplinary Studies in Literature and Environment* 3 (2): 101–120.

Bennett, David. "Getting the Id to Go Shopping: Psychoanalysis, Advertising, Barbie Dolls, and the Invention of the Consumer Unconscious." *Public Culture* 17 (1): 1–25.

Bertocchi, Sophie and Bruno Thibault. *J.M.G. Le Clézio.* Nantes: Éditions du Temps, 2004.

Bissessur-Asgarally, Sarojini. "Le Clézio: Mythologies et philosophies de l'Inde." *J.M.G. Le Clézio Prix Nobel de Littérature: Hommages, témoignages, analyses.* Spec. issue of *Italiques* 2009: 44–54.

Boncenne, Pierre. "J.M.G. Le Clézio s'explique." *Lire* 32: 20–40.

Borgomano, Madeline. "*La Quarantaine* de Le Clézio et le vertige intertextuel." *Cahiers de Narratologie* 13: 2–9.

Bosia, Michael. "AIDS and Postcolonial Politics: Acting Up on Science and Immigration in France." *French Politics, Culture & Society* 27 (1): 69–90.

Brée, Germaine. *Le Monde fabuleux de J.M.G. Le Clézio.* Amsterdam: Rodopi, 1990.

Brown, John. "A New Book of Flights: Immigration and Displacement in J.M.G. Le Clézio's *Poisson d'or.*" *World Literature Today* 71 (4): 731–735.

Buell, Lawrence. *The Environmental Imagination.* Cambridge, MA: The Belknap Press of Harvard University Press, 1995.

Cadorel Raymond. "Le Mexique dans l'œuvre de Le Clézio." *Récifs* 7: 63–91.

Calloway-Thomas, Pamela Cooper, and Cecil Blake. *Intercultural Communication* . Boston: Allyn and Bacon, 1999.

Castles, Stephen. "International Migration at the Beginning of the Twenty-first Century: Global Trends and Issues." *International Social Science Journal* 52 (165): 269–281.

Cavallero, Claude. "J.M.G. Le Clézio et la question de l'engagement." *Horizons Le Cléziens: Actes du colloque de Grenade.* Ed. Maria Luisa Bernabé-Gil. Toulouse, France: Inter- Lignes, April 2009. 195–216.

———. "J.M.G. Le Clézio et le sable des mots." *Tangence* 82: 121–134.

———. "J.M.G. Le Clézio: Le voyage vers l'origine." *French Studies in Southern Africa* 34: 31– 43.

———. *Le Clézio, Témoin du monde.* Paris: Editions Calliopées, 2009.

Chanda, T. (2001). La langue française est peut-être mon véritable pays, entretien avec J-M Le Clézio. *Label France* (45) 2001.

Chomsky, Noam. "Ideological Conformity in America." *The Nation* (Jan. 27, 1979): 77–81.

Chomsky, Noam and Edward Herman. *Manufacturing Consent: The Political Economy of the Mass Media.* New York: Pantheon, 2002.

Clavareau, Agnes. "Lecture Mythique de *Désert* de J.M.G. Le Clézio." *Mythe-Rite-Symbole* (1985): 395–412.

Clifton, Don. "Progressing a Sustainable World: A Socio-ecological Resilience Perspective." *Journal of Sustainable Development* 3 (4): 74–96.

Cohen, Lizabeth. *A Consumers' Republic: The Politics of Mass Consumption in PostwarAmerica.* New York: Vintage, 2003.

Cole, Nicki. "Ethical Capitalism and Its Cultural Logic." *Consumers, Commodities, and Consumption* 9 (2): n.p.

Collins, Eva and Kate Kearins. "Delivering on Sustainability's Global and Local Orientation." *Academy of Management Learning & Education* 9 (3): 499–506.

Cooley, Aaron. "Failed States in Education: Chomsky on Dissent, Propaganda, and Reclaiming Democracy in the Media Spectacle." *Educational Studies* 46: 579–605.

Cox, David. "Consumerism Triumphs in *The Joneses*." *The Guardian.* www.guardian.co.uk/film/filmblog/2010/apr/26/consumerism-the-joneses.

Crawford, Robert. "Selling Modernity: Advertising and the Construction of the Culture of Consumption in Australia." *Antipodean Modern (ACH)* 25: 114–143.

Cunningham, Anne. "Autonomous Consumption: Buying Into the Ideology of Capitalism." *Journal of Business Ethics* 48: 229–236.

Damamme-Gilbert, Béatrice. "Les enjeux de la mémoire dans *Onitsha* et l'Africain de J.M.G. Le Clézio." *Australian Journal of French Studies* 45 (1): 16–32.

Dauvergne, Peter. "The Problem of Consumption." *Global Environmental Politics* 10 (2): 1–10.

Dean, Jodi. "Enjoying Neoliberalism." *Cultural Politics* 4 (1): 47–72.

Dean, Thomas. "What Is Eco-criticism?" www.asle.org/site/resources/ecocritical-library/intro/defining/dean.

De Cortanze, Gérard. *J.M.G. Le Clézio: Le Nomade immobile.* Paris: Gallimard, 2002.

De Souza, Carl. "Le Clézio in vivo." *J.M.G. Le* Clézio Prix Nobel de Littérature: Hommages, témoignages, analyses. Spec. issue of *Italiques* 2009: 18–20.

Devillo, Lorenzo. "L'Errance dans *Aracoeli* de Morante, *Le Chercheur d'or* de Le Clézio et *Moon Palace* d'Auster." *Compar(a)ison* 2: 43–53.

DeWeese-Boyd, Ian and Margaret DeWeese-Boyd. "The Healthy City Versus the Luxurious City in Plato's Republic: Lessons About Consumption and Sustainability for a Globalizing Economy." *Contemporary Justice Review* 10 (1): 115–130.

Dey, Tarcis. "J.M.G. Le Clézio: Le Chercheur d'Or." *Nouvelle Revue Française (NRF)* 388 (1986): 77–83.

Dickinson, Greg. "Selling Democracy: Consumer Culture and Citizenship in the Wake of September 11." *Southern Communication Journal* 70 (4): 271–284.

Di Scanno, Teresa. *La Vison du monde chez Le Clézio: Cinq études sur l'œuvre.* Paris: Nizet, 1983.

Dormoy, Nadine and Liliane Lazar, eds. *A Chacun sa France.* New York: P. Lang, 1990, 121–133.

Dormoy, Nadine. "J.M.G. Le Clézio ou la transcendance de l'instant." *Dalhousie French Studies* 19: 85–95.

Doucey, Bruno. *Pawana* (Supplementary Materials). Paris: Gallimard, 2003.
Dufay, François. "JMG Le Clézio: 'on ne peut pas faire barrage au métissage.'" *L'Express.* www.lexpress.fr/culture/livre/jmg-le-clezio-on-ne-peut-pas-faire-barrage-au- metissage_587614.html.
Duncan, Grant. "After Happiness." *Journal of Political Ideologies* 12 (1): 85–108.
Dutton, Jacqueline. *Le Chercheur d'Or et d'Ailleurs: l'Utopie de J. M. G. Le Clézio.* Paris: Harmattan, 2003.
Edgley, Alison. "Manufacturing Consistency: Social Science, Rhetoric and Chomsky's Critique." *Westminster Papers in Communication and Culture* 6 (2): 23–42.
Ehrenfeld, David. *The Arrogance of Humanism.* Oxford: Oxford University Press, 1978.
Espejo, Maria. "*Désert* de Jean-Marie Gustave Le Clézio: Analyse d'éléments descriptifs et interprétation écocritique." *Çédille* 5: 329–346.
"Every Word Contains the World." April 26, 2009. *La New-Yorkaise.* 7 Jul. 2009. http://lanew- yorkaise.com/?p=452.
Fanchin, Gérard. "Le Discours Littéraire: Finalité Esthétique et Visée Pragmatique." *French Studies in Southern Africa* 31 (2002): 16–26.
Fenelon, James and Thomas Hall. "Indigeneous Peoples and Globalization: Four Cases of Resistance and Revitalization." American Sociological Association Meeting, August 14–18, 2004, San Francisco, Copyright of Conference Papers-American Sociological Association.
Garcin, Jérôme. "Rencontre avec J.M.G. Le Clézio, à l'occasion de la parution de *Ourania* (2006)." *Le Nouvel Observateur* 2–8 février, 2006.
———. "Voyage en utopie: un entretien avec J.M.G. Le Clézio." *Le Nouvel Observateur* 2–8 Feb. 2006.
Garsdal, Lotte. "Le Mythe littéraire et la coloration mythique selon Le Clézio." *Pre publications* 181: 20–28.
Gatta, John. "Rediscovering the Earth." *Sewanee Review* 112 (4): 618–624.
Gulubovic, Zagorka. "Philosophical Principles as a Foundation of the Concept of Globalisation." *Synthesis Philosophica* 47 (1): 19–33.
Hamilton, Joan. "Nature 101." *Sierra* (Nov.–Dec. 2000): 1–6. www.sierraclub.org/sierra/200011/nature.asp.
Harrington, Katharine. "Writing between Borders: Nomadism and Its Implications for Contemporary French and Francophone Literature." *Contemporary French and Francophone Studies* 10 (2): 117–125.
Hayes, Lydia. "Desert." *Middle East Journal* 64 (1): 149–150.
Heise, Ursula. "The Hitchhiker's Guide to Ecocriticism." *PMLA* 121 (2): 503–516.
Hertich, Alexander. "*Ourania.*" Rev. of Ourania by J.M.G. Le Clézio. *French Review* 81 (3):628–629.
"Histoire du pied et autres fantaisies, de J.M.G. Le Clézio." *L'Express.* www.lexpress.fr/culture/livre/histoire-du-pied-et-autres-fantaisies-de-j-m-g-le- clezio_1045905.html.
Holzberg, Ruth. "Le Clézio et Le Voyage Linguistique vers l'Extase." *Bulletin* (1976–1977): 89–105.
Horkheimer, Max and Theodor Adorno. *Dialectic of Enlightenment.* New York: Continuum, 2002.
Houseman, Gerald. "Joseph Stiglitz and the Critique of Free Market Analysis." *Challenge* 49 (2): 52–62.
Hume, Margee. "Compassion without Action: Examining the Young Consumer's Consumption and Attitude to Sustainable Consumption." *Journal of World Business* 45: 385–394.
Jaggi, Maya. "J.M.G. Le Clézio: 'Being European, I'm Not Sure of the Value of My Culture, Because I Know What It's Done.'" *The Guardian* www.guardian.co.uk/books/2010/apr/10/le-clezio-nobel-prize-profile
Johnson, Loretta. "Greening the Library: The Fundamentals and Future of Ecocriticism." *Choice* (Dec. 2009): 7–13.

Johnson, Patricia. "Adam Pollo and the Greek Connection: The Mythological Dimensions of Le Clézio's *Le Procès-Verbal.*" *Classical and Modern Literature* 4 (1): 5–14.

Jollin-Bertocchi S. and Bruno Thibault. *J.-M.G. Le Clézio.* Nantes: Éditions du Temps, 2004.

Jollin-Bertocchi, Sophie. *J.M.G. Le Clézio: L'Erotisme, les Mots.* Paris: Kimé, 2001.

Kadioglu, Sevket. "J.M.G. Le Clézio: Refus de l'Eurocentrisme et l'appel de l'ailleurs." *Journal of Faculty of Letters* 24 (2): 123–138.

Kennis, Andrew. "Theorizing and Historicizing the Media Dependence Model." Paper presented at the annual meeting of the International Communication Association, Marriott, Chicago, IL, May 21, 2009. www.allacademic.com/meta/p301211_index.html.

Knapp, Bettina. "J.M.G. Le Clézio's '*Désert*': The Myth of Transparency (The Questing Fictions of J.M.G. Le Clézio)." *World Literature Today* (September 1997): 703–708.

Koechlin, Timothy. "Stiglitz and his Discontent." *Review of Political Economy* 18 (2): 253–264.

Kronegger, Marlies. "From Profane Space to the Sacred Place or Center in *Désert* by Le Clézio." *The Elemental Passion for Place in the Ontopoiesis of Life.* Ed. Anna-Teresa Tymieniecka (1995).

Kyria, Pierre. "J.M.G. Le Clézio, trois ans après." *Combat* (Le journal de Paris) 67: 9–11.

Labbé, Michelle. *Le Clézio, l'Écart Romanesque.* Paris: Harmattan, 1999.

Lambert, Hervé. "Fuite et nostalgie des origines." *Sud* 85–94.

Lang, Kurt and Gladys Engel Lang. "Noam Chomsky and the Manufacture of Consent for American Foreign Policy." *Political Communication* 21: 93–101.

Langman, Lauren and Douglas Morris. "Globalization, Cyberspace, and Identity." *Information Technology Education and Society* 3 (2): n.p.

Lazar, Liliane. Rev. of *Révolutions*, by J.M.G. Le Clézio. *French Review* 78 (3): 622–623.

Le Clézio, J.M.G. *Ailleurs: Entretiens sur France-Culture avec Jean-Louis Ezine.* Paris: Diffusion le Seuil, 1995.

———. Coeur brûlé et autres romances . Paris: Gallimard, 2000.

———. "Dans la Forêt des paradoxes (texte intégral)." *J.M.G. Le* Clézio Prix Nobel de Littérature: Hommages, témoignages, analyses. Spec. issue of *Italiques* 2009: 74–85.

———. *Désert.* Paris: Gallimard, 1980.

———. *Desert.* Trans. C. Dickson. Jaffrey, NH: David Godine, 2009.

———. "Errance et Mythologies." *Magazine Litteraire.* 362: Feb. 1998.

———. *Étoile Errante.* Paris: Gallimard, 1992.

———. *L'Extase Matérielle.* Paris: Gallimard, 1967.

———. "Fantômes dans la rue." Paris: Elle, 2000.

———. *Fever.* Trans. Daphne Woodward. New York: Atheneum, 1966.

———. *Haï: Les Sentiers de la Création.* Geneva: Éditions d'Art Albert Skira, 1971.

———. *La fête chantée.* Paris: Le Promeneur, 1997.

———. *La Fièvre.* Paris: Gallimard, 1965.

———. *La Guerre.* Paris: Gallimard, 1970.

———. "Lavez l'injustice faite aux Chagossiens." Oct. 17, 2009. *Le Monde.* 7 Jul. 2009. http://inventerre.canalblog.com/archives/2009/10/22/15523424.html.

———. *Le Chercheur d'Or.* Paris: Gallimard, 1985.

———. "Le Génie Datura." *Les Cahiers du Chemin.* 14: 95–129.

———. *Le livre des fuites: roman d'aventures.* Paris: Gallimard, 1969.

———. *Le Procès-Verbal.* Paris: Gallimard, 1963.

———. *Les Géants.* Paris: Gallimard, 1973.

———. "Les littératures de langue française à l'heure de la mondialisation." Keynote Speech. Montreal, Canada. Oct. 17, 2008. Radio Canada, Radio.

———. "Lettre d'Albuquerque." *Autrement* 69: 22–24.

———. *L'Histoire du pied et autres fantaisies.* Paris: Gallimard, 2011.

———. *L'Histoire du pied et autres fantaisies.* France 5. Interview. www.youtube.com/v/Ervhm0YI29U&showsearch=0.

———. *L'inconnu sur la terre.* Paris: Gallimard, 1978.

———. *La ronde et autres faits divers*. Paris: Gallimard, 1982.
———. *La Quarantaine*. Paris: Gallimard, 1995.
———. *Mondo et autres histoires*. Paris: Gallimard, 1978.
———. *Mondo & Other Stories*. Trans. Alison Anderson. Lincoln: The University of Nebraska Press, 2011.
———. "Quel avenir pour la Romaine." Jan. 7, 2009. *Le Monde*. 7 Jul. 2009. http://les4saisons.over-blog.com/article-33381375.html.
———. *Mondo et Autres Histoires*. Paris: Gallimard, 1978.
———. *Ourania*. Paris: Gallimard, 2006.
———. *Pawana*. Paris: Gallimard, 1992.
———. *Pawana*. Trans. Christophe Brunski. *AGNI Online* (2001): 1–14. www.bu.edu/agni/fiction/print/2001/53-clezio.html.
———. *Poisson d'Or*. Paris: Gallimard, 1997.
———. *Raga: approche du continent invisible*. Paris: Seuil, 2006.
———. *Terra amata*. Paris: Gallimard, 1967.
———. *Terra Amata*. Trans. Barbara Bray. London: Hamilton, 1969; New York: Atheneum, 1969.
———. *The Book of Flights*. Trans. Simon Watson Taylor. London: Vintage Books, 1972.
———. *The Giants*. Trans. Simon Watson Taylor. New York: Atheneum, 1975.
———. *The Prospector*. Trans. Carol Marks. Boston: David R. Godine, 1993.
———. *The Round & Other Cold Hard Facts*. Trans. C. Dickson. Lincoln: University of Nebraska Press, 2002.
———. *Voyages de l'autre côté*. Paris: Gallimard, 1975.
———. "What Is Literature?" Lee Hall Auditorium, Mississippi State University. 30 Mar. 2009. Mississippi State University Television Center, DVD.
———. "The World Has No Center." *NPQ* 26 (3): 78–81.
Lee, Sue-Im. "'We Are Not the World': Global Village, Universalism, and Karen Tei Yamashita's Tropic of Orange ." *Modern Fiction Studies* 53 (3): 501–527.
Léger, Thierry. "Pour un métissage culturel et littéraire dans *Ourania* de J.M.G. Le Clézio." *J.M.G. Le Clézio dans la forêt des paradoxes*. Eds. Bruno Thibault and Keith Moser. Paris: L'Harmattan, Collection Études transnationales, francophones et comparés, 2012: 263–272.
Leopold, Aldo. *Almanach d'un comté des sables*. Paris: Aubier Montaigne, 1996.
Le Goff, Alain. *Pawana* (Supplemantary Materials). Paris: Gallimard, 2003.
Leichenko, Robin and William Solecki. "Exporting the American Dream: The Globalization of Suburban Consumption Landscapes." Ed. Stephen Roper. *Regional Studies* 39 (2): 241– 253.
Levy, Karen D. "Elsewhere and Otherwise: Lévinasian Eros and Ethics in Le Clézio's *La Quarantaine*." *Orbis Litterarum* 56 (4) (2001): 255–275.
———. "From Mauritius to Cawnpore: The Permutations of Myth and Memory in Le Clézio's Fiction from *Le Chercheur d'or* to *La Quarantaine*." (25 pages) in The *Selected Proceedings of the Sixth Conference of the International Society for The Study of European Ideas,* published on CD-ROM by MIT Press, Spring 2001.
———. "Intersected Pasts and Problematic Futures: Oedipal Conflicts and Legendary Catastrophes in *Onitsha* and *Etoile Errante*." *The International Fiction Review* 25 (1–2): 36–49.
———. "The Elusive Gold of J.M.G. Le Clézio: The Problematic of the Self-Portrait in *Le Chercheur d'or* and *Voyage à Rodrigues*." *The French Novel from Lafayette to Esvignes*. Eds. Bell, Lintz, and Poe. New Paradigm Press: 1995, 183–198.
———. "To Approach, to Welcome, to Contest: Levinasian Teaching and the Feminine in Le Clézio's Mauritian Sagas." *Orbis Litterarum* 61 (6) (2006): 488–513.
Lie, Rico. *Spaces of Intercultural Communication*. Cresskill, NJ: Hampton Press, 2003.
Macé-Scarron, Joseph. "Histoire du pied et autres fantaisies, de J.M.G. Le Clézio." *Le Magazine Littéraire* Oct. 24, 2011. www.magazine-litteraire.com/content/critique-fiction/article?id=20320.
Mezade, Jean-Paul. "Le voyage à rebours." *Sud* 85–86; 149–154.

Miall, David. "Representing the Picturesque: William Gilpin and the Laws of Nature." *Interdisciplinary Studies in Literature and Environment* 12 (2): 75–93.

Michel, Jacqueline. "Epreuves du livre. Réflexions sur *Etoile errante* de J.M.G. Le Clézio." *Lettres Romanes* 4: 279–286.

Miller, Robert. "Le Malaise du sacré dans *Onitsha* et *Pawana* de J.M.G. Le Clézio." *Nouvelles Etudes Francophones* 20 (2): 31–42.

———. "*Onitsha* ou le rêve de mon père: Le Clézio et le postcolonial." *International Journal of Francophone Studies* 6 (1): 31–41.

Minow, Nell. "Interview: Derrick Borte of *The Joneses*.'" *Movie Mom*. http://blog.beliefnet.com/moviemom/2010/04/interview-derrick-borte-of-the.html.

Model, David. "The Applicability of Herman and Chomsky's Propaganda Model Today." *College Quarterly* 8 (3): 1–6.

Moser, Keith. "The De-centered Humanism and Cosmic Engagement of J.M.G. Le Clé zio: Posing Questions in an Age of Suspicion." *Sprachkunst* 42 (1).

———. "J.M.G. Le Clézio's Urban Phantoms and the Paradox of Invisibility." *Modern Language Review* 106 (3): 724–744.

———. "Le paradoxe du langage ou le 'terrible privilège' de l'humanité selon J.M.G. Le Clézio." *J.M.G. Le Clézio dans la forêt des paradoxes*. Eds. Bruno Thibault and Keith Moser. Paris, France: L'Harmattan, Collection Études transnationales, francophones et comparés, 2012: 211–220.

———. "Penser et vivre l'interculturel: La naissance de la FIP à Maurice." *Les Cahiers Le Clézio* 3–4: 41–46.

———. *"Privileged Moments" in the Novels and Short Stories of J.M.G. Le Clézio: His Contemporary Development of a Traditional French Literary Device*. New York: The Edwin Mellen Press, 2008.

———. "Rending Moments of Material Ecstasy in the Meditative Essays of Two Nobel Laureates: Le Clézio and Camus." *Romance Notes* 49 (1): 13–21.

Motte, Warren. "Ten Fables of the Novel in French of the 1990's." *World Literature Today* 75 (3–4): 84–88.

Mouat, Ricardo. "Literature in the Global Village: Skármeta's *Match Ball*." *Revista de Estudios Hispánicos* 33: 133–141.

Mullen, Andrew. "The Propaganda Model After 20 Years: Interview with Edward S. Herman and Noam Chomsky." *Westminster Papers in Communication and Culture* 6 (2): 12–22.

Mullen, Andrew and Jeffery Klaehn. "The Herman-Chomsky Propaganda Model: A Critical Approach to Analysing Mass Media Behaviour." *Sociology Compass* 4 (4): 215–229.

Munro, Donald. "Dark Comedy *Joneses* Parodies Obsession with Stuff." *The Fresno Bee (CA)* April 15, 2010.

Naturel, Mireille. "Ailleurs et altérité dans trois romans contemporains: *L'Amant, Le Chercheur d'or, La Goutte d'or*." *Etudes Francophones* 13 (1): 29–42.

Newman, Lance. "Marxism and Ecocriticism." *Interdisciplinary Studies in Literature and Environment* (ISLE) 9 (2): 1–25.

Novinger, Tracy. *Intercultural Communication: A Practical Guide*. Austin: University of Texas Press, 2001.

Onimus, Jean. "Angoisse et Extase Chez J.M.G. Le Clézio." *Etudes* 358 (4): 511–524.

———. *Pour lire Le Clezio*. Paris: PUF, 1994.

Oppermann, Serpil. "Ecocriticism: Natural World in the Literary Viewfinder." *Journal of Faculty of Letters* 16 (2): 29–46.

———. "Seeking Environmental Awareness in Postmodern Fictions." *Critique* 49 (3): 243–253.

Pfaff, William. "The Fall: Original Sin & Free Market Capitalism." *Commonweal*, October 10, 2008: 7.

Pickard, Richard. "Magic Environmentalism: Writing/Logging (in) British Columbia." *A Sense of Place: Re-Evaluating Regionalism in Canadian and American Writing*. Eds. Chris Riegel et al. Edmonton: University of Alberta Press, 1997: 95–112.

Pieterse, Jan. *Global Mélange: Globalization and Culture*. Rowman & Littlefield, 2003.
Popkewitz, Thomas. "Globalization as a System of Reason: The Historical Possibility and the Political in Pedagogical Policy and Research." *Yearbook of the National Society for the Study of Education* 108 (2): 247–267.
Racevskis, Roland. "J.M.G. Le Clézio's *Terra Amata*: A Micro-Fictional Affection for the Real." *Romantic Review* 90 (3): 409–416.
Rao, SS Prabhakar. "'Nomad Novelist' J.M.G. Le Clézio: The Integrative Voice." *The Icfai Journal of English Studies* 4 (1): 54–56.
Ravoux-Rallo, Elisabeth. "Se voiler d'encre: sur *Haï*, de J.M.G. Le Clézio." Ed. André Tournon. *Croisements Culturels*. Ann Arbor: Michigan Romance Studies, 1987: 81–88.
———. "Vers les icebergs: un art poétique." *Sud* 85–86: 63–67.
Real, Elena. "Un Espace pour le Vide." *Sud* (1970): 181–184.
Ridon, Jean-Xavier. "J.M.G. Le Clézio: Between Here and There, a Displacement in Memory." *World Literature Today* 71 (4): 717–723.
Rigby, Kate. "Chapter 7: Ecocritism." *Literary and Cultural Criticism at the Twenty-first Century*. Ed. Julian Wolfreys. Edinburgh: Edinburgh University Press, 2002: 151–178.
Rochefort-Guillouet, Sophie. *Dissertations sur la recherche du bonheur*. Paris: Ellipses, 2005.
Roussel-Gillet, Isabelle. *J.M.G. Le Clézio: Ecrivain de l'incertitude*. Paris: Ellipses, 2011.
———. "Le Clézio, passeur au monde: L'Ecriture et le passage des seuils." *Nouvelles Etudes Francophones* 22 (2): 152–163.
Rueckert, William. "Literature and Ecology: An Experiment in Ecocriticism." *The Iowa Review* 9 (1): 71–86.
Sack, Robert. "The Consumers World: Place as Context." *Annals of the Association of American Geographers* 78 (4): 642–664.
Salles, Marina. *Le Clézio: Notre Contemporain*. Rennes, France: PUR, 2006.
———. *Le Clézio, peintre de la vie moderne*. Paris: L'Harmattan, 2007.
Samuelsson, Lars. "Reasons and Values in Environmental Ethics." *Environmental Values* 19: 517–535.
Sandner, David. "'Habituated to the Vast': Ecocriticism, the Sense of Wonder, and the Wilderness of the Stars." *Extrapolation* 41 (3): 283–297.
Schweitzer, Marlis. "Patriotic Acts of Consumption: Lucile (Lady Duff Gordon) and the Vaudeville Fashion Show Craze." *Theatre Journal* 60 (4): 585–608.
Seaman, Donna. Rev. of *Désert*, by J.M.G. Le Clézio. *Booklist*, Jul. 2009: 30.
Shanahan, Daniel. "Articulating the Relationship Between Language, Literature, and Culture: Toward a New Agenda for Foreign Language Teaching and Research." *Modern Language Journal* 81 (2): 164–174.
Smith, Stephen. "Le Clézio's Search for Self in a World of Words." *Modern Language Studies* 10 (2): 49–58.
Spencer, Robert. "Ecocriticism in the Colonial Present: The Politics of Dwelling in Raja Shehadeh's Palestinian Walks: Notes on a Vanishing Landscape." *Postcolonial Studies* 13 (1): 33–54.
Steigerwald, David. "All Hail the Republic of Choice: Consumer History as Contemporary Thought." *The Journal of American History* (Sep. 2006): 385–403.
Stiglitz, Joseph. *Globalization and Its Discontents*. New York: W. W. Norton & Company, 2002.
———. "Globalization and the Economic Role of the State in the New Millennium." *Industrial and Corporate Change* 12 (1): 3–26.
———. *Making Globalization Work*. New York: W. W. Norton & Company, 2007.
Taran, Patrick. "Human Rights of Migrants: Challenges of the New Decade." *International Migration* 38 (6): 7–46.
Tarrant, Michael. "A Conceptual Framework for Exploring the Role of Studies Abroad in Nurturing Global Citizenship." *Journal of Studies in International Education* 14: 433–451.

Tatic, Kasim. "Globalization, Competiveness, and Environment." School of Economics and Business, Sarajevo Bosnia and Herzegovina. Published paper. www.hrcak.srce.hr/file/33801

Thibault, Bruno. "'Awaité Pawana': J.M.G. Le Clézio's Vision of the Sacred (The Questing Fictions of J.M.G. Le Clézio)." *World Literature Today* (March 1997): 723–729.

———. "Immigration et Individuation: L'Archétype de l'Anima dans *Désert* De J.M.G. Le Clézio." *Romance Notes* 11(4) (2000): 361–371.

———. *J.M.G. Le Clézio et La Métaphore Exotique.* New York: Rodopi, 2009.

———. "J.M.G. Le Clézio." *The Journal of Twentieth-Century/Contemporary French Studies* 2 (2): 365–376.

———. "Le Chant de l'Abîme et la Voix Chamanique Dans *Le Procès-Verbal* et Dans *Voyages de L'Autre Côté.*" *Symposium* 53 (1): 37–50.

———. "La Métaphore Exotique: l'Ecriture du Processus d'individuation dans *Le Chercheur d'or* et *La Quarantaine* de J.M.G. Le Clézio." *French Review* 73 (5) (Apr. 2000): 845–861.

———. "Méditation et Education: L'Archétype de l'Initiation Dans 'Lullaby' de J. M. G. Le Clézio." *Symposium* (March 2001): 1–12.

———. "Du Stéréotype au mythe: l'écriture du fait divers dans les nouvelles de J.M.G. Le Clézio. " *French Review* 68 (6): 964–975.

Thiher, Allen. "Jean-Marie Gustave Le Clézio. *Cœur brûle et autres romances.*" *World Literature Today* 75 (2): 138–139.

Thompson, William. "Voyage and Immobility in J.M.G. Le Clézio's ' *Désert* ' and ' *La Quarantaine.* ' (The Questing Fictions of J.M.G. Le Clézio)." *World Literature Today* (September 1997): 709–716.

Tsai, Wan-Hsiu Sunny. "Patriotic Advertising and the Creation of the Citizen-Consumer." *Journal Media and Communication Studies* 2 (3): 76–84.

Ugochi, Njemanze. "The Challenges of Globalization and the Use of Children's Literature in Achieving Cultural Literacy in Nigeria." *Studies in Literature and Language* 1 (4): 49–54.

Van Acker, Isa. "Errance et Marginalité chez Le Clézio: *Le Procès-verbal* et *La Quarantaine.*" *Nouvelles Etudes Francophones* 20 (2): 69–78.

Vital, Anthony. "Toward an African Ecocriticism: Postcolonialism, Ecology and *Life & Times of Michael K.*" *Research in African Literatures* 39 (1): 87–106.

Von Werlhof, Claudia. "The Globalization of Neoliberalism, its Consequences, and Some of its Basic Alternatives." *Capitalism Nature Socialism* 19 (3): 94–117.

Wachtel, Charlie. "Q & A With Director of *The Joneses.*" *The Film Crusade.* www.filmcrusade.com/qa-director-derrick-borte-of-the-joneses.

Walker, David. "Du détail au totalitarisme: variations sur le commerce conquérant chez Le Clézio." *J.M.G. Le Clézio dans la forêt des paradoxes.* Eds. Bruno Thibault and Keith Moser. Paris, France: L'Harmattan, Collection Études transnationales, francophones et comparés, 2012: 111–124.

———. "Setting the record straight: J.M.G. Le Clézio." *Outrage and Insight: Modern French Writers and the 'fait divers.'* Oxford: Berg, 1995: 233–250.

Waelti-Walters, Jennifer. *J.M.G. Le Clézio.* Boston: Twayne Publishers, 1977.

———. Interview with Jennifer Waelti-Walters, October 12, 2009. *Le Clézio, Portrait of a Gentle Writer.* December 18, 2009. www.npr.org/templates/story/story.php?storyId=95615028.

———. "Narrative Movement in J.M.G. Le Clézio's Fever." *Studies in Short Fiction* 14 (3): 247–254.

Weisbuch, Robert. *Chronicle of Higher Education* 26 Mar. 1999: B4.

Westerlund, Fredrik. "La vie urbaine-mort urbaine: La ronde et autres faits divers de Jean-Marie Gustave Le Clézio." *Moderna Sprak* 92 (1): 71–80.

———. *Les Fleuves dans l'œuvre Romanesque de Jean-Marie Gustave Le Clézio.* Diss. The University of Helsinki, 2011.

Westling, Louise. "What Would be an Ecological Humanism?" *PMLA* 114 (5): 1103–04.

Wickramasekara, Piyasiri. "Globalisation, International Labour Migration and the Rights of Migrant Workers." *Third World Quarterly* 29 (7): 1247–64.

Woollen, Geoff. "Father Figures." *Modern & Contemporary France* 13 (4): 497–500.

Yen-Yu, Sheng. "Ravaging the Earth, Wasting our Patrimony." *Postcolonial Green: Environmental Politics and World Narratives.* Eds. Bonnie Roos and Alex Hunt. University of Virginia Press, 2010: 83–101.

Yillah, Dauda. "Envisioning Difference in Le Clézio's Onitsha." *French Studies* 62 (2): 173–87.

Young, Dannagal. "Sacrifice, Consumption, and the American Way of Life: Advertising and Domestic Propaganda During World War II." *The Communication Review* 8: 27–52.

Zanganeh, Liza Azam. "Une œuvre mal comprise aux Etats-Unis." *Le Monde,* 11 October 2008: 23.

# Index

# About the Author

**Keith Moser** is assistant professor at Mississippi State University. After publishing his first book, entitled *'Privileged Moments' in the Novels and Short Stories of J.M.G. Le Clézio: His Contemporary Development of a Traditional French Literary Device* (2008), Dr. Moser has contributed several essays to peer-reviewed publications, such as *Romance Notes, Dalhousie French Studies, Modern Language Review, Les Cahiers Le Clézio, French Cultural Studies, Janus Head, Sprachkunst,* and *The EFL Journal.* Although the majority of his research focuses on Le Clézio, he has also published material related to Albert Camus, Marcel Proust, Jean-Paul Sartre, Claude Lanzmann, Fatima Besnaci-Lancou, Dalila Kerchouche, and Zahia Rahmani. Moser's research areas are truly interdisciplinary, as evidenced by his essays concerning interculturality, literary representations of bullying, and teaching literature in the World Language classroom. Moser recently co-edited a collection of essays with Bruno Thibault (*J.M.G. Le Clézio dans la forêt des paradoxes,* 2012). He also organized the first campus visit in the United States for the 2008 Nobel Laureate in Literature, J.M.G. Le Clézio, at Mississippi State University from March 28–April 4, 2009. Additionally, Dr. Moser served as an invited volunteer for the *Fondation pour l'interculturel et la paix* (Foundation for Interculturality and Peace), co-founded by J.M.G. Le Clézio and Issa Asgarally, to help launch this humanitarian organization from the island nation of Mauritius in May 2010.

www.ingramcontent.com/pod-product-compliance
Lightning Source LLC
Chambersburg PA
CBHW071528110726
47908CB00003B/982

* 9 7 8 0 7 3 9 1 9 7 5 9 2 *